Out of the Long Dark

Popular Music History

Series Editor: Alyn Shipton, journalist, broadcaster and former lecturer in music at Oxford Brookes University

This new series publishes books that challenge established orthodoxies in popular music studies, examine the formation and dissolution of canons, interrogate histories of genres, focus on previously neglected forms, or engage in archaeologies of popular music.

Published:

Handful of Keys: Conversations with Thirty Jazz Pianists
Alyn Shipton

The Last Miles: The Music of Miles Davis, 1980–1991
George Cole

Jazz Visions: Lennie Tristano and His Legacy
Peter Ind

Chasin' the Bird: The Life and Legacy of Charlie Parker
Brian Priestley

Forthcoming:

Lee Morgan: His Life, Music and Culture
Tom Perchard

PREZ: The Life and Music of Lester Young
Dave Gelly

Sunshine and Shade: The Life of Sonny Criss
Nic Jones

Lionel Ritchie: Hello
Sharon Davis

Gone in the Air: The Life and Music of Eric Dolphy
Brian Morton

In Search of Fela Anikulapo Kuti
Max Reinhardt and Rita Ray

Out of the Long Dark
The Life of Ian Carr

ALYN SHIPTON

equinox

London   Oakville

Published by
UK: Equinox Publishing Ltd., Unit 6, The Village, 101 Amies St.,
London SW11 2JW
USA: DBBC, 28 Main Street, Oakville, CT 06779

www.equinoxpub.com

First published 2006

Library of Congress Cataloging-in-Publication Data

Shipton, Alyn.
Out of the long dark: the life of Ian Carr/Alyn Shipton.
    p. cm -- (Popular music history)
Includes discography (p.), bibliographical references (p.), and index
ISBN 1-84553-222-8 (hb)
1. Carr, Ian. 2. Music critics--England--Biography.
3. Jazz musicians--England--Biography. I. Title. II. Series.
ML423.C2854S55 2006
781.65092--dc22
                        2006006882

British Library Cataloguing-in-Publication Data
A catalogue record for this book is available from the British Library.

ISBN-10   1 84553 222 8   (hardback)
ISBN-13   978 1 84553 222 2   (hardback)

Typeset by S.J.I. Services, New Delhi
Printed and bound in Great Britain by Lightning Source UK Ltd., Milton Keynes
and in the United States of America by Lightning Source Inc., La Vergne, TN

contents

list of illustrations

introduction and acknowledgements

Every other year in the late 1960s and early 1970s, for a week in May, the nave and chancel of St. Andrew's parish church in Farnham, Surrey, turned into the country's leading concert hall for young musicians. The Farnham Festival, the brainchild of my school music master, the late Alan Fluck, brought young players from the surrounding area into direct contact with the leading composers and players of the time. Thus it was that as a primary school pupil of seven, I clip-clopped my way through the percussive burglar's footsteps of Thea Musgrave's *Marco The Miser,* with the composer in attendance. Later Malcolm Arnold conducted our school orchestra through one of his specially written *Little Suites,* and we gave premieres of new works by, among others, John Addison, Don Banks, Alan Rawsthorne, and Richard Rodney Bennett.

Alan Fluck's vision was about breaking down musical barriers. Along with a classical education, he gave me and my contemporaries every encouragement to play and hear jazz, folk and rock music. Five friends and I formed a jazz group at Farnham Grammar School, and played our way through stock arrangements, as well as going to hear as many bands as we could in concert, including Humphrey Lyttelton and Alex Welsh, as well as Bruce Turner and Kathy Stobart.

In 1969, when I was fifteen, the Farnham Festival announced that one of its major commissions that year would be a huge jazz cantata by the pianist Michael Garrick, who then lived locally in Camberley. At the time, as well as being a prime mover in the poetry and jazz movement, Michael was the pianist in the Rendell-Carr Quintet, a cutting-edge band that my contemporaries and I constantly read about in the music press, but had never heard at first hand. So it was a thrill to discover that Don Rendell and Ian Carr themselves would be in the Michael Garrick Sextet for their concert in St. Andrew's church, along with the choir of Farnborough Grammar School in which some of my friends were singers.

By special dispensation, the members of my little group were allowed to take the day off from school and sit in on all the rehearsals for Garrick's new work. For the concert itself we sat in the very front row, trying to learn all we could from watching and listening to Don, Ian, Mike and their colleagues, Art Themen on tenor, John Marshall on drums and Coleridge Goode on bass. They played with a brash confidence, and the memory of Ian's flugelhorn cutting through the dusty atmosphere of the old church above the swish of Marshall's ride cymbal still makes the hairs on the back of my neck stand up. Along with my enthusiasm for traditional and mainstream jazz, I became an immediate convert to what was going on in the British modern scene. My weekly haul of new and second-hand records from the local shops, where I traded my used discs for new ones, stretching my pocket money and part-time job earnings to buy everything I could, suddenly became packed with music by Joe Harriott, Amancio D'Silva, Mike Westbrook, and above all, the Rendell-Carr and Garrick groups.

If there is a reason beyond the music for this, it is that the members of Michael Garrick's group were incredibly nice to us. They did not shrug off our teenage enthusiasm with the hardened carapace of unpleasant professional cynicism which Ronnie Scott later presented to me when I was a fledgling journalist, nor did they look down on our efforts to learn and absorb from them, as well they may have done, given our very amateurish beginnings. When I later played with Don Rendell in the resident big band at the Ritz in the 1990s, he greeted me with warm enthusiasm, and the same spark of interest that he had shown back in 1969. In our many meetings over the years, Michael Garrick has been similarly encouraging. But overall, it was hearing Ian Carr that inspired me. Awkward, bearded, implacably Northern in our safe Southern world, there was a rugged lyricism and beauty in his playing that I had never previously heard in live jazz.

When the Rendell-Carr band broke up, my friends and I followed Ian's career with Nucleus avidly. Our shared copy of *Elastic Rock* was almost worn out on the sixth form gramophone, and our school drummer Phil Lockhart began to wear vests and neckscarves like John Marshall's, even though he still modelled his playing (and his kit) more after our other idol of the time, Ginger Baker. As every new Nucleus disc appeared, we not only bought it, but listened avidly and discussed the nuances of each track over endless supplies of Nescafé and buttered toast.

Being caught up in Ian's story in this way, as I suspect many of my generation were, means that it's not always easy to be objective. In the past, I have tended to write about American jazz, often visiting and interviewing the founding fathers of the music on home turf, but nevertheless writing from the safe distance that the Atlantic creates between our two cultures. Although jazz is an international language, the American dialect has tended to predominate, and I have been captivated by its intoxicating shades and nuances. But in the last few years, both delving further into the academic study of oral history while reading for my PhD at Oxford Brookes University and simultaneously working with George Shearing on his autobiography, I have realised that as an English writer, my attentions should be equally devoted to the strong British accent in jazz.

The contribution of British musicians, and the development of the music in the UK have often helped the main current of jazz to take some surprising turns, and Ian Carr has been there for more than a few of them, from the pioneering Newcastle bebop band the EmCee Five to the Rendell-Carr Quintet, from the free jazz of John Stevens and Trevor Watts to the roaring big bands of Neil Ardley and Stan Tracey, and from the timely world-music-meets-jazz experiments of Joe Harriott, Amancio D'Silva and Guy Warren of Ghana to the early days of jazz-rock fusion in Britain with Nucleus. Students from his various educational activities are now making the running in British jazz themselves, while Ian has shifted his main attention from playing not just to writing books about jazz, but being actively involved in making prize-winning documentary films as well.

So when John Smallwood proposed to me the idea of writing a book about Ian, I accepted with alacrity. As I began to explore Ian's story I found interesting parallels with my own. My mother's family had academic and social connections with Durham, where my great-grandfather Samuel Blackwell Guest-Williams had been head of Durham School, a Dean of the Cathedral and rector of the nearby village of Pittington. In the same era, Ian's great-grandfather had been principal of St. Bede College. One of my great uncles had been a student at Ian's university, King's College, in the early days of its federation with Durham, and he and his brother later lived in Christleton Old Hall in Cheshire, not much more than a stone's throw away from Eaton Hall, where Ian underwent his army officer training.

Furthermore, Ian and I have both done our time as boy choristers, while simultaneously discovering the joys of recorded jazz. By the 1990s, of course, we were both regular presenters on BBC Radio 3, and have subsequently shared much information on aspects of jazz history. Ian was a vital contributor to several of my programmes, including a long series on jazz education, and so I hope this book goes some small way to repay the debt I owe him, both for fostering much of my initial interest in jazz, and keeping me abreast of many of the developments that have taken place in the music since.

Why the title, *Out of the Long Dark*? Ian's composition of that name was written in response to a Gerald Laing sculpture, called *Conception*. It describes in music the journey of a successful spermatozoa en route to fertilise a human egg. But its title, together, I think, with the music itself, conceals several more layers of meaning. The piece was written at the end of a long bout of depression, and celebrates Ian's emergence from it. This is a recurrent theme in his life, with numerous periods of long dark, and successful re-emergences, notably after the tragic death of his first wife Margaret, and — artistically — at the end of the Rendell-Carr period which led to Nucleus. But there are more instances — ranging from Ian's travels as an aimless and penniless teacher of English as a foreign language, through the France, Corsica and Italy of the late 1950s, which led to his emergence as a trumpeter on his return to the North-East, to the dark and light of his successful battle against cancer in the 1980s.

Ian himself has been central to the preparation of the book, helping me with dozens of obscure queries, and with the supply of pictures and press cuttings. In addition to letters, and detailed double checking of transcripts (plus a draft discography which I prepared as a research tool but which now appears in full form in the book), Ian has subtly pointed me towards sources I might not have thought of, or known about, and introduced me to many of his friends and colleagues. Several of my own interviews with him, done over a twelve year period, have found their way into the book, but throughout the process, he has respected my independence as a biographer, and not sought to influence any of my conclusions or critical observations.

John Smallwood began work on this book at least fifteen years ago, gathering interviews and press reports about Ian that have all gone into the preparation of the final text. At the end of the 1990s, he turned his voluminous files and his tape collection over to me, and I have supplemented that work with a research programme of my own. I should acknowledge John's generous support for the project and also that of Andrew Simons, of the National Sound Archive at the British Library, who commissioned me to conduct some of the interviews in the book for the library's jazz oral history programme. I must also acknowledge Mike Gott and Andy Gray at BGO records, who have not only done a superb job of reissuing the majority of Nucleus and Rendell-Carr material, but who also were kind enough to ask me to write liner notes for the series, which evolved in parallel with this text. At the same time, I should mention Brian O'Reilly and the team at Hux Records, who similarly involved me in the production of their BBC Nucleus sessions album *The Pretty Redhead*.

Several of my BBC colleagues have been involved in the gathering of interviews for the book. In particular I should single out Derek Drescher, who produced the Zyklus session mentioned in the text for Radio 3's *Impressions*, (which I co-presented with Brian Morton,) and who reintroduced me to Neil Ardley, with whom I'd previously worked in connection with his career as a science writer for children. Part of my interview with Neil that appears in the book was done as background for that *Impressions* broadcast. Derek has also been a companion at several recent Nucleus concerts, as has his fellow producer Felix Carey, with whom I made the series on jazz education that involved Ian. Other help has come from Terry Carter at BBC Birmingham and Oliver Jones at the World Service. For Terry, I worked as the writer and researcher on Barbara Thompson's Radio 3 series on *Jazz Rock in Britain*, and I'm grateful to Barbara and Jon Hiseman for their contributions to that project, some of which I have drawn on here. Oliver and I have shared many an adventure around the world in making *Jazzmatazz* for six years, and our guests on the programme during that time have included many of the participants in this book, including Ian himself.

I would like to thank Sandy Carr, George Foster (who kindly supplied various recordings for me) and John Latimer-Smith for help in the final stages of preparation of the text, and Tony Williams of Spotlite Records for discographical assistance. Other specialist input to the recordings list is acknowledged on page 171.

Finally I should mention Janet Joyce and Val Hall at Equinox, who have worked with me through thick and thin on many books, and to whom I especially grateful for taking on this book. With all the hoopla arising from Gilles Peterson's 'Impressed' and 'Repressed' CD series, and a renewed interest in UK jazz of the 60s and 70s, I hope the time is right to look in more detail at the career of someone who has been at the core of British jazz development for almost half a century.

Alyn Shipton
Salviac, France, 2006

1 northumbrian sketches

'It's the landscape I remember the most. Fabulous countryside, yellow flowers, fantastic trees, forests, woods, streams, dangerous rivers in which people occasionally drowned, wonderful swimming, and then in the winter, frozen bushes and trees dripping with frost. My composition *Northumbrian Sketches* is about that landscape. South Durham, North Yorkshire. Very beautiful counties. Of course the industrial area comes into it, but I have terrific memories of childhood, of summers and winters in these landscapes. Very beautiful physical memories.'[1]

When you've grown up in such a place, wild, rural, and romantic, it stays with you all your life. Although Ian Carr was born in Dumfries, in Scotland, on 21 April 1933, it is the Northumbrian landscape, where he spent the most formative years of his childhood, that has remained rooted in his imagination. Despite the attempts of public school and the army to smooth out his accent into standard English, Ian's speech still retains the rise and fall of the North-East, and the same distinctive individuality has pervaded his musical work in becoming one of Britain's leading jazz trumpeters, bandleaders and composers. Even though, in common with all jazz players, Ian has looked to the United States for a measure of inspiration, and found it in the trumpet-playing and musical diversity of Miles Davis or the pianistic lyricism of Keith Jarrett, his own music nevertheless retains as strong a local accent as his speech.

Not only did the region inspire his *Northumbrian Sketches* suite, a piece originally titled after its final movement *Spirit of Place* and written for the 1986 Bracknell Festival in memory of the North-Eastern writer Sid Chaplin, but it also inspired the title track of the Nucleus album *Roots*, and lies deep behind many of Ian's Shakespearean compositions, with their innate sense of Englishness.

After an anonymous early childhood in South Shields, in the industrial North-East of England, where his father, Thomas Randall Carr, was a commercial traveller for the soap company, Thomas Hedley, Ian moved at the age of seven with his mother and brother into an isolated rural house, and his love affair with the countryside began.

Morey Cottage, some distance from a road, with no running water or electricity, was two miles from the village of Whorlton, close to the Tees and just east of Barnard Castle. When his father came back from serving in the Royal Air Force at the end of the war in 1945, the family moved a short distance away into the village of Gainford, which is equidistant between Barnard Castle and the industrial town of Darlington. Both these villages are in County Durham, close to its southern border with North Yorkshire, and the landscape is almost as wild and romantic today as it was then. Indeed, Whorlton, in particular, has changed little from this late Victorian account of the place:

'The village of Whorlton occupies a beautiful situation, about three miles east-south-east from Barnard Castle; the Tees with its overhanging cliffs, thickly fringed with trees, passing near it on the south. On the opposite bank is the village of Wycliffe, and a fine range of country extends in every direction. The Tees is here crossed by a fine iron suspension bridge, which was erected in 1830-31, from designs and under the direction of the late Mr. Green, architect, of Newcastle. The span between the points of suspension is 180 feet.'[2]

Such a poetic description might suggest that the love of literature which has suffused Ian Carr's musical career, and which also led to him becoming one of Britain's most distinguished biographers and writers on jazz, was initially inspired by the same surrounding landscape. Yet it was the effect of a short period a little earlier than his move to Whorlton, when he was living with his paternal grandfather in a bungalow near Blackpool in 1939, that kindled his love of letters.

Henry Carr, Ian's grandfather, had been a scientist and the headmaster of a state school, in which he built up a science curriculum well before this was the norm in English education. As a young man, he had attended Armstrong College, the forerunner of King's College, Newcastle, before being appointed to his headmastership at twenty-eight. Being such a high-flier eventually took its toll, and he retired early, giving him plenty of time to read, and to nurture his working knowledge of several languages, notably French and German. He had married the daughter of Dr. Thomas Randall, the one-time Principal of Bede College, and it was from both sides of this generation of the family that Ian took his full baptismal name, Ian Henry Randall Carr.

In retirement at Bispham, outside Blackpool, Henry Carr welcomed his grandson at the start of the war, when the boy was evacuated from the potential target zones of the industrial North-East to the quiet of the Lancashire coast. Although the old man, with his thatch of white hair and moustache, would tut-tut over the latest illustrated news of the war in *Picture Post*, he saw to it that Ian had no light reading matter of his own, no comics, and no saccharine children's stories. Instead, the boy read and learned by heart tales from the Bible or Greek mythology, had practical instruction from his grandfather in science, and began to acquire the rudiments of French.

This fuelled a delight in literature which has never left him, and encouraged his imagination to roam freely. His flights of fancy were further spurred on by the vivid stories and poems his grandfather would recite in front of the fire, not least, W. S. Gilbert's lurid ballad about cannibalism, *The Yarn of the Nancy Bell*, which became a particular favourite. The poem is related by an old salt, who gradually reveals that he survived a shipwreck by eating his fellow survivors. The six-year-old Ian's eyes would stretch in awe at the gruesome ending:

'Then only the cook and me was left,
And the delicate question, "Which
Of us two goes to the kettle?" arose,
And we argued it out as sich.

'For I loved that cook as a brother, I did,
And the cook he worshipped me;
But we'd both be blowed if we'd either be stowed
In the other chap's hold, you see.

'So he boils the water, and takes the salt
And the pepper in portions true
(Which he never forgot), and some chopped shallot.
And some sage and parsley too.

'"Come here," says he, with a proper pride,
Which his smiling features tell,
"T'will soothing be if I let you see
How extremely nice you'll smell."

'And he stirred it round and round and round,
And he sniffed at the foaming froth;
When I ups with his heels, and smothers his squeals
In the scum of the boiling broth.

'And I ate that cook in a week or less,
And — as I eating be
The last of his chops, why, I almost drops,
For a wessel in sight I see!

'Oh, I am a cook and a captain bold,
And the mate of the *Nancy* brig,
And a bo'sun tight, and a midshipmite,
And the crew of the captain's gig!'[3]

It was not only such vivid first-hand experiences of literature and language that Ian absorbed during his short stay with his grandfather.

The bungalow, called Cornerways because it stood at the junction of two roads, also contained a piano. Ian was strictly forbidden to touch this pride and joy of the household, a condition he tacitly accepted until one day his Auntie Audrey, who taught the piano for a living, turned up with one of her prize pupils. The boy, Gordon Coleman, who was three years older than Ian, proceeded to play extremely well, and received much applause from the assembled company. Ian still believes that it was the passionate jealousy this inspired, swearing to himself that one day he would outdo this prodigy, that lay behind his later decision to opt for music as a career and strive to reach the top of his profession. As it turned out, the boy he heard was to become one of Britain's leading light-music pianists and arrangers, under the name Gordon Langford, so he was quite an exceptional talent to have encountered, but this was not something Ian knew at the time, when he resolved to outdo him.

Yet despite the jealousy that her pupil inspired, Ian formed a close bond with his Auntie Audrey, who lived in London. 'She was a pillar of strength,' Ian recalls. 'She was married to a Russian jew, with whom she had three sons. He was a printer, but no good as a businessman, so she had to work to keep the family together. She taught and looked after them all. It was a very intellectual family, and they lived in a shabby house because she didn't have time to clean it. But they had a perfect library and a perfect collection of records. She played the piano very well herself, and knew all about the arts. In fact, she had been on a trip to Russia with Bertrand Russell in about 1935 to see what it was like. She was such a spirited woman that in her early twenties she had ridden her bike from the North to London, which took her two or three days. Audrey was a teacher all of her working life. When she retired, she began to travel abroad, working as a tutor with families. She had been to Turkey and had picked up Turkish. Then she went as a tutor to a rich Italian count, to teach his son, where she learned Italian. She also spoke Russian, as well as good French and Yiddish. But she was like a mother to me. I could talk to her about anything, and she was very broadminded. She understood what I did, liked music and everything I aspired to.'[4]

After a few months at Cornerways, during which his father was first posted away from home with the RAF, Ian rejoined his mother and his younger brother Mike, who having been born in December 1937 had been deemed too young to leave his mother to go to Lancashire. For a few months they were together in digs on a farm in North Yorkshire, but towards the end of 1940, they moved into Morey Cottage, which sat in its own little valley, surrounded by fields, with a beck close by that sparkled its way down to the Tees. The road to Whorlton passed by about half a mile up a hill to the front of the house, which was reached by a long unmade track that petered out as it got near to the building.

Ian's mother Phyllis was virtually a single parent during the war years, and although his sister Judith, the family's youngest child, was born in 1940, there was subsequently a coolness between the Carr parents. Thomas Carr suffered the indignity at the end of the war of being told by Hedley's that he was too old to have his old job back, and so he went into business with a friend to start a new food importing firm, which became better established as the decade went on. Consequently, after his return to the family, a lot of Ian's father's energy went into this business, and even though there were occasional family holidays to the

Ian and his parents, Thomas and Phyllis Carr, circa 1935. (Ian Carr)

picturesque Yorkshire fishing village of Staithes, or to relations near Bath, Thomas Carr was a distant and preoccupied figure.

In later years, Ian's parents were barely on speaking terms with each other, although in the mid-40s the church and politics brought them together. In keeping with the aspirations of a self-made man of the period, Thomas Carr was somewhat right-wing in his outlook, telling his friends he was a liberal, but at the same time complaining that the Liberal party had gone soft, and so he was compelled to vote Conservative. His wife, by contrast, was a Tory for quite different reasons, believing quite simply that Conservatives were 'a nicer class of people'. She did not wish to be identified with workers in cloth caps, and her social climbing ambitions were projected onto the aspirations she had for her sons. Although this later led to a gulf between Ian and his mother, it was her initial push that helped to launch his musical career.

Some aspects of Phyllis's family were larger than life, seeming almost to have come directly from the *Yarn of the Nancy Bell*. Her father (whose surname was, coincidentally, also Carr) had been a lighthouse-keeper, and a chief engineer in the merchant marine. He habitually slept with a revolver under his pillow, as well as occasionally having his wife watched by detectives while he was away at sea. He was horrified by physical deformity of any kind, and was known hurriedly to change seats in a railway carriage if anyone with so much as what he regarded as a minor defect entered the same compartment. He had died mysteriously at sea a few weeks before Phyllis was born.

However her mother (Ian's grandmother) had an equally extraordinary background, in that she ran a tailor's shop in Bond Street. A generation earlier, this London shop had been visited by the future Napoleon III of France, and in due course, Ian's great-grandfather was whisked off to Versailles to become the emperor's head tailor.

Despite being thrown on his mother's company in Whorlton, there was always an emotional reserve between her and Ian, which had begun when he was little more than a toddler, following the doting closeness they had enjoyed together during his early childhood. This coolness lasted all her life. With Phyllis preoccupied with a new baby, Ian and his brother mainly occupied their time with one another, playing around the cottage in the Whorlton countryside, because its isolation meant there was seldom anybody else around. The boys got on well together as small children, and were to continue to be close colleagues as young adult musicians, both in Ian's student band, and in Mike's first major professional group, the EmCee Five.

Ian was later to describe Whorlton as a first-hand lesson in the power of nature and the four seasons. The contrast between summer and winter in the North-East of England is extreme. On the one hand, there was the parched summer landscape, so dry that the trees withered in the fields, the well at the cottage dried up, and water had to be carried from the nearby spring that was itself reduced to a trickle. In winter, the bitter cold cut through everything, and when it snowed, the track to the house became impassable, leaving the children unable even to walk the two miles to school. In baked summer or frozen winter, a car could be driven across the fields to the house, but the merest hint of rain and its tyres would sink deep into the mud, and sacks would have to be put underneath the wheels to give enough traction for the vehicle to escape.

Yet, isolated though the cottage was, for much of the year the Carr boys were fully involved in the life of the village, where they went to school, and Ian, in particular, began to pursue the musical dream kindled by his jealousy of Gordon Langford. 'I had piano lessons from quite early on, when I was about nine, I should think,' he recalled. 'My brother and I sang in the choir in Whorlton, and the vicar, who was called Porteous, gave piano lessons. He had a bald crown and curly ginger hair round the edge. His long fingernails clacked on the keys and he smoked while he played. Little puffs came out of his nose like a dragon. And the little puffs always smelt very nice, which is probably one of the reasons why I smoked too early. I always sang by ear, and I never really learned to read music for the piano. I just did it with my ear. Even when we recorded with the EmCee Five in 1961, I couldn't really read.'[5]

Despite his lack of sight reading, Ian was one of the outstanding singers in the choir, taking many of the treble solos in anthems or carols, and in common with many of his generation of British jazz musicians, the church choral tradition became part of his musical consciousness. Among his contemporaries, both John Surman and Keith Tippett, for example, similarly absorbed the harmonic structure of *Hymns Ancient and Modern*, the pointing of the psalms, and the well-known settings of anthems, until they were as natural as breathing.

Ian was to continue as a chorister when the family moved to a terraced house in Station Road, Gainford. As he grew older, the choir became a place to meet the village girls, some of whom Ian admired from afar, staring at their tanned brown knees in the space between the hymnbooks and the hassocks in the opposite choir stalls. The choir was also a great social leveller, singing by invitation at the local landowners' imposing houses at Christmas and Easter, in addition to carolling around the more modest dwellings of the village. As well as the boys and girls of his own generation, Ian sang alongside senior choristers, such as the postmaster, who was a bass and smelt of the Capstan cigarettes he habitually smoked, or the church cleaning lady, who shattered decorum on the choir outings by getting tipsy and performing her party piece, *Stop Your Tickling, Jock, In Case You Turn Me Frock*.

Ian was twelve when his father returned from the war, and although Thomas Carr had forgone a formal education himself, walking out on his parents when he was sixteen, he was at pains to see that his own sons fared better. So he arranged for Ian to sit the entrance examination for Barnard Castle School, a local fee-paying public school, which he attended from September 1945. Barnard Castle — known locally as Barney — is listed as one of the fifty most historic towns in England, with a 12th century castle; the remarkable Bowes Museum of Art, built in the style of a French Renaissance chateau; and a host of small specialist shops, many of them ancient, including some that formed part of the setting for Charles Dickens' novel, *The Old Curiosity Shop*.

'My social life in Gainford was dominated by three things, family, school and village life,' Ian remembers. 'Gainford was a social village like a cake, layer upon layer. My family was, I suppose, lower middle class. Slightly better than the workers, as it were, and inferior to the rest of them. Some of the houses in the village were stately and grand, and to the Eastern end were the beginnings of a council estate, which was a new development. The village had three pubs, but above all a billiard hall, which we frequented a lot. But having lived in Whorlton, we still roamed all around the surrounding countryside, which was absolutely gorgeous. We swam in the river, or boated in a little collapsible boat we had, and we did some things I'm not so proud of today, like shooting at birds with air pistols. It was farming country and I had a lot of friends who were farmers.

'Life in the village itself was very sporty. We played cricket on the village green, football in the winter, and there was a tennis court. But actually, in that period after the war, life revolved around the church, where I was confirmed on 3 May 1945.'[6]

St. Mary's, Gainford, is a smallish church, seating about 150, and built in the gothic revival style in 1853 on the site of an earlier building. It has an open-beamed wooden ceiling, and attractive Minton floor tiles in the chancel. The main form of the building is that of a simple hall, with an octagonal turret forming a small belfry in the South-West corner. In other words, it is a perfectly typical Victorian parish church of a type which exists across the length and breadth of Britain. But to the Carr family it became the centre of weekend activity. Ian and Mike were choristers, and their parents and younger sister Judith were all members of the church.

The vicar, Eric Harry Wale, a tall, thin-faced, though otherwise stoutish man, with tortoiseshell spectacles, became a mentor to Ian. He had served as a sapper in World War One, and was happy to regale the boy with stories of life in the trenches, which fuelled a later interest in all things to do with the 1914-18 war. He also lent him many books, and threw open the vicarage for Ian and his fellow choristers to play table tennis.

At the same time, Ian took part in village amateur dramatics, with walk-on parts in *The Importance of Being Earnest* and *Without The Prince* (a pre-Stoppard experiment in writing a play about Shakespeare's *Hamlet*). The village also offered the opportunity for Ian and Mike to continue with the piano lessons they had started with the Rev. Porteous, when a builder's wife called Mrs. Charge took them on. The sepia photo above the piano of her brother, who had been killed in the Great War, not only provided Ian with something to look at as he plodded through his exercises, but further fuelled his interest in that war. Owing to this interest, before he left school Ian joined the local branch of the Royal Observer Corps, which both offered an official-looking blue uniform to its cadets, and gave young enthusiasts the opportunity to follow up spotting aeroplanes by actually flying in them. Ian took his first flight in an RAF trainer on 29 August 1951.

Overall, his school life was in many ways a reflection of the village. For a start, it was very sporty, and the games master Mr. Parry was a specialist in swimming, not only sending winning teams to competitions with other public schools, but ensuring that the majority of the boys were competent swimmers, and passed their exams in life-saving. Track and field training was equally significant, and for a time, school and home life ran parallel, as Ian's father, or his best friend Dump Morrison's father, would take the boys to amateur athletics meetings at the weekends, where Ian performed well in sprinting and the high jump.

The academic side of school was not so straightforward, and although Ian was always placed in the 'a' stream, he initially made no effort at any of his subjects except English. One day his English master, Mr. Southwood, suggested publicly to the class that he should give the Carr boy more marks for a piece of work, 'because he's no good at anything else'.[7] Stung into action at the age of sixteen, Ian eventually managed nine School Certificate subjects including one distinction and seven credits.

Not surprisingly it was in English that he received his highest mark, and moving into the sixth form, this was not only the subject in which he continued to excel but also the one in which he found a mentor, in the form of the senior English master, Arnold Snodgrass. Blessed with a thunderous voice and an intimidating persona, Snodgrass combined being an excellent classroom disciplinarian with the ability to inspire and motivate his young charges.

'He was an absolutely terrific man,' recalls Ian. 'He opened a whole series of doors for me into the visual arts, into literature and into jazz. He'd corresponded with Robert Graves, the poet, and he was an Oxford contemporary of W.H. Auden. He'd also written a novel, although he wouldn't let me read it! Having been at Oxford during the Depression, the economic situation meant that when he graduated, he couldn't get a job. He told me he went for eighty interviews before he came to Barnard Castle School, where he then worked all his life, eventually becoming Second Master. I owe him a huge debt for the way he helped me get on. He had a very wide view of culture, and introduced me to poets, particularly Pope, and Shakespeare. To introduce boys of sixteen to Shakespeare is not the easiest thing in the world, but he made *Henry IV Part I* fun, and so interesting! My love of Shakespeare has continued all my life, and it was started in the right way by him.'[8]

Under Snodgrass's influence, Ian also discovered the paintings of Dali and Picasso, the novels of Graham Greene, and contemporary films, such as *Citizen Kane*. Inspired by Snodgrass's enthusiasm for drama, Ian acted at school, extending the range of his village amateur theatricals with a role in Sheridan's *The Rivals*. The boys were regularly taken to plays at Richmond Repertory Theatre in Yorkshire, and also to Newcastle, where in May 1952 they saw a particularly memorable production of *King Lear*.

His teacher's remarkable powers of inspiration did not only apply to Ian. Another pupil who ultimately adopted a literary career as a result of them is the Oxford-based poet and fellow of New College, Craig Raine, who reports: 'At Barnard Castle I was taught by an absolutely remarkable English teacher, Arnold Snodgrass, a friend of W. H. Auden at Oxford. There was no question that he altered my mindset on things and made me very critical. I remember when I was eleven or twelve, we had a book to read in class, John Buchan's *Prester John*. He ridiculed it mercilessly and we all defended it because we thought it was exciting.'[9]

Raine, in common with other Barnard Castle boys, benefited from Snodgrass's constant encouragement to his students to write poetry. Every effort brought the urgent endorsement to 'keep on doing it!', as a result of which Ian himself produced a love lyric dedicated to Mary Herbert, a fellow singer in the choir, part of which ran:

'With flashing eyes that my advances scorn,
With pride that pricks my heart just like a thorn,
I see her vision stand before me yet.'

Apparently Mary herself rather liked it, and revelled in the flattery of having a poem written about her, especially after her mother discovered a copy tucked under her pillow. Snodgrass was pleased, too, in this instance because Ian was attempting a complex verse form, although he was just as encouraging when it came to satirical verse, or even doggerel, given that his creative philosophy was, 'it's probably better to write one smutty limerick than to read the whole of Milton's *Paradise Lost.*'[10]

This urge to be original, rather than to be derivative, to make something out of nothing, and to live a creative life, ultimately became the guiding philosophy for Ian's entire career. It saw him through depression — the 'long dark' — of his adult life, and it prompted him to work diligently as a trumpeter, composer, bandleader, and author.

As he has already hinted, it was not just a love of literature and a lifetime's philosophy that Ian took from Snodgrass. It was also a new kind of musical enthusiasm, to which he could apply his mentor's urge to be creative: 'He was a jazz fan,' says Ian. 'In the 1930s, he'd seen both Duke Ellington and Louis Armstrong when they came to England, and he had records by them and other artists. He'd play me *A Monday Date*, by Louis Armstrong and Earl Hines and ask what I thought of it, or lend me other discs by the Hot Five or Hot Seven, for me to take away and let him know later what I made of them.'[11] Soon jazz was Ian's major passion, shared at home with his younger brother, who had also become a pupil at the school. At weekends they would take the bus into Darlington to buy discs, or borrow them from other interested friends.

'We got records,' remembers Ian. 'I think the first we ever got was a 78: Fats Waller's *Jingle Bells*. My father liked Fats Waller. *My Very Good Friend The Milkman* was on the other side. And then we got *Hamp's Boogie Woogie*. We were not surfing the internet but surfing the radio for jazz from abroad in those days. So that's how we first heard *Hamp's Boogie Woogie* and things like that, and then slowly we got more sophisticated in our tastes. We were hooked on the blues. We liked all that early stuff, Pine Top Smith, Sister Rosetta Tharpe and Marie Knight — gospel music. Boogie woogie we liked a lot. These are great foundations. People that began with bebop often didn't get that, and you can hear it in their playing that they didn't.'[12]

Two school friends from Newcastle, Marcus Price and David Bell, shared Ian's enthusiasm, and together they swapped records, and compared notes on their musical heroes. 'They got me onto Muggsy Spanier and Woody Herman, believe it or not,' he confirms. 'I was seventeen when I heard Woody Herman's *Original Apple Honey* and all that kind of thing. That's what we got from those rather hip businessmen's sons.' Ian's diaries confirm that every Saturday, in addition to expeditions to buy records, he also became an avid listener to BBC Radio's *Jazz Club*. But any amount of discs and broadcasts are scant preparation for hearing jazz played live in the flesh.

'There were visiting people,' Ian remembered, the excitement noticeable in his voice as he spoke. 'To Darlington came that Australian Jazz Band. Graeme Bell! And my mother took us there. It wasn't full when we arrived. It was in a dance hall. And as we walked across the dance floor to get a seat somewhere — my mother followed by us two boys — the band wolf-whistled her! She got all flustered. Then, later, I saw Bob Barclay's Yorkshire Jazz Band, which had Dickie Hawdon on trumpet. One of the things I remember about that — these things are very important — was the marvellous sound of cymbals, and the terrific sound of the brass with that band. That really stuck with me. We were hearing all those things, and we were hungry for anything.'[13]

As time went on, there were other bands that came to the North East, including Humphrey Lyttelton's group, which was still staunchly revivalist in the early 1950s, and the Carr brothers went along to hear as many of these visitors as they could.

Following these trips to hear live bands, it was not a big step from experiencing jazz on disc and in person to wanting to play it. For Mike Carr it was a matter of developing the skills he had been learning for years at his piano lessons, in order to become an aspiring jazz pianist. His progress was very rapid, and in his early teens, he even sat in at Cook's Ferry Inn for the interval pianist Alan Clare during a recording of a BBC *Jazz Club* programme that took place when the boys' father took them to London to see relatives.

Ian's transition was less straightforward. It involved taking up a new instrument altogether, and according to his diary, the momentous event that started his playing career took place on 30 July, 1951, when he was eighteen. 'I'd always wanted a trumpet,' he says. 'I'd heard Humphrey Lyttelton and Louis Armstrong, and I liked it. I got a bugle mouthpiece, and I'd fit that mouthpiece into anything and play it like a trumpet. In our village there were piano teachers, but there was no trumpet teacher or anything like that. Eventually my mother took pity on me and she went to an auction of furniture, where there was an old trumpet-cornet, a Boston, silver plated, with *ne plus ultra* engraved on it. And so she picked it up for me and bought the Harry James trumpet tutor. With those two things, I taught myself to play.

'In the early pages of the book there was a picture of a piano keyboard, and although I was a slow reader of music, I knew what the notes on the piano were. In the book, they'd illustrated the trumpet fingering next to seven notes on the piano, in other words, just one octave of fingering. So I learned that, and of course for years I used wrong fingerings for the rest of the notes that weren't listed there, just as other self-taught jazz trumpeters such as Bix Beiderbecke did. For example, the correct fingering for a trumpet D – a concert C – is valves one and three for the lower D on the stave, and just the first valve for the higher one. But I used one and three for the higher note for years, because that's what the book told me to use for the lower D on the stave, and of course, it didn't have a picture for the higher one, so I just assumed it was the same. As a result, for a long time I played with entirely wrong fingering. Years later I learned the proper techniques, but every time I play, even today, I still see a piano keyboard in my head.'[14]

Because Ian had used his exceptional ear to get by as a chorister and would-be pianist, he did the same thing as a trumpeter, the difference being that at eighteen, he was intellectualising the reasons for not learning to play properly, or to read music. This was not, however, without the weight of quite powerful opinion in his favour. The recently published history of jazz, *Shining Trumpets*, by Rudi Blesh, mandatory reading for any schoolboy jazz fan, extolled the 'inward precious quality to be heard, felt, and sensed' in the music of the New Orleans players who had invented jazz. 'That some of the players could not read,' Blesh wrote, 'does not point to musical ineptitude on their part. On the contrary, they were exceptional men with the gift of skilled creative improvisation.'[15]

With the benefit of hindsight, Ian can now see the folly in accepting such views as the basis for his approach to playing, but at the time he did not see that there might be another point of view.

'I didn't realise it at all,' he told me. 'I was a complete natural. For a long time I thought that if you analysed, you'd lose your spontaneity and everything, and I was very foolish because when you analyse consciously, it then becomes part of your subconscious and you just go on again.'[16] Yet, in terms of practical experience, the Carr brothers were actually giving themselves a musical education that was every bit as valuable as detailed analysis of transcribed solos or written scores. They learned by trial and error how to play much of the music in their record collection by ear, working out from the discs the melodies, the accompanying harmonies, and even some of the solos that they heard. 'My brother was very much more able on the piano than I was,' says Ian. 'And so he would work out what all the harmonies were and things like that, and he would help me with the melodies. Nowadays, although I've got no great technical skill with the piano, I know far more about harmony and things than I did then.'[17]

To those around them, and particularly their mother, the Carr boys' playing seemed exceptionally good. So, on 10 July 1952, Phyllis Carr entered her sons for the local round of a national talent competition at the Darlington Hippodrome. It was fronted by the bandleader Carroll Levis, who had been touring the circuit for years, combining a variety show by his recent so-called Discoveries with the opportunity for raw and inexperienced local talent to become the 'Discoveries' of the future. During the early 1940s, his music director, who rehearsed the pit band for each and every young hopeful, had been the famous jazz pianist, Marian McPartland, who recalls: 'There'd be a juggler, a dancer and a singer, and then I'd play a selection on the piano. After that, the talent show would begin.'[18]

'We went there,' remembers Ian, 'and it was a revelation. It was full of seedy out-of-work actors that were organising it, and the Master of Ceremonies was Barry Took. These seedy actors would show us their reviews and photographs. It was not a very brilliant show. It had a terrible drunken old man singing *That Lucky Old Sun*. I can't remember what the others did. Anyway we got to go to the final in London at the Paris Cinema, Regent Street. There was an orchestra there, and the drummer played for my brother and me. For our bit we played a Louis Armstrong tune called *Hotter Than That*. We were introduced as "two young gentlemen on the stairway to stardom". The headmaster at Barnard Castle School had a very serious talk with me before we went there and he said, "Whatever you do, do not wear the school blazer." We had no intention of wearing the school blazer, not least because I'd recently been told off for wearing loud jackets at school. Anyway we went down there and did it, and it was fun. What's more, it went out on the radio, so I'd actually done a broadcast within a year of getting my trumpet. That's amazing really, because I'd only been playing a few months, and my brother was still in short trousers.

'We'd learned *Hotter Than That* off the record. It's not the easiest of things. I didn't do the vocal chorus, which is really sophisticated, singing twelve bars of three four over nine bars of four four. We just played the tune and I played a solo on it. My brother was pretty advanced in those days, for someone about thirteen years old.'[19]

Later that same summer, Ian and his younger brother were often to be found playing at jam sessions in Darlington, and even as far afield as Newcastle. And that is where their playing really took off after September that same year, when Ian left school and started life as an undergraduate.

2 from king's college to queen's commission

Today the Armstrong College campus, built in 1871, is at the heart of the University of Newcastle upon Tyne, but in 1952, when Ian began his university career there, its buildings formed the major part of King's College, which had been founded in 1937 as a division of Durham University. For almost thirty years from that foundation, the University of Durham operated a split-site federal system, with its several colleges in the city of Durham itself constituting one half of the federation, and King's in Newcastle being the other.

Ian had family ties to both sections of the University, his great grandfather having been principal of St. Bede College in Durham, whereas his grandfather, Henry Carr, had read for his BSc at Armstrong College, before it was renamed King's. It was decided in the family that he ought to try initially for a place at Bede. 'It was,' recalled Ian, 'a little bit posher.'[1] Nowadays, the college is amalgamated with the former women's teacher training college of St. Hild, but in the 1950s, the stern Victorian gothic of St. Bede's main block stood on its own in the lively thoroughfare of Gilesgate, near a marble factory, and close to the historic home of the Durham Light Infantry. The little lane that ran past the campus is still known as Bedebank. Today, almost all the surrounding buildings have gone, and the college itself has survived a ruthless programme of road improvement only because it stood far enough back not to be flattened when the A690 was made into a dual carriageway and Gilesgate split into two halves by a vast roundabout.

However all this was in the future when Ian's father drove him to Durham for the interview with the college principal, Canon Brigstock. 'My father said, "Make sure you say to the principal that your great grandfather sat in the chair he's sitting in!"' Ian remembers. 'But I couldn't bring myself to say that.'[2] Nevertheless, standing stiff in his best suit, Ian was ushered in to the very room where his great grandfather had presided over the college many years before. Canon Brigstock was, as earlier generations of the Carr family had been, a deeply religious man, and so when the principal read out a section of Ian's headmaster's report, the would-be student knew his goose was cooked as far as this application was concerned.

'He has the reputation for being able to play dance music fairly well,' ran the commentary. Ian immediately saw red. Not only did the report apparently fail to mention his talent for English literature, but his headmaster had confused dance music, which was very *infra dig*, with the *bona fide* jazz that Ian and Mike were trying to play. What is more, dance music in any form was usually anathema to gentlemen of the cloth in early 1950s England. 'Christ, that was the wrong thing to say!' he blurted out.

The Canon smiled knowingly, but, as Ian was to reflect whenever he later thought about the incident, 'He wasn't thinking smiles. He was offended because I'd said, "Christ!" in front of him.' In due course, a formal letter of rejection arrived.[3]

As things turned out this was just as well, because Ian's experience at King's could not have been more different. Instead of being seen by the principal, he was interviewed by Professor John Butt, who was head of the English department. The questions were all about literature, and Ian's enthusiasm obviously shone through, because he was promptly offered a place to read English, (with the proviso that along with his studies, he had to take an advanced course in Latin, which he had given up at sixteen). It was an extremely good moment for a would-be student of this particular subject to be enrolled in this particular college. The English literature department at King's in the early 1950s consisted of an exceptional group of scholars, and in addition to Professor 'Twickenham' Butt, who was already recognised as Britain's leading authority on the poems of Alexander Pope, the eminent critic Frank Kermode was also among the tutors, before his move to Cambridge. For the next three years, Ian would immerse himself in the study of literature, with subsidiary courses in ethics, as well as art and architecture.

Once again, fate took a hand, and just as Arnold Snodgrass had fostered Ian's early interest in Shakespeare and Pope, he now found a literary mentor in the form of his tutor Peter Ure. Author of several books on Yeats, and a celebrated Shakespearean text editor, Ure transferred his passions to Ian, notably a love of Yeats, which was to inspire compositions such as *Crazy Jane* on the Rendell-Carr *Phase III* album. As well as developing Ian's thirst for literary exploration, Ure encouraged Ian's own ambitions as a writer, criticising his poetry, and often inviting him over to his house for a glass of beer or sherry, to discuss his latest work.

This was no matter of mere favouritism, because not long into his college career, Ian had become literary editor of *Northerner*, the university magazine, and was not only writing his own stories, articles and poems for its pages, but encouraging his contemporaries to do so as well. Among them were Norman Sherry, later to become famous as the biographer of Joseph Conrad and Graham Greene, and the poet Stanley Broderick. Several cover designs were by the artist Ian Stephenson, who was studying at the affiliated King Edward VII Art School, from where he went on to become a founder member of the Durham University fine art department.

In between editing the literary pages of the magazine, and proposing motions for the debating society such as 'Poetry is the Harlot of the Arts', Ian also threw himself into a lively correspondence with other up-and-coming writers. These included the poet Christopher Logue, some eight years older than Ian, who was living in Paris, and who sent over copies of journals such as *Points* or *Merlin*, which included new work by Samuel Beckett and other expatriate writers. Never one to mince his words, Logue produced an apoplectic response to an edition of *Northerner* that Ian sent him in return, which included several pieces by Stanley Broderick. 'Get hold of Broderick, this slimy lump of fossilised dog vomit, take him by one of his loose ears, put him on a raft with a half-northwesterly gale, and shove him out to sea,' ran the letter.[4]

Other students involved in the literary sphere of college included the playwrights Stanley Eveling and David Mercer. King's always retained strong local links with Newcastle, but Eveling recalled that in common with many locals, he went there, 'not because it was the best place for me to go, but because that was where we went...Geordies of the vintage and class to which I was tethered never supposed that they would become anything. The best we could manage was a dodge and a wheeze, a way of not being noticed while we could earn ourselves a crust and do very little.'[5] Eveling was one of the generation of returning servicemen who, during the immediate postwar period, were guaranteed a university place assuming they held the minimum qualifications. In his view and that of many Geordies who had taken the King's shilling, it was better to be paid a pittance of a grant to read books for three years than to go into the kind of dead-end job that seemed to be the lot of most working-class Novocastrians. The presence of many such ex-servicemen, intermingled with a new university intake straight from school, gave the student population a more than usually diverse mix of age and experience.

Yet, as Ian's contemporary, the former dental student Richard Cook recalls, in practical matters, the shadow of World War Two still lay long over everyday life. Nothing had yet happened to give this new decade, the 1950s, a character and individuality of its own. 'It seemed to belong to or be an afterthought of the Forties,' he wrote. 'A pinched and mean time. There was still food rationing, though flour, eggs, soap, milk and clothes had been de-controlled.'[6] With beer at one shilling and sixpence a pint (seven and a half pence in today's money), a student could live a social life of a sort, but only up until 10 pm. when the strict licensing hours ordered all bars and pubs to close.

With everything shut, there was not much to do but go back to one's lodgings and read. At first, Ian found the transition from the more ordered life of school quite difficult. 'It was a terrible change,' he maintains, 'because you were just left to your own devices. I'd never been on my own so much.'[7] Being alone in Newcastle after the open countryside of Gainford was also quite a shock. In Eveling's memorable description: 'The grass was having a rotten time and mostly trampled down and covered with bits of other things. The rooms we were stuffed into were having a hard time with their bits of hard time furniture, chairs with broken legs, beds with their damp, grey flock mattresses. Even the trees were down to their last black branches.'[8]

Ian did not have rooms in college, but lived in digs in a house in town, not too far away from his studies. Having led the comfortable life of a public school boy, and coming from the country, his main memory of moving to the city is the total contrast of being constantly impoverished throughout his time at University. 'Although I got a grant,' he confirms, 'it was not a very large one, and my father was supposed to top it up. But he never did, or hardly ever. I remember one day, that first winter, cycling through the snow to his office and confronting him.

'"Look, you have to give me some money!" I said. And he did, but only a fiver or so, to tide me over. I was really hard up, and yet when I pawned the watch he'd given me for passing my School Certificate, he was really shocked. Consequently, I always had to take vacation jobs between each term, working in a tobacco warehouse and for other local firms.'[9]

Although Ian had been a naturally athletic schoolboy, competing in running, jumping and boxing events, it would have been hard to discern this from the appearance he fostered as a student. 'I was cultivating long hair, ragged clothes, not eating enough and smoking myself to death,' he remembered, somewhat wryly. But these affectations were nothing compared to his idea of carrying around a shooting stick – a sort of portable seat on a spike – much used by those who followed field sports. 'That's a bit Freudian, isn't it,' remarked Norman Sherry, already a man of the world, who had been in Burma with the army, and was a few years older than Ian. Despite never having heard of Freud, Ian laughed off the remark, and became fast friends with Sherry, sharing his delight in Joseph Conrad, and keeping in touch in later years as the older man's career took him eventually to become Distinguished Professor of Literature at San Antonio University in Texas.

'He was one Geordie of impeccable working class credentials who became quite famous,' remembered Eveling. 'He was very small, with a large black moustache.'[10]

Sherry, like Ian, was involved in a multitude of extra-curricular activities, but it dawned on both of them as the Easter vacation of their

Three Novocastrian intellectuals in London: (l to r) Ian, Norman Sherry, Gerald Laing. (Ian Carr)

final year began that they would have to do some frantic last-minute revision. There were to be nine three hour papers in the final examinations, and Ian's tutor had predicted he would get a 2-1. Owing to the late start of his final spurt of serious work, he only managed a 2-2, but at the same time Sherry, widely regarded as one of the year's most brilliant students, only managed a 2-1, instead of the expected first class honours. To Sherry's chagrin, his fiancée, Sylvia, achieved the highest first class mark for ten years.

Being immersed in English literature, and covering everything from Anglo-Saxon to Middle-English, novels of all ages, and poetry from Shakespeare to Yeats, left a lasting impression on Ian. But his university years were also memorable to him for two entirely different reasons. Firstly, with the help of a girl called Edith, he discovered sex, and the two of them conducted a steamy affair. Ian's passion was so great that he cycled the length of Hadrian's wall to see her one vacation, sleeping in a barn on his way to her parents' home at Whitehaven in Cumbria, which was more than seventy-five miles from Newcastle.

Secondly, he was able to indulge in his equally fervent passion for jazz, and to play with a number of like-minded enthusiasts in what amounted to his first proper group.

To most people in Britain in the early 1950s, jazz, if it meant anything at all, was the sound of Humphrey Lyttelton and George Webb's rugged revivalism, or the somewhat suaver Dixieland presented by the BBC on Mark White's *Jazz Club*. Indeed, King's College boasted its own 'trad' band. Nationally, and particularly in London, the impact of Charlie Parker, Dizzy Gillespie and Thelonious Monk had been felt and appreciated by a few cognoscenti, but was hardly common knowledge. Writing about discs by Lee Konitz and Frank Rosolino for the *Northerner*, Ian might have been reviewing Icelandic folk music, for all the day-to-day impact it had on the majority of his fellow students. Consequently, Ian, and his brother, who — although he was not yet a student — made every effort to be around and about among the student community in Newcastle when he was not at school, cast about as widely as possible to find some kindred spirits.

They were immediately fortunate in recruiting a rhythm section. Eric Beetham, from the school of dentistry, played competent drums, and John Udy, who had been evacuated to Canada during the war to attend the same school as Oscar Peterson, before returning to Newcastle to read town and country planning, was a fine bassist. The quintet was rounded out by Don Armstrong, who was not a student at King's, but who played clarinet and tenor saxophone. The band appeared in some of the university revues, and at rag week, where their bebop playing was regarded as another of the crazy student stunts for fundraising.

It seems remarkable, but despite only three of its members being students at the college, the quintet actually represented King's in the annual national inter-university jazz band competition, which in 1954 was held at Liverpool. Ian recalls: 'We were the only modern group, and so we couldn't really compete, because everyone else was playing trad. Nevertheless, we played. We brought the house down. A fellow student from Newcastle, Adrian Henri, who later became one of the "Liverpool poets" was there with his purple shirt and his suede shoes, [and got] so excited that he was hanging by his hands from the theatre balcony, waggling his feet and kicking his legs about excitedly in time to the music. That's how unusual modern jazz was. People call today's music modern jazz, it's not modern, it's contemporary. Modern jazz was bebop and so on. That's the way it was.'[11]

Compared to the burgeoning nightlife of the Newcastle to which Ian returned in the 1960s, there were no jazz clubs or coffee bars with live music during his undergraduate years. Playing was mainly a hobby and the opportunities for public performance were few. There were, however, occasional visits by bands from elsewhere, during which Ian and Mike could hear how other Britons were tackling the modern repertoire. 'Mostly the live things you heard were trad,' recalls Ian, 'but when I was in college, Tubby Hayes came up, and Ronnie Scott. I know Tony Crombie came up. It was the Tubby Hayes nine-piece band with Dave Usden on trumpet, who died in the 70s. And so we saw that. We knew about Don Rendell, and we saw Don [as it was] getting into the 50s.'[12]

Having graduated and then taken an extra year to qualify as a teacher, Ian was rudely jolted out of the Bohemian life he had espoused as a student when he was called up for his National Service in September 1956. Looking back on it, Ian is sure that this was entirely beneficial to him. His literary output was, he admitted, 'a few stricken verses about a horrific universe, seen through the eyes of a drunken, ill-informed, underfed undergraduate.'[13]

Whether it was the army's talent for spotting potential leaders, or simply its insistence of physical and mental fitness, or the way that when its men are thrown together in artificial conditions they forge strong friendships, the army was to be one of the three main formative influences on the young adult Ian Carr. University had been one, with its literary networking, and core of solid reading and aesthetic appreciation. The third was to be a two-year peregrination around Europe at the end of National Service, but in my view, the army was the most significant of the three. It drew out of Ian a basic self-reliance that he was to fall back on again and again during his years of professional bandleading.

'The army was right for me at that time,' he told me, when we discussed this. 'I'd been a student that was deliberately in rags, with long hair, smoking too much, and not being athletic at all, because I'm naturally athletic, (which) was a very foolish thing to do. The army was great...because I had to change my image and everything, and also I made very good friends. I had a lot of confidence. My grandfather had made me feel important. I realise that now. He made me feel really important. And so, (when) I went into the army, I took a commission, and I went into a regiment that was a very great historical regiment. But you had to assert yourself there. Because unless you were the son of a famous father that they knew, they were going to treat you like shit. And the last thing I was going to allow was to be treated like shit.'[14]

This bald summing-up rather commutes a sequence of events. Ian's initial training was as an ordinary recruit, at Strensall, Yorkshire. It was only after six weeks of basic training, with his newly close-cropped hair, constant physical exercise, weapons drill, and cheek-by-jowl living, that Ian was sent to Aldershot for the War Office Selection Board. Having passed, there followed a four-month period of officer training at Eaton Hall, near Chester, the family estate of the Dukes of Westminster. Hopeless, or hapless, at drill, and described more times than he cared to remember by his RSM as 'a long streak of piss,' Ian was finally passed out as an officer. His eventual success may have had a lot to do with a lecture he was forced to give as part of his training, and for which he elected to speak on the subject of 'morale'. Finding the army's basic notes on the subject risible, he delivered a lecture that systematically took apart the official documentation and offered some more constructive definitions.

Now a second lieutenant, Ian elected to join either the Durham Light Infantry, or the Royal Northumberland Fusiliers, both regiments which in those days retained strong connections to the areas where he had grown up and been educated. His posting turned out to be to the latter, who were on a tour of duty in Ulster, at the Palace Barracks, Belfast, during the very early post-war period of 'the troubles'. In his new uniform, a single pip on each shoulder, and travelling for the first time on a first-class ticket, Ian embarked on the boat train:

'When the adjutant met me off the boat, he quizzed me all the way about important Novocastrians I might know, and every query drew a blank. Then he became deeply suspicious, and he said, "Well I hope you've got decent headgear, and not one of those fucking silly little corduroy caps." Which was exactly what I had.

'So I said, "Of course, not!" And I threw it away as soon as I could, and got a trilby.

'He took me without much ceremony to the officers' quarters. I was shown my room, and told to come down to the anteroom at twelve-thirty, before lunch. So I came down and opened the door, and it was like tearing the scab off a wound. The room was full of cigarette smoke, and the snarl of genteel conversation, of men languidly holding gins and tonics, purring away. I stood there, and I was ignored. Really, I was not used to that, ever. So I saw some subalterns standing by the fire, and I just went straight up to them and said, "Hello, I'm Ian Carr, who are you?" And Gerald Laing was there, (who became my great friend – my greatest friend actually) and he was shocked that anyone would just do that. It was so beyond the protocol. It was so wrong. But he admired it. So we were friends from day one, and that helped. He looked a very unprepossessing guy. He looked to me toffee-nosed, snobbish. He had a Dachshund in his arm, and I thought, "Oh, God. Bloody typical."'[15]

Later, seated next to Laing at dinner, where it is forbidden to talk shop until after the loyal toast, Ian heard him indulge in a long witty monologue about Winnie the Pooh, keeping the junior officers around him in fits of laughter instead of their usual taciturn silence.

The ice broken in this dramatic way, Ian became a platoon commander in X Company, commanded by Major Freddie Ward, who became his military mentor in the transition from a raw recruit to an effective officer. He was forced to find the quick and effective route to every decision concerning the thirty men in his charge, and in the six months or so before the unit was posted to Germany, Ian described himself as typifying the new subaltern: 'ignorant, avidly curious, desperate to prove themselves and greedy for experience.'[16] But in addition to mastering the job, patrolling during day and night, crawling around the borderlands looking for IRA terrorists, and the constant training, inspections and weapons practice, some of the most enduring friendships of Ian's life were forged. Among them were John Latimer Smith, later to become his first publisher, and, of course, Gerald Laing.

'We really got to know each other one night when Ian was duty officer and had to sleep on a camp bed in the orderly room,' recalls Laing. 'We started talking then, and we haven't really stopped since. I was a regular and he was a national serviceman, but that wasn't a barrier between us. I wanted out of the boring box, and what Ian fed me, which helped immensely, was a reading list and an attitude. That attitude is something he's kept faith with all these years, which is that art really exists, that it's something great and tangible. In the photos of those days in the army, he looks almost like a political commissar. In a remarkably short time, Ian had got hold of the situation, and he became very highly respected. What was unique about him in the regiment, was that he was respected for who he was, for himself as a person, not for his soldierliness. This was, I think, a characteristic that helped him immensely as he later emerged into being a jazz musician.'[17]

Ian remembers it a little differently: 'I'm older than him, and I was extremely well-educated...but he had read very little, so I was a source of information about what to read, and things like that. I helped him a lot then. In later life – he's incredibly well-read now – he helped me a lot. Some of my best work was done to accompany his sculptures in an exhibition, and on *Out of the Long Dark* there are four [of those] pieces, particularly the title track, which I don't think I could ever have bettered.'

Laing was a man of passionate enthusiasms. He had earlier been consumed by a devotion to the ballet and still owned a pair of shoes belonging to the dancer Belinda Wright. In Ulster, he had turned his formidable energies to learning to paint. 'Gerry used to go [with me] to get art lessons,' Ian told me. 'We used to go in Belfast to an old man – Boyd Morrison he was called – who'd been part of the Bloomsbury set. And he actually did a drawing of me which I've got in my workroom. In 1957, I think this was, and he said "It's for the frontispiece

Gerald Laing, still Ian's best and oldest friend. (Ian Carr)

of your first book!" It's that kind of drawing. Something like Rupert Brooke...Boyd Morrison. He's dead now of course, long dead.'[18]

Gerald Laing may have later inspired Ian's music, whilst John Latimer Smith was to encourage both his literary and musical endeavours, but there were other officers in the Royal Northumberland Fusiliers who shared Ian's musical passions at the time. 'There's a guy whom I'm still very friendly with now called Derek Buckingham, who ended up as a major, who was [then] a captain or a full subaltern. He played guitar. We had another friend, Peter Adams, who was half Norwegian. He played guitar, [and was] also a captain. We used to have jam sessions in the mess, and when I had to sell my Boston trumpet-cornet to help to pay for the tailor's bill for my dress suit, I used to borrow a cornet from the bandmaster.'[19]

Although several of Ian's colleagues in the officers' mess were aware of his interest in jazz in general and playing the trumpet in particular, his commanding officer, the colonel of the regiment, was unaware of this decadent obsession.

'We had the brigadier for a ceremonial dinner one night,' laughs Ian, 'and the regimental band played behind screens. Nice tunes from the musicals. At the end of the meal the custom was to walk out of the door, walk round to the other door, and languidly stand there listening to the band, looking at it, from the other side of the room. I walked round, and the door was framed by the colonel on one side and the brigadier on the other. When the music stopped, the bandmaster, Mr. Stone, came with a little cushion with a cornet on it between them, and said, "Fancy a blow, sir?"

'So I went in and played *St. Louis Blues*, and the brigadier loved it, so the colonel couldn't say anything. Then the brigadier said, "How about *Tiger Rag*?" and things like that. The colonel didn't say much at all.

'A few days later I got an invitation to dinner at the colonel's. He wanted to brainwash me, because I was supposed to be the evil influence on the subalterns, making them rebel. They weren't very rebellious. Or I was thought to be the evil influence on Gerald, who was already fed up with the army. He'd had enough. He's got a military tradition. His father was in the regiment before he was, but actually he wanted to get out. So I went to dine with the colonel.

'He just tried to rile me, saying he thought we should bring back flogging, and then at one point he said, "Well, I don't think an officer and a gentleman plays the trumpet." I can't remember exactly what I replied, but I might have said "I feel I agree with you" or something like that.'[20]

Ian had developed sufficient *sang froid* in his few short months in the army not to rise to the bait, but meanwhile Laing's behaviour was starting to become decidedly odd as his dissatisfaction with the regiment grew. He once ran round the mess barking like a dog, even nipping at the adjutant's ankles. On another occasion he rode a motorbike into the building, revving his engine close to a desk where Ian was working, and filling the place with exhaust fumes. Fortunately the sojourn in Ulster was almost at and end, and in November 1957, the regiment set off for a new posting to Germany. This was to have a beneficial effect on Gerald and Ian's lives in general, on their artistic endeavours, and on their friendship, but first there was the logistical question of getting the men and their families moved across the channel.

'I was left in charge of the rear party for that, which was a very responsible command,' Ian remembers. 'I had to bring them all over – men, women and children. One colonel called John Webb, thanked me profusely for bringing over his wife and kids. And my platoon sergeant, Gipsy Smith, was so emotional he wept, when I brought his people over.'[21]

In Germany, Gerald Laing went for more painting lessons from a local German artist, and Ian used to go too. Their cultural horizons were broadened as a result, which was not true of the assistant adjutant, for whom the words 'artist' and 'homosexual' were interchangeable. He, in common with other members of the mess, was convinced that Ian's wayward influence was having a bad effect on Laing, and that his artistic endeavours were to be stamped out at all costs. 'I've got nothing against art, but queers are bad!...I mean it!...Disgusting!' railed the adjutant.[22]

In due course Ian was to leave the army before Laing, following a skiing accident during a winter warfare course at Winterburg. After convalescence in hospital in Münster, he returned to his B.A.O.R. base, and wrote to the War Office asking to be demobilised in Germany. His request was granted at the start of September 1958, and with his two years' statutory service under his belt, Ian left the army on a train to Paris for a further two years of itinerant wandering. Being released from institutional life for the first time since he had started school was a shock to his system, and he reacted by rebelling and dropping out from society.

Nevertheless, his army service had sown some seeds for his future life in jazz which should not be underestimated. Not least was the fact that in the early 1950s, the Ministry of Labour and Musicians' Union were still keeping American jazz musicians out of Britain, except on the basis of exchange work permits. The same was not true of Germany, however, which had a thirst for American culture in the postwar years, and welcomed U.S. jazz musicians with open arms. His army service, and particularly the relatively free coming and going allowed to officers as opposed to other ranks, meant that Ian could take every opportunity to seek out and hear jazz played by the men and women who had created it.

'We saw Lionel Hampton there, and various things like that,' he recalled. 'And we even went to one show where there were some girl dancers, plus a pianist who was the first to learn *Rhapsody in Blue* by ear in New York. He was the first guy to get it. His name was Charlie Bourne and because they were pretty, we brought the girls back to the officers' mess, but I got Charlie Bourne to stay the night.[23] I got him a room in the mess, and he had breakfast. He had some kind of weird religion. He had bacon and eggs and he said, "See those bacon and eggs? That's God right there." He was an incredible stride piano player, a white man, with a really good piano style.

'But my introduction to modernism had been the Modern Jazz Quartet when I was at college. We tried to play cool jazz, and theirs was the kind of jazz we were trying to play. God knows what it sounded like!...but I didn't hear very much cool jazz in Germany with my contemporaries. It was more the swing thing. Of course, to see Lionel Hampton live was a hell of an experience.

'His was one of the first if not the first big name American bands that I saw in the flesh. And the thing was that he played fantastically. He was a swing player, but he was a modernist too. He's timeless, really, Hampton. And he was such an enthusiast. He had reinforced tom-toms, and he used to jump on them and dance on them at some point. Then at the end, by which time he'd already done an encore with the band, the audience were still crazy for the music, so he sent the band off, and just with the rhythm section he played another half an hour...and it was really staggeringly good. Really interesting. It made an impact on me in Germany.'[24]

3 on the bum

The army Land Rover bounced over the German cobbles *en route* to the railway station. A corporal was driving Lieutenant Carr there for the last time, after he had said his farewells to his men and the officers' mess and was heading for Paris and freedom. The vehicle stopped and as Ian swung himself down, the corporal set down his suitcase. With a perfunctory nod, he turned and was gone. Ian bent to pick up the case, but as he did so, a gloved hand closed over his, prised his fingers away and hoisted up the bag.

It was Major Gerry Rickman, the senior colleague to whom Ian had acted as assistant in the months following his accident, who had come down especially to see Ian off. Rickman carried the bag over to the platform, and saw Ian onto the train.

It was a touching farewell to an army career that had combined plenty of pointless exercise with a practical training in self-containment, prompt decision-making, and getting on with other people. As I have suggested, it was to be a great resource for Ian in the years to come, but that is not how it seemed to him at the time.

Describing his army career, Ian likes to use a metaphor that concerns an old man who farmed on the opposite shore of the Tees from Gainford. There was no bridge from his farm to the village, except for a high trestle structure that carried a mineral railway line from one tall bank to the other. The river ran fast and shallow many feet below, with plenty of dangerous rocky rapids, and there was only a tiny one foot-high barrier between the tracks and the sheer drop. Every night, the old farmer used to walk across this railway bridge to have a drink in the village pub.

After a pint or two, the old man would rant and rave and blaspheme, until he was roaring drunk. How on earth, wondered his fellow drinkers, did the old fellow ever get back across the bridge? One night, two of the regulars decided to follow him. They watched as the old man struggled up the embankment to the railway line. Then they looked on in astonishment as he fell to his knees and began to crawl across the bridge, a sleeper at a time. As he reached the first sleeper, he muttered, 'The Lord's good!', and as his hand stretched to the next, he muttered just as strongly 'But the Devil's not so bad!' And so it went on, a sleeper at a time, until he was safely across. Then he turned to where the two watchers had concealed themselves and yelled back across the water, 'And now you can both go to hell!'

'I think of that as being exactly like my time in the army,' says Ian. 'For two years I'd been walking a tightrope between what I wanted to do and what other people wanted me to do. Now, as I left on the train for France, they could all go to hell!'[1]

When he arrived in Paris, Ian's rusty School Certificate French was only just up to the job of communicating. As he stayed on in France, he became fluent, but his early days were quite tough. In addition, he had just £30 in the world, after leaving the army, and he made considerable inroads into that on his first night, when the 'modest' hotel an army friend had recommended turned out to be very expensive.

'That first night, I was exhausted, and worried and frightened, because actually I wasn't very brave. It had taken all my nerve to go on the bum,' he remembers. Soon, he found himself a far cheaper hotel, the Providence, which cost 400 old francs, or around eight shillings, a night, but not before his first night's sleep in the French capital had been shattered by the noisy lovemaking of a couple in a room across the courtyard from the expensive hotel. Looking out of his top-floor window, Ian discovered that they were performing in full view of their neighbours, and leaving nothing to the imagination: 'I thought, bloody hell! This must be what it's like every day in Paris!'[2]

Although very few days lived up to the erotic excitement and frustration of that first night, Ian did quickly get to meet some of the characters who were living on the fringes of the city's literary and Bohemian circles. Notable among those who became his friends were the American poet Piero Heliczer and his girlfriend Olivia d'Hauleville. They made a living selling copies of the *Paris Review* to crowds in fashionable left bank cafés, while writing experimental poetry and experiencing the city's climate of free love. Their circle also included the ex-GI writer Kenneth Tindall and his Norwegian girlfriend Tove, James and Gloria Jones, Allen Ginsberg, Gregory Corso and William Burroughs.[3] 'I met them on the street,' recalls Ian, 'and we became very friendly. Heliczer was a strange little guy, but very nice, and Olivia wrote poetry under the name of 'Om'. I was writing poetry again at the time myself, trying once again to do literary things.'[4]

To finance himself, Ian set up as a freelance teacher of English, and for a few weeks he managed a hand-to-mouth existence, soaking in the atmosphere of the city. In particular there was the opportunity to hear jazz – or at least there would have been if one had the money to pay the cover charges at the various clubs dotted around Paris. Most famous, and presenting well-known American guests, was Le Chat Qui Pêche just off the Rue de la Huchette.

'I had no money, of course, so I stood outside the door, and kept pushing it open to listen,' recalls Ian. 'Some guy just inside kept shutting it again, until another man came and stood beside me and started pushing it open with me. I thought, "This is a good guy, somebody like me!" So we became friends. He was the Colombian abstract painter Alberto Gutiérrez, who is now very well-known and whom I remained in touch with. At that time he was a qualified doctor who had gone on the bum a bit like me, although he was a rather posher bum than I was.'[5]

It was Gutiérrez who helped Ian fund his move from Paris at the end of the month, after he had finally realised he could not live on air, and had gone to see the assistant director of education about a job as an English language teaching assistant. After all, he was a qualified teacher and had just finished two years as an army officer, so he appeared to be an ideal recruit. As it turned out, M. Renard, in the French education department, was wondering what to do about several cancellations about which he had just been notified as the schools and colleges returned to work that September. So he simply suggested to Ian that he choose the place he would most like to go, from the list of vacancies. Ian selected Nice, because it was not only the best paid, but a real contrast from England, Belfast and Westphalia, where Ian had spent all of his life so far. 'It paid 62,000 old francs a month,' he noted. 'My board and lodging for a month was 11,000. So in other words, I got to live in a room in the college, had fantastic food, and received 51,000 francs a month to play with.'[6]

The college was L'école des Instituteurs, a teacher training establishment, and Ian's job was to give twelve hours of conversation classes per week. He saw the job as not just teaching English but 'teaching England', in other words conveying ideas about topics of interest and importance in Britain that would make good talking points. Bringing his military diligence and responsibility to the job, Ian turned it into a success, becoming popular with the Principal because of his application to the task. He also organised a jazz appreciation group and put on the occasional concert as well. 'I was interested in getting involved, because I was learning French at the same time,' he points out. 'At first my students would say things in French that I didn't understand, and they would laugh about it, which was bloody irritating. But soon I knew what they were saying, and it was a two-way process.'[7]

The college was situated close to the Rue Stephen Liegeard, in the higher reaches of the city, around three kilometres from the town centre and the coast, and overlooking a serene inland valley in the foothills of the Alpes Maritimes. There was a brightness about the place and an abundant vegetation that contrasted dramatically with the grubby browns and greens of Westphalia. As the cockerels crowed in the mornings from the smallholdings in the valley, the smell of fresh bread and coffee was in the air, and the light twinkled on the establishment's ultimate luxury, a swimming pool. Ian organised his formal teaching so that his twelve hours were crammed into two days, leaving him the rest of the week free. And to bolster his flagging finances, he took some private pupils as well. One, a businessman, paid him in meals, taking Ian to every different restaurant in the area so that he could experience French cuisine at its best. Another, a lady called Madame Jeannin, treated Ian like a second son, and invited his parents to stay with her when they came out to France on a short visit. When he visited the city over twenty years later with the United Jazz and Rock Ensemble, Ian called on her, and she recognised him immediately. They went out for lunch and thereafter remained close correspondents until her death in the late 1980s.

Ian's most memorable visitor in 1958, however, was Gerald Laing, who was still in the army, and who came down for a few days on a pass. Lured South by Ian's accounts of the place, Laing arrived with high hopes of a romantic painting holiday, filled with wine, women and song, In the event, it poured with rain, and apart from a vain attempt to set up his easel in a downpour, Laing spent the time eating and drinking voraciously, and introducing Ian to the whores of the Rue de France. Ian's first experience of professional sex was not helped by his formal teacher's attire of tweed jacket and cavalry twill trousers, which he felt made an already somewhat embarrassing and awkward experience the more so. Nevertheless, he was to visit the street again from time to time, in between more innocent flings with local girls.

'Ian had wangled me a temporary job teaching English at the École,' recalled Laing, 'which just about paid for my lodging in return for offering some English conversation. I rather liked the class because it was full of French women, but it was somewhat disastrous educationally because I was in the throes of discovering T.S. Eliot. All my class really wanted to know was how to say "Where's the station?" But I was offering them a critical commentary on *The Waste Land*!'[8]

During his visit, Laing lodged close to the college with a peasant woman called Madame Couvin, who also owned and operated an olive press. She let him stay for a modest rent, and was generally very kind, but although she was still alive when Ian returned to Nice in the late 1970s, she failed to remember their acquaintanceship from the 1950s.

One extraordinary experience during Ian's time in Nice was his visit to the writer W. Somerset Maugham at the Villa Mauresque at Cap Ferrat, the rocky promontary to the East of the city. One of Ian's students was writing a thesis on Maugham, whose books Ian had read extensively during his student years. Could Ian, perhaps, help his student meet the great man?

Ian's personal interest in writing short stories was such that he had his own reasons for wanting to meet one of the finest literary miniaturists of the age, and so he wrote to the author, requesting a meeting. Back came a reply, with a note saying that Maugham would be delighted to meet both teacher and student, and that if they cared to present themselves at the bridge that led across to the Cap Ferrat, his car would pick them up and bring them to the house. In fact, when the appointed day came, the student failed to turn up, so Ian went on his own, and was received by Alan Searle, Maugham's secretary. 'He was a very civilised man, with grey crinkly hair, a purple sweater and grey flannels,' recalls Ian.

In the house were remarkable paintings and art treasures. A picture of a woman from Picasso's blue period hung in the hallway and elsewhere were various examples by Gaugin and other French masters. Searle ushered Ian into the drawing room, which he described as follows:

> It was all shades of brown, including Maugham, who was in it, because he was shades of brown as well. He was very sunburned, his hair was sandy, and even when he smiled, his teeth were brown. I didn't see him until he moved. From his books I'd got the impression that he would pounce on you, but he wan't like that at all. Very gentle, with a terrible stammer. I felt like finishing his sentences for him. We had a long conversation, and then he offered me 'whisky on the rocks', which was not an expression I knew, even from the army. It was just scotch and ice, of course, and I felt great sitting there chatting to him over a drink. Then his secretary came in again, and ushered me away, but they asked me to come back at the same time the following week.
>
> I did just that, and more or less the same routine happened, except Searle took me upstairs to show me Maugham's study. It was full of exercise books in which he'd written all his works. The texts were on the right hand side in blue ink and the corrections were on the left-hand facing pages in red. From his desk you could see one of Gaugin's paintings of Tahitian women let into what had once been a window frame. Searle told me the previous visitor to the study had been Winston Churchill, just a few days before. He'd insisted on climbing all the stairs, although Maugham himself stayed downstairs, and at the top, Churchill who was by then in his final years, nearly had a heart attack.

I felt strange being a guest there immediately after him and being taken to see the same things.

Then there was another whisky, and I went home. The following week I came back, and this time Searle took me round the garden, which had a glorious array of plants begind the house. He said, 'Mr. Maugham wants to know why you wear a beard, because you've got such a beautiful face.' That was the moment whe I twigged what was going on. I thought they had invited me because I was an interesting conversationalist, but it wasn't that at all. So I refused their invitation to dinner, and that was that.'[9]

Later, as various biographies of Maugham appeared, it became obvious that Alan Searle was rather more than his secretary, and indeed the author scandalised literary society, already aware of his homosexual predilections, by trying to adopt Searle as his 'son'. Thus, as it turned out, Maugham did not have a very great effect on Ian's ambitions to be a short story writer.

As a postscript to this episode, a few days after his final visit to the Villa, Ian saw Churchill being driven to watch a cycle race on the Promenade des Anglais. Slumped in his seat as his limousine drove behind the crowds, the old statesman sat up poker straight and waved his cigar as soon as he came in sight of the public.

Ian's stay in Nice lasted almost a year, until the college closed for the summer in June 1959. During that time, he comfortably immersed himself in French life and become reasonably proficient at the language. He had also managed to keep abreast of what was going on in the jazz world, because of the insatiable French appetite for the music. One disc, in particular, made a lifelong impression on him.

'I just wandered into a record shop one day on a street that was going down towards the sea,' he recalls, 'and found Miles Davis's record of *Walkin'*. And I thought, "Oh, that's interesting. I'll take it back to the college and have a play." Actually I still find it fascinating to hear, now. I still find it stunning, and still hear new things in it. One of the most interesting is Horace Silver's comping...the way he changes it with the different soloists. When he gets a solo at the end, after all that complexity, his solo is the simplest solo you could ever imagine. It's perfect. And you think, "God, simplicity works". Because after all that incredible brilliance, we don't need any more brilliance. What we need is something that goes straight to the heart and is simple. So that's what I got from it, and it is something that stayed with me in my own music.

'I didn't know of course that these two tracks had been called already classic tracks. Although they're studio albums, the band has the same dynamism as if they're playing live. When I play it [today] to Guildhall students, they can't believe how dynamic it is. Everything counts on those records...What they're playing is two blues – a medium one and a fast one. [The other track recorded at this session on 29 April 1954 was *Blue 'n' Boogie*.] The whole of the tradition of the blues is there. So you've got the blues. You've got the feeling, and at the same time you've got an incredible kind of ecstasy. It's very ecstatic, that music. And you can hear them listening. When one person finishes, the next one picks up on the last phrase usually and goes straight in. When you're in Miles Davis's band, you're very much aware that he's listening to you, because Miles Davis was a great listener. And when he's listening, people are really doing their very utmost. The nice thing is that the climax of both of those tracks is the saxophone solo on *Walkin'* by Lucky Thompson, who was at the height of his powers. It was much clearer to me than Charlie Parker had been a few years earlier...it wasn't until later I really began to understand Charlie Parker.'[10]

The formative influence of this particular session on Ian's own musical development was considerable, and it is undoubtedly also the point which initiated his serious interest in Miles Davis, something that was later to lead to researching and writing his biography of the trumpeter. *Walkin'* is an object lesson in the creation and release of tension, and when I discussed it with the bassist Percy Heath, who played on the disc, he recalled how Lucky Thompson had kept blowing beyond the normal playing time of a single, but that Bob Weinstock, the producer, had kept the tapes rolling despite the timing on his stopwatch, because the tension was building up so well.[11] When I suggested to Ian that it was this element of *Walkin'* in particular that had underpinned much of his own music of the next two decades, he agreed: 'Well, you learn. That's drama, you see. When you're playing a piece and improvising on it, you've got to create and release tension all the time. And when you're preparing a programme, the programme has to do the same thing. You've got to create tension and then release it, or create it in a different way, which is a different kind of tension. You've got to do that all the time. And this is drama. For example, I haven't listened to Oscar Peterson in years, but...the drama of Oscar Peterson's trio is phenomenal. Phenomenal. And it's really cunningly organised. And you can't buy that. That's really important. He plays solo, and then suddenly the rhythm section comes in, ...and it's really terrific!'[12]

During his last weeks in the army, Ian had acquired a trumpet from a fellow soldier, and begun practising again. Consequently in Nice, with his £15 Boosey and Hawkes instrument in hand, he soon hooked up with a pianist in the city who'd previously worked with Chet Baker. Together, they jammed regularly, and ended up playing quite a lot of sessions. There, and later in Italy during the final stage of his travels, Ian attempted quite complex music, learning all the time. 'I was doing it all by ear,' he remembers. 'Somebody showed me the lead sheet of *Oleo* by Sonny Rollins, which I play now from memory, of course, but I couldn't get that ruddy part at all. I could make out what each note was, but I couldn't sight read the rhythms. Now of course, it's all different. But even now – and not only for me – even now things become clearer at certain points in your life.'[13]

Battling to learn complex rhythms, and absorbing lessons from records, Ian had sufficient free time in Nice to draw a lot of things together in his playing in a way that he had not managed to do since university. Ironically, however, it was when he eventually left Nice to join an army friend for a job in a Corsican holiday camp, that he ended up becoming a professional trumpeter for the very first time.

As soon as he arrived by boat from Nice at Calvi, on the northwest corner of Corsica, Ian found that the summer job he was supposed to get had fallen through. For a few days, he slept rough, helped out by a loan from his friend, until he landed a job as a barman at the Club Olympique at Pinède, just along the coast from Calvi. The club still exists today, with its seaside bungalows, its tennis courts and beaches for windsurfing and sailing. In the 1950s, however, it was a hotbed of after-hours excitement, 'a rare and raving place where anything could happen', as Ian describes it.[14] A jazz band played every night for dancers, featuring a black percussionist called Armani, together with trumpet, saxophone, piano, bass and drums. One night, the drummer went berserk, and after running to the front of the stage and exposing himself to the crowd, he began hitting his drums so maniacally that the curtain swiftly came down and he was carried off. Fortunately the band's trumpeter doubled on drums, so he took over at once for the next set, and Ian was immediately drafted in to play trumpet.

Hence, in July 1959, in the unlikely setting of a Corsican holiday village, Ian became a professional jazz musician for the first time.

He got on well with the rest of the band, and his playing developed accordingly. But now he was playing for a living, and being a man who did nothing by halves, he wanted as many opportunities to blow as possible. His fellow musicians – already seasoned professionals – couldn't understand it, and they remonstrated with him that both they, and the Club Olympique, would prefer it if he worked exclusively for them.

This was impossible for Ian, once the latent musical creativity in him had been released. He found that there was a *manouche* guitarist, Etienne 'Sarane' Ferret – a cousin of Django Reinhardt, and a member of the famous *gitane* Ferré family – playing at another club a little further up the coast, and after his own job was over, he took off there every night to sit in. For a few weeks, this carried on, but the rest of the Club Olympique band with whom Ian worked complained more and more, so he decided the only thing to do was to leave the group.

Meanwhile, his social life on Corsica had taken a turn for the better. Playing in the evenings left him free to be out and about in the daytime, and he made friends with the Australian painter Malcolm Hawsley and his wife, Shirley Deane, who was a writer. Through them he met the Australian poet David Reece. The Hawsleys had a proper sea-going yacht, the *Jack London*, which had all its cabins faired in below decks, a sleek racing line and a wooden exterior finish. Reece was a harsh but fair critic of Ian's efforts at poetry, and the four of them endlessly discussed the creative muse. Ian believes that it was their hard-nosed blunt Australian attitude, and their somewhat swashbuckling approach to the sea, that helped him shed a lot of his British inhibitions and shyness. His reward was to become a featured character in the book that Shirley Deane wrote about the period.[15]

Then, the yachtsman Eric Hesselberg, who had been Thor Heyerdahl's navigator on the Kon-Tiki expedition, arrived in the harbour at Calvi, looking for crew. After returning to Norway from his expedition with Heyerdahl, Hesselberg had built his own motor-sail yacht, *Tiki*, and brought her down to the Mediterranean through the canals of France. Ian remembers her as rather high out of the water, and prone to rolling in bad weather, but a good seaworthy vessel.

Ian himself had sailed in the army. As a forces member of the Belfast Yacht Club he had done some ocean racing around the Irish coast, and he had kept up his skills on the lakes of Germany after his posting to the Rhine. Consequently he accepted the offer of a job as crewman, and set off with Hesselberg and his Swedish girlfriend, to sail round the Mediterranean. Being a celebrity, and the author of the book *Kon-Tiki and I*, Hesselberg not only had enough royalty income to finance his nomadic life, but he had a constant stream of visitors. He kept a copy of the Heyerdahl movie on board to show to interested audiences wherever he landed, as a way of making a small additional income.

Hesselberg was an amateur guitarist, and so he and Ian played together to while away some of their longer voyages, and they also tried their hand at jointly writing a book. Hesselberg was a fascinating character, having spied for the Allies during World War Two, and he was a very experienced sailor, looking older than his forty five years, with a balding pate, long grey hair and beard, and a vast six-foot-four frame.

A few days after Ian joined him, they set sail for Italy, but the Mistral, which was blowing hard, forced them to put in to Macinaggio on the north-eastern tip of Corsica, where they remained weather-bound for a fortnight. Trying to cross the Ligurian Sea was not straightforward and once again weather forced them to put in to port, this time on the prison island of Pianosa, where the convict population was distinguished from the civilian islanders by its white uniforms. Another two weeks passed and they finally crossed to Italy, and tied up in Livorno, where they stayed put for several months. Ian began to learn Italian from reading the papers and harbourside conversation, and he also met the restauranteur Vincenso Catarsi, at Vada, down the coast to the South, where a band played regularly. Ian jammed with them, and formed a strong friendship with Catarsi, who during the several months Ian was in the area never let him pay for food or drink, and was later to invite the EmCee Five to be his guests and play there to entertain his diners.

As he had done in Nice, Ian began teaching English, this time for the Berlitz school in Livorno, and he spent his spare hours soaking up the literary atmosphere of the place, which was considerable, as not only was it the location for Smollett's tomb, but the town had associations with Byron and Shelley. He put all his remaining energy into writing a novel, and this moved on apace when Hesselberg left Ian in sole charge of the boat for six weeks over Christmas 1959. On Christmas Eve, alone in the boat on the quayside, Ian sang lustily along with the carols on the BBC World Service.

Yet the six weeks without Hesselberg's vital and energetic presence caused Ian to reflect on what he was doing with his life: 'I was trying to be a writer. I wrote a lot of poems, which I still have, and some short stories that I don't think were any good anyway. But I simply wasn't making it as a writer. Nobody published anything that I wrote, and I got fed up with that. I got depressed, and I thought to myself, ''The only honest thing you really do is music. Because you've never seen yourself as a musician. You do it just because you love it. So maybe that's what you should really do.''

'At the time, people were casting aspersions on jazz, and so I wasn't sure whether I should really devote my life to it. I thought about it a lot, and I thought about all the people that I admired and liked. Of course I know far more about them now than I did then, but I thought it was a noble thing to be involved with. I perhaps didn't say noble to myself at that time. I just thought, ''I must get into this more deeply''. My brother had been writing to me all the time, saying he'd got this incredible quartet. He was playing vibes and piano, and he said, ''The trumpet player isn't very keen, so will you come back?" So I decided to come back.'[16]

When a beautiful yacht tied up alongside *Tiki*, its owner in due course introduced himself to Ian, and offered him a job crewing back to Monte Carlo. The newcomer was called Walter Whisker, and his boat had previously belonged to the Hollywood star Tyrone Power. Whisker was a flamboyant character, who took Ian to the races in Pisa where he won his harbour dues on the horses, and as soon as Hesselberg returned, Ian moved to Whisker's yacht, and after some repairs to the engine, they set off. The voyage was eventful, with a few close calls in terms of foul weather, dodgy navigation and Whisker's somewhat casual attitude to mooring, but in the end, Ian got back to southern France, borrowed a few pounds from Madame Jeannin to help with provisions, and caught the train for the long journey back to England. With very few clothes to his name, a ragged cut-down macintosh, and a straggly beard, he was a long way from being the trim army officer who had set out on his travels a couple of years before.

4 stephenson's rocket – the emcee five

Although Mike Carr was just over four and a half years younger than Ian, he was conscripted for his national service at the same time in 1956, being posted to Cyprus with the RAF during the period that Ian and the Royal Northumberland Fusiliers were in Northern Ireland and Germany. Being a keyboard player and already somewhat gregarious, Mike spent much of the spare time during his posting playing jazz with his fellow conscripts. In addition, the British bases in Cyprus received a fair contingent of visiting musicians with whom it was possible to jam after hours. Among those whom Mike remembers meeting at this stage were the trumpeter Kenny Wheeler (who was later to become a friend and colleague of Ian's) and the saxophonist Bobby Wellins. All of this woodshedding during his time in the Air Force did much to develop Mike's playing skills and confidence as a soloist.

Having played together in and around Newcastle during Ian's time at King's College, it was natural that the Carr brothers would want to resume their association in due course, and during their National Service quite a number of letters passed to and fro, between airman and fusilier, talking of when and how they would get together again once they had left the forces. Then, of course, the plan was interrupted when Ian set off on his travels. However Mike, by contrast, returned to Newcastle almost immediately after he was demobbed in 1958. He got himself a day job and set about playing as much jazz as he possibly could during his evenings and weekends. For most of this time, he worked as a sales representative for Mars Bars, and became a local talking point, owing to the fact that he would turn up for gigs in his company van, his set of vibes nestling in a bed of confectionary samples.

Nonetheless, his intense playing experience meant that when, in March 1960, the heavily bearded Ian eventually returned from his time on the bum, Mike had gathered around him a quartet of some of the finest musicians in the North-East. Despite the letters that had passed between the brothers, it was now by no means an automatic assumption that Ian would find a place in the line-up, as this was a tight-knit group with a burgeoning original repertoire, built around the hard bop style pioneered by Clifford Brown, Horace Silver and Art Blakey.

The key to any band's success in those days was to have a regular gig, and the EmCee Four, as Mike's quartet was called, played every Saturday night at the Marimba Coffee House in Newcastle city centre. Unrestricted by pub licensing hours, the Coffee House put on its jazz from midnight to three o'clock the following morning, which had the added advantage that musicians who worked in the city's dance halls were able to play there after they finished their regular jobs at around 11.30 pm.

Originally, when the quartet was formed in 1959, in addition to Mike Carr on piano and vibes, the rest of the line-up consisted of saxophonist Gary Cox, drummer Ronnie Stephenson, and bassist Malcolm Cecil, who moonlighted each week from his military posting at the RAF's Catterick Camp, some fifty miles or so southwards down the A1, to play with the band. Cox and Stephenson had been living in a caravan on a site outside Newcastle, and they first met Cecil quite by chance when he stayed there in another van with the legend 'Bag's Groove' painted on the outside. The quartet's name derived from the combined initials of Mike Carr and Malcolm Cecil.[1] A veteran of Dizzy Reece's band, Cecil was the most experienced of the four. He had worked nationally in the Jazz Couriers with Ronnie Scott and Tubby Hayes, and was a member of the London-based Dill Jones trio immediately prior to his National Service. He was ultimately to become a significant figure in the popular music world, becoming firstly a pioneer of synthesizers, and secondly, after emigrating to the United States in 1967, a long-term colleague of Stevie Wonder.

Following Cecil's discharge from the RAF, from which he returned to his life in London as a freelance bassist, his place in the EmCee Four was taken by John O'Carroll, who, in common with Cox and Stephenson, played with Don Smith's dance band at the Oxford Galleries, meaning that the three of them came to the Marimba well warmed up, and aching to cut loose on playing jazz after an evening of strict tempo ballroom fare. This was the line-up of the EmCee Four at the time when Ian arrived back in the city.[2]

The leading light in establishing professional modern jazz in Newcastle was the entrepreneur Mike Jeffreys. He had been an economics student at King's College, but dropped out of the course in order to spend more and more of his time wheeling and dealing on the local music scene. His particular enthusiasm was for rhythm and blues, and in due course, this led to him becoming the manager of the Animals in September 1963 – the experience he had gained by that time in the clubs and dancehalls in and around Newcastle giving him a sure-footed grasp of the business, such that he did a deal with the Yardbirds' manager, Georgio Gomelsky, to bring that hard-edged rhythm and blues band up to play on his Northern circuit, while the Animals had the run of the Yardbirds' regular Southern gigs. This was a key move in establishing the national success of both bands. Later, in partnership with Chaz Chandler, he was to manage Jimi Hendrix, after the guitarist moved to Britain in the mid-1960s.

But at the start of the decade, all this was in the future. Jeffreys had been running Sunday night traditional jazz sessions in Newcastle for some time (indeed the Animals' vocalist Eric Burdon had begun his musical career as a trad trombonist with the Pagan Jazzmen in some of these very events), and he gradually expanded his activities, with the financial assistance of a Mr. Capstaff, to bring modern jazz to the Marimba on Saturdays. Very shortly after Ian's return to the North-East, Jeffreys found a new venue at what was to become the Downbeat in Carlisle Square, and moved the late night Saturday sessions there. Consequently, it was at the Downbeat that Ian took his chances to try and join the band.

In Mike Carr's opinion, Ian still had a long way to develop in order to reach the standard of the others, because even though he had played occasionally in Corsica, Italy and France, he lacked the solid, constant experience that Mike had built up during and after his National Service, and he had yet to benefit from the positive input of Gary Cox and Ronnie Stephenson, both of whom had taken Mike's musical education in hand.

'I'd learned a lot from Malcolm Cecil,' Mike recalls, 'and from Gary Cox as well, because both of them knew a lot about chord changes and harmonies. It brought me up musically, so to speak, playing with them. But when Ian arrived, he wasn't fluent. He didn't know the changes to a lot of what we played.'[3]

But what Ian lacked in experience, he made up for in enthusiasm and commitment. He recognised that what he was hearing in Newcastle was easily on a par with the best of what he had heard in Europe, and he desperately wanted to be a part of it. 'They told me,' he laughed, 'as soon as I could play the theme of Clifford Brown's *Joyspring*, I could join the group, thus making it a quintet. I soon managed that, and so began one of the most exciting times of my life.'[4]

As it turned out, Mike and the others had already harboured ambitions to turn the EmCee Four into a five-piece band, but had had trouble finding a trumpeter who matched up to their skills, or who shared their commitment. 'Some time before Ian's return, we had gotten ourselves a trumpeter,' remembers Mike, 'who was a Scottish fellow named Douggie Smith. He was actually quite a good player, but he wasn't really a great enthusiast. He was sort of in it for fun, and all he wanted was to come down on a Saturday night and get a few quid and a couple of beers.'[5] Ian, for all his temporary musical shortcomings, more than made up in enthusiasm and passion for Smith's limited level of involvement. Soon he was working hard at acquiring better musical skills, learning to sight-read (a process that took him quite a few years to master) and beginning to write music.

One gig a week, however, was not going to transform Ian's fortunes. To make a living, and finance the purchase of his new Conn Victor trumpet, he took a job as an English master at John Marlay School, and although Ian has seldom discussed what he did as a teacher, the film director and erstwhile jazz trumpeter Mike Figgis, who was one of Ian's first pupils there, recalls his fiery and inspirational enthusiasm for English literature.[6]

Perhaps the main reason Ian doesn't recall much about this teaching post was that he was permanently exhausted. The EmCee Five not only played each Saturday from midnight until three in the morning, but the

The EmCee Five at the Downbeat. (Jim Perry)

band also fitted in a midweek rehearsal at the Downbeat on Wednesdays, which also ran from midnight until dawn. Eyes bleary with sleeplessness, Ian and Mike would set off afterwards for their day jobs, with their ears still ringing with the band's latest music, while the three dance band players went home to bed before their nightly gig. For a fledgling teacher, albeit one who had an encyclopaedic knowledge of Shakespeare, backed up with the leadership experience of an Army commission, it was tough to be suffering from systematic sleep deprivation, albeit self-imposed.

However, as Ian threw himself into the life of the band, it took a quantum leap forward. 'The EmCee Five's success,' wrote the critic Alun Morgan, 'lay in the fact that it was playing the music of the day, rather than trying to recreate a past style. In 1960, bands like the Max Roach/ Clifford Brown group or the Jazz Messengers were well represented in the jazz stores, and the EmCee Five gave Newcastle jazz enthusiasts the opportunity to share, at first hand, the atmosphere and feeling of this vital music.'[7]

The band, however, also had a strong local accent, because amid the contemporary standards, it constantly challenged itself with newly-composed music. Mike and Gary Cox were both writing something for the quintet almost every week. and soon Ian was trying his hand at composition as well. 'There was always the feeling of breaking new ground,' says Ian, 'invading the unknown and constantly growing. I had a lot of technical catching up to do, and I could barely read music at all. Mike, Gary and Ronnie Stephenson were the spearheads, and I hung in there with desperate intent.'[8]

As the band's first year as a quintet went by, it achieved a very high level of internal cohesion, and the individual members worked hard to play to one another's strengths. This was helped by the buoyant, joyous atmosphere of their weekly gig, surrounded by the enthusiastic twenty-somethings of the coffee-house *demi-monde*, an experience Ian has described as 'sweating, beaming, ecstatic music-making'.[9] In retrospect, the group's cohesion also has a lot to do with the fierce drive of its rhythm section, which is immediately apparent on its first discs, made privately at the Morton Sound studios in Newcastle in June 1961.

I suggested to Ian that having such a strong rhythmic platform had been vital in the success of the band: 'Yes, it was fantastic,' he agreed. 'Although then I did not hear the drums. I felt them, I mean my time was good. Nowadays I know what to listen to for drums, and when they're not working, I know why they're not working. But when I listen to those tracks again, the grace of what Ronnie Stephenson does...I find it's beautiful the way he plays the drums, in a very musical way. I took the music for granted.'[10]

Indeed, the band set such standards that both Ian and Ronnie Stephenson would use them as the yardstick for all their subsequent musical experiences. When, in much later life, they were both working in Germany, they met and compared notes on what both considered to have been a formative experience. 'We measured everything that followed in our careers,' Ian confirms, 'against the dynamism of those nights with the EmCee Five.'[11]

Before long, word had spread about this quintet that was making such waves at the Downbeat club, and because the gigs started so late, other musicians who visited the Newcastle area to play dancehall or concert dates were able to come along after hours. For example, when the John Dankworth Orchestra played in town, John and Kenny Wheeler were among the band-members who turned up to listen and sit in. Occasionally, visiting American musicians made the pilgrimage as well, although these were few and far between in the early 1960s because of the complex exchange arrangements required by the Musicians' Union and Ministry of Labour to issue work permits. Without a British 'exchange' act going to the United States to perform on a 'tit for tat' basis, it was prohibited for Americans to play in the U.K. Things became a lot easier as the sixties progressed and the 'British invasion' of rock and pop bands became popular in the States, but in 1960-61 American jazz players were in short supply outside London, because of the limited reciprocal demand in America for British acts.

However, all the survivors of the EmCee Five remember the day the Count Basie band came to town in June 1960, when, after their concert, most of the musicians made their way to the Downbeat. I had a similar experience while playing at Ronnie Scott's in 1982, and looked up through the gloom to see the shadowy figures of my heroes from that same band making their way to the bar, after they had finished performing at the Royal Festival Hall. It's hard to describe the combined sensations of fear and adrenaline that pulse through your system on stage, when you know such a collection of marvellous musicians is listening, yet from their recollections of what happened in Newcastle twenty years earlier, this is exactly what Ian and his colleagues felt.

They need hardly have worried. First Thad Jones played a tune or two, and then Joe Williams sang a blues. After that, trombonist Al Grey and saxophonist Frank Foster sat in, and before long Grey was grinning broadly in his inimitable toothy fashion and complementing 'this great little drummer', Ronnie Stephenson.

Foster was equally enthusiastic, and locked horns in an epic battle with Gary Cox. It was, as Ian recalls, an extraordinary experience for young musicians in their twenties to be jousting with such experienced jazz warriors. 'Eventually,' he remembered, 'Frank Foster turned to Gary and said, "Boy, you're too good for me. I'm gonna do what John Coltrane and Johnny Griffin do to me. I'm gonna carve you."

'Gary, who was very competitive, said "Okay, come on then!"

'Frank called *Sweet Georgia Brown*. He snapped his fingers at an outrageously fast speed and said, "This tempo, a solo each, then we'll trade eight bars first of all, then fours, and then twos."

'They went into it, and Gary played a fantastic solo, and then they got to the exchanges, the eights and the fours, and Gary was still hanging in there. Frank was ripping through the chord changes like a knife through butter. As they got further into the fours, Gary started to fumble, and he really fumbled once they started trading two-bar phrases. When they finished, he came off muttering, "I've been shamed!" He wouldn't play again all night. But in fact it was a great honour to have been carved by such a leading saxophone player, somebody who, as he said, could hold his own against Griffin and Coltrane. That's how good the EmCee Five was.'[12]

There's more than a hint of the excitement of the band's live sound on its first recordings, made, as I mentioned, in a local studio in June 1961. Gary Cox's blistering soloing is apparent on his own *Lefty's Tune*, a contrafact of *Strike Up The Band*, and the ensembles are tight-knit in the style of a contemporaneous Horace Silver quintet. Mike Carr's bluesy solo playing adopts stabbing hard-bop right-hand runs with punctuating left hand chords, and Ronnie Stephenson switches adroitly from brushes to sticks for his exchanges with the front line. If there is a weakness on this and Horace Silver's *Blowing The Blues Away*, from the same date, it is in Ian's own soloing, which, while it shows he was beginning to learn how to use space and long notes to create atmosphere, is for the most part rather jerky and stilted, with some phrases borrowed from mid-50s Miles Davis, but not yet sufficiently knitted into a convincing style of his own.

The discs are, however, the first opportunity to hear Ian's playing on record, although they were soon superseded by a vastly better session made in London the following December. This came about through the good offices of a local businessman and enthusiast, Geoff Harrison. On first hearing the band, he recognised its unique qualities, saying, 'Newcastle in the late 1950s had a special feel about it. The drabness and austerity of the immediate post-war years was beginning to be replaced by a new optimism and excitement. A new social, cultural and political order seemed to be in the making, and it was as part of the heady atmosphere of those times that a number of musicians, led by pianist Mike Carr, brought to the city the revolutionary new jazz music, bebop.'[13]

Harrison knew, however, that despite a considerable measure of local success, to 'make it', the band would sooner or later have to break into the London jazz scene. Indeed, Ronnie Stephenson had already decided to do just that, leaving the North-East to join John Dankworth's Orchestra, but he was to return to the EmCee Five line-up one more time, as a result of Harrison's visit to London to see the record producer and entrepreneur Denis Preston.

Dapper, bespectacled and with a trim beard, Preston was a former violinist who was highly musically literate and had been involved in jazz record production since the late 1940s, when he produced George Shearing's London trios with Jack Fallon and Norman Burns. Fond of whisky and high living, as a contemporary press report put it, he 'combined considerable technical expertise with business flair and a flamboyant personality.'[14] He had previously joined forces with the enthusiasts Max Jones and Albert McCarthy to contribute to their short-lived postwar journal *Jazz Music*, and had also got involved with the Radio Rhythm Club, but his most significant contribution to British jazz was to separate the role of the producer from that of the record company itself.

Up until 1956, when Preston opened his Lansdowne Studios in the Holland Park area of West London, a producer was either a relatively lowly minion in a large company such as Decca or EMI, or a go-it-alone independent, who carried all the associated risks of sales, stock management, production and distribution. The blind drummer Carlo Krahmer and his business partner Peter Newbrook, were the epitome of this latter type of producer/proprietor. Their Esquire label, managed on a shoestring and tidal wave of enthusiasm, had been the home for most British modern jazz pioneers since the late 40s.

Preston, however, believed that by producing first-rate recordings in his own studio he could license the results to the highest bidder. He consequently set up his Record Supervision management company, and made a great success of doing just this with its mid-50s 'Jazz Today' series, mainly consisting of traditional style discs that were licensed to Pye's Nixa subsidiary, and which became a significant factor in the careers of Chris Barber and Acker Bilk. He also took over the production of Humphrey Lyttelton's Parlophone recordings, effectively working as a freelance producer within EMI. That relationship developed further in 1959, when he initiated the 'Lansdowne Jazz Series' for EMI's Columbia and Parlophone imprints, and by 1961, with the series well-established, he was on the look out for new talent from the more modern areas of jazz.[15]

'A very apprehensive young man knocked on the door of Denis Preston's Lansdowne Studios and asked to see the great man,' recalls Geoff Harrison, of his visit South. 'I handed him a privately produced LP made by Mike [the July 1961 recordings] and endured an eternity of apparently indifferent silence whilst the unfamiliar sounds of *Preludes* and *John O'Groats* filled the studio. I waited for him to pass judgement, wondering nervously whether the refusal would be gentle or brutal. Having heard four tracks, he turned to me and asked whether the guys would consider recording for him.'[16]

Harrison could hardly contain his excitement. He found the nearest phone booth and called Mike Carr to relay the news. A few months later, the band came to London on 14 December 1951 to make a 45rpm EP, which Preston entitled *Let's Take Five*. For the session, Ronnie Stephenson came back into the band, having by this time already joined John Dankworth, and John O'Carroll's place was taken by Dankworth's bassist, Spike Heatley. One side of the 7-inch disc consisted of two compositions by Mike Carr, and the other was entirely taken up by a six-minute version of Gary Cox's *Preludes*. The band plays throughout with pent-up energy, and a self-confidence that rivals the best American groups of the period. Heatley and Stephenson prod away at Mike Carr, who responds with some fluent right-hand solos and ever more urgent comping. Most noticeable is the dramatic improvement in Ian's playing. His muted lead on Mike's *The One That Got Away* is followed by an edgy muted solo of great poise, and the use of space in his open solo on *Stephenson's Rocket* displays a maturity that was entirely missing from that summer's demo disc. The stellar performance, however, is *Preludes*, opened by Ian's slinky, sinister, open horn and Heatley's bass, and developing on a modal basis through a series of short independent sections. The horn figures behind the piano solo are reminiscent of Miles Davis's sextet on *Kind of Blue*, but the tempo changes and moodswings of the piece are entirely original and Ian's bustling solo in the centre segment announces to the world a talent worth taking notice of. Denis Preston, too, took note of the trumpeter in this uncompromising Northern quintet, which recorded entirely original compositions for him, and this was to stand Ian in good stead in the future.

Preludes had been written for a Tyne-Tees television programme the previous year, in the series *Your Kind of Music*. At Ian's suggestion, Gary Cox composed the piece as a short suite of related sections around the theme of T.S. Eliot's poem of the same name, and it was premiered on screen in late 1960, before becoming a regular part of the quintet's repertoire. Ian's main memory of the television broadcast is the series host Spike Milligan, a former jazz trumpeter himself, asking for a blow on Ian's horn. 'I've only had syphilis and gonorrhoea,' he remarked, as he pressed his lips eagerly to the mouthpiece.[17]

The press thought highly of the new EP, and the EmCee Five soon found it had strong advocates in the form of critics Charles Fox and Alun Morgan, as well as pianist and broadcaster Steve Race. Writing in *Jazz Monthly*, Morgan observed: 'One of the most immediately striking aspects of the music is the intelligent, helpful support provided by Mike Carr. Ian Carr and Gary Cox have already reached an incredibly high standard and if I were a well known West End jazz musician, I think I would be extremely worried by the frightening level of competence and invention shown by this out-of-town band. Cox is all over his instrument like a seasoned professional (he deservedly earned the praise of the Basie musicians when he played at a jam session with Frank Foster and Al Grey in June, 1960); Ian Carr has more to say on trumpet than almost any other British jazz musician and I am of the opinion that the standard of jazz (I don't mean "Trad") in this country is now second only to that in America.'[18]

At the time of its recording date for Denis Preston, the EmCee Five also played at Ronnie Scott's Club, still based in those days at its original address in Gerrard Street in Soho, and many musicians on the London scene came along, interested to hear this dynamic band from the North-East. More memorable for Ian was a session the band played subsequently at the Flamingo, around the corner in Wardour Street, a venue that manager Sam Kruger had built into a home for modern jazz players such as Tony Kinsey, Tommy Whittle and Bill le Sage. 'Everybody came down,' Ian recalled, 'including the legendary drummer Phil Seamen. He was very excited and wanted to play with us, to sit in for Ronnie. He heard us play first, then he had a handful of yellow pills, and a handful of blue pills. He had a Coca-Cola bottle which was mainly whisky with just a drop or two of coke in it, and he drank that. Then he had a fix in his arm and smoked a joint. He came over to me and said, "I really feel like playing now." In fact he played terribly. He was just too high, but on a good night he was a truly marvellous player!'[19]

London was not the only far-off place to which the EmCee Five took their music. In the summer of 1961, Ian had contacted Vincenso Catarsi and persuaded him to book the band to play for a week in Tuscany, in the idyllic surroundings of the coastal town of Vada, South of Livorno. With a local drummer Dave Fox in place of Stephenson, the rest of the original line-up played at Catarsi's beach-side restaurant and finished the trip with a concert a few miles away at Viareggio, sharing the programme with the Italian band led by saxophonist Gianni Basso and pianist Oscar Valdambrini. There was much mutual enthusiasm between the English and Italian musicians for one another's work, and the trip was a success.

Back in Newcastle, however, a phase was inevitably drawing to a close in Ian's life. If he was going to make it as a musician, he would have to follow Malcolm Cecil and Ronnie Stephenson to London. Having tried the itinerant literary life and failed, this second attempt at an artistic career would not so easily evade him. When an offer came in the spring of 1962 to come South to join the Jamaican-born flautist and alto saxophonist Harold McNair, Ian accepted. But he did so on the grounds that he would see out the academic year at John Marlay School, and move South in the summer. There were to be a few more months of fun, playing with the EmCee Five, and revelling in the music of what John Dankworth once called 'the Kansas City of the North'.

Dankworth's joking title was not too far off the mark. Traditional jazz was well represented in the city by the Panama Jazzmen and the Vieux Carré band, and, at a time when Humphrey Lyttelton was leading a national movement away from traditional jazz to the small group swing of the American Midwest, the Newcastle exponents of this were Mighty Joe Young's mainstream band. When it came to the bluesier side of Kansas City's spectrum, the best-known example amid Newcastle's music of the early 1960s was to be the Animals. While the EmCee Five was at its zenith, however, the Animals had not yet acquired their final line-up, nor the name by which they would become famous. The precursor of the group was a rhythm and blues quintet led by Eric Burdon and Alan Price called the Kansas City Five. Ian, and other members of the EmCee Five often sat in with their more blues-orientated counterparts, adding spontaneous riffs, or making up head arrangements of Ray Charles numbers. And in return, Eric Burdon brought his atmospheric singing to EmCee Five gigs, turning up to charm the coffee bar for the princely sum of fifteen shillings. The relationship was to bear further fruit as the decade wore on, as we shall see, but its most immediate effect in 1961 was that Burdon, a former graphic artist, designed the cover of the EmCee Five's EP.

Jazz was also the favourite music of the growing community of Tyneside artists and literati. Gerald Laing was briefly home in the city after leaving the Royal Northumberland Fusiliers in 1960, before taking up a place at St. Martin's School of Art in London, and he was a regular at Ian's gigs. The abstract expressionist painter Scott Dobson, between sloshing paint over several canvases at a time, wrote a jazz column for the *Evening Chronicle*, and John B. Walters, at that time a local secondary school teacher but later to become famous, first as a trumpeter with Alan Price, and then as John Peel's BBC radio producer, wrote on jazz and blues for the *Newcastle Journal*, as well as giving evening classes on jazz history. His short, perceptive pieces of criticism occasionally focussed on the gritty urban realism of the EmCee Five or Eric Burdon, and he found qualities to praise in both, writing of Burdon as displaying 'the authority and defiance of a young city Negro', and of the EmCee Five 'breathing life' into the 'staid and cosy' London jazz scene.[20]

As for the city's other writers, the best-known was the novelist Sid Chaplin. A former miner, and an influential figure among the 'angry young men' of 1950s English writing, he published his novel of urban alienation, *The Day of the Sardine* in 1961. His hero, Arthur Haggerston, makes his progress into adulthood in a Novocastrian world dominated by dull, repetitive industrial employment and equally unfulfilling street violence. Yet Chaplin was far from alienated himself, and was a powerful force for good in the sweeping changes that were about to overtake his beloved city. As the funding for culture in Britain became a pilot scheme for devolution, he was one of the progenitors of the regional arm of the Arts Council, Northern Arts, which was also established in 1961, and he was a fervent jazz fan, not only having made the pilgrimage to a then very un-touristy New Orleans, but becoming a regular at the Downbeat.

'He was,' wrote Ian, 'a kind of social and artistic catalyst, a general inspiration to his associates, and he seemed to know every nook, cranny and historical wrinkle of Newcastle.'[21] A friendship flourished between Chaplin and Ian, who still possesses a signed first edition of *The Day of the Sardine*, and who later made plans to write Chaplin's biography.

'He was like a father to me,' Ian recalled. 'He was an incredibly gentle man, totally without malice, with fantastic story-telling ability. I used to go for long walks with him, and as we walked, he would give me the history of everything we were looking at, whether we were in the town or the country. Our friendship lasted a long time. After I had been ill in 1983, I wanted to write a book, and my then wife, Sandy, suggested I do a biography of Sid, because we were so close. I went up to see him, interviewed him, recorded tapes, and drove through the snow round the areas where he used to live, taking photographs while he talked into the tape machine. But my agent never could get anyone interested in publishing it, because he was stereotyped as "a north country novelist". So I had to phone him and say we couldn't get a publisher, and I'd have to abandon the project. But in a way it galvanised him, because talking to me about his early days set him off, and he recorded a lot of the memories he had never set down. Nevertheless, I continued to feel guilty that the project never happened, and three years later, the news came that he had died. I poured a lot of the emotions I felt into *Old Heartland*, my commission for string orchestra, which came about almost at the moment he died.'[22]

Back in the 1960s, Chaplin was one of a number of people Ian sounded out about putting Newcastle more firmly on the map as a cultural centre. He convened a meeting at his mother's house for various local movers and shakers, including the councillor Ted Fletcher, who at one point came up with the suggestion that the EmCee Five should be publicly funded to the tune of £70.00 per man each week to keep the band in the North-East. Another attendee was the councillor T. Dan Smith, later disgraced for his role in the John Poulson affair, but in 1961 still a visionary councillor, wont to read his own poetry on the virtues of pulling down the slums of Scotswood Road. The strong and genuinely felt emotions of his poetry appealed to Ian, but Chaplin was more cynical, murmuring that if Smith's preferred high-rise solution was really about the creation of 'vertical villages', then by rights they would have a pub and a church stuck on top!

Although little came of Ian's attempts to galvanise local writers into action, one outcome of his proselytising efforts was the setting up of a Newcastle Jazz Committee. The particular event that inspired it was the City Council's decision to hold an Arts Festival in 1961, on the programme for which jazz was only reluctantly given a place at the last minute, despite there being more than 100 regularly working jazz musicians in the area. With John Walters as its chairman, and a selection of other dignitaries among its members, its role was described in the local press as that of 'a pressure group to fight ignorance, bigotry and the people who refused to allow jazz to take its rightful place in the artistic life of the community'.[23]

But time was running out for Ian to put the committee and its promises to the test. As term ended in July 1962, he set off for London, to join Harold McNair. The EmCee Five played a farewell set for him at Mike Jeffreys' new club, the A'Go Go on Percy Street, and rather like a long-term employee being presented with a gold watch after fifty years' service, the band gave Ian a pewter mug inscribed with all their names, including that of the young drummer Johnny Butts, who had taken Ronnie Stephenson's place, and who, like Ronnie, was ultimately to leave the North-East to join John Dankworth. Tragically, he was killed in a freak road accident in Burmuda, just four years later.

We do, however, have one memento of how the band sounded with Butts on drums, because when Harold McNair came to Newcastle in October 1962, the EmCee Five got together just one more time to record live at the A'Go Go. Midge Pike from McNair's band played bass, but the remainder of the quintet's dynamism, drive and flair are undimmed. Butts's snare work on *John O'Groats* drives the band along, and brings a different character to the rhythm, but the abiding impression is that this short-lived group was one of the great undiscovered treasures of modern British jazz.

5 affectionate fink – harold mcnair and 1960s london

Harold McNair was one of the most charismatic figures on the British jazz scene of the early 1960s. Two years older than Ian, he was already a vastly more experienced jazz musician, having started out in his native Jamaica with the Kingston All Stars in the late 1940s, before moving to the Bahamas, where he became quite a well-known tenor saxophonist. Being Jamaican, he could travel from there to work in Cuba at a time when few Americans were able to visit the island, and he was also permitted to perform in the United States. After occasional visits to Florida, he played in New York at the beginning of 1960, before deciding to try his hand in Europe. In the late spring of 1960, now focussing on the alto saxophone, he worked successively in Stockholm, London and Paris. During his time in the French capital he played with both the mercurial Algerian-born pianist Martial Solal, and with the doyen of expatriate Americans, drummer Kenny Clarke.

When Quincy Jones went on the road in Europe later in 1960 with the band from the failed Harold Arlen musical, *Free and Easy*, McNair joined the line-up on tenor saxophone, in a reed section which featured him alongside Phil Woods, Jerome Richardson, Budd Johnson and Sahib Shihab. By the time he returned to London to join Stan Tracey's quartet at Ronnie Scott's that summer, he was a seasoned international professional, already acknowledged as a distinctive soloist, particularly on the alto, but even more so on the flute. He 'incorporated all of the jazz flute techniques prevalent at the time and added his own perfect blend of lyricism and driving swing,' wrote flute historian Peter Guidi,[1] explaining why McNair quickly became a celebrated member of the inner circle of the London jazz scene.

Although he was not a well-known American musician, he was nevertheless welcomed as a soloist at Ronnie Scott's at a time when the club was regularly featuring such transatlantic stars as Don Byas, Dexter Gordon, Zoot Sims and Lucky Thompson, not to mention the Belgian tenorist Bobby Jaspar.[2] Reviews of McNair's work confirm that he really was a soloist fit to be compared to these major league players, one writer succinctly pointing out that 'McNair on tenor saxophone conveys an irrepressible urgency and drive which seems unstoppable, whilst his flute work, whether indulging in Roland Kirk-like antics or simply singing a lyrical ballad, is amongst the finest upon that instrument anywhere in jazz.'[3]

Before Ian Carr, complete with his new Conn Victor trumpet, arrived in London in July 1962 to join McNair's band, the saxophonist had fitted in a quick return to the Caribbean, a few short trips to New York, and several recording sessions. His British debut on disc (made in August 1961) was with Tony Crombie's quintet, with the former EmCee Five bassist Malcolm Cecil in the line-up as well as Ian's future Nucleus colleague, pianist Gordon Beck. This session was followed up with a number of other records, including his first single under his own name, made for Fontana during a live quartet session at Ronnie Scott's in November 1961, which featured McNair on alto and flute, with pianist Terry Shannon, Jeff Clyne on bass and Phil Seamen on drums.

Shannon was still on piano when Ian joined the band nine months later. The bassist was by then Phil Bates, who had worked with a variety of bands from John Dankworth's orchestra to Sandy Brown's Jazz Band. The drummer was from South Africa, and tended to indulge in competitive jousts with McNair, 'dropping bombs' and frequently playing quite intrusively.

With nowhere to stay in London, Ian roomed with McNair himself, and no longer supported by a teacher's income, attempted to live on what he could make from gigs. Although the band managed to obtain some quite high-profile work, there was not a lot of it, and for the four months or so that Ian was in the line-up, he was often reduced to living on next to nothing. In addition to that, he was surprised how different McNair's musical attitudes were to those of the EmCee Five. 'Gary and Mike had been bringing in new things for us to play almost every week,' he recalled. 'When I came to London to join Harold, I was disappointed. His band had no vision like that, and didn't have its own compositions. It was not as good as what I'd left. That shocked me.'[4]

Ian nevertheless found himself greatly impressed by McNair's own sound. 'He was a great player, both on alto or tenor sax and flute, that's for sure,' he confirmed. 'But I didn't really like the group much,

The Harold McNair band in Newcastle: (l to r) McNair; unknown, drums; Midge Pike, bass; Mike Carr, piano; Ian. (Jim Perry/Ian Carr)

especially after Terry Shannon left and we had a whole succession of piano players. Then Phil Bates left to be replaced by Midge Pike, who was a very good South African bass player, and he came with us on the Northern tour, during which we recorded with the EmCee Five.'[5]

One immediate effect of Ian joining the quintet was that some of his former band's repertoire, if not its insatiable quest for new material, rubbed off on his colleagues. 'EmCee Five enthusiasts will be glad to hear that Harold McNair is eager to use themes and arrangements by this group for his new quintet,' ran one press report.[6] But overall McNair's instrumental virtuosity, and his over-reliance on his own powers as an improviser, mitigated against the band taking on more structured material, originals or fresh arrangements. 'Harold had no idea of musical direction,' remembered Ian, 'which meant that one minute he would "do" a Charlie Parker, then he'd play a few standards, then move on to a flute feature, and things like that.'[7]

Prodded by Ian into thinking about changing his repertoire a little, McNair finally approached an American friend of his, who was serving with the USAF in Britain, to see if he would produce some arrangements for the band. 'He was a white guy, this Air Force sergeant,' said Ian, 'and he came round with this pile of arrangements he'd written out. At that point I really couldn't read music well at all, and here were all these complex-looking written charts. So I rang Kenny Wheeler, to ask if he'd help. I knew him through my brother, because after they'd first met in Cyprus while Mike was in the RAF, he'd come up a number of times to see us in the EmCee Five. Kenny agreed to show me how to read these tunes, so I went over to meet him at his studio one afternoon, and he took me through them. They actually turned out to be awful! If I'd known, I wouldn't have wanted to put in the time on them, but thinking they were good originals, I was keen to try them out. Despite the quality of the music, I thanked Kenny for helping me, and I wanted to give him a pound, which was quite good money in those days. Naturally, being Kenny, who is a very retiring kind of person, he didn't want to take it. But I insisted, saying, "You have to take this pound, because I might want to ask you for help again, and I couldn't feel free to do so unless you accept this payment". So in the end he took it, and he ended up not only being a real help to me, but a good friend too. He's a fantastic musician, of course, but a very nice guy as well.'[8]

Given that Ian had had piano lessons as a child, it seems strange that his reading was so poor. But he was essentially a self-taught trumpeter, and up to this point he still relied more on his ears than his eyes for his playing of both instruments. Nevertheless, it was during his time with McNair that he seriously began to address the problem of reading music, and to try and overcome what he believed was a psychological block that dated back to his childhood experiences of classical music. His reading did not magically improve overnight, but at least his arrival in London gave him the impetus he needed to start serious work on it.

Although he was swiftly disillusioned by his experiences in Harold McNair's band, and knew he would soon have to move on, the London jazz world into which Ian had arrived in 1962 was an intoxicating array of new sounds and opportunities compared to the North-East.

The scene centred on Ronnie Scott's club, still in its original premises at 39 Gerrard Street in Soho, and presenting as many visiting American soloists as money and the Musicians' Union would allow, backed by Stan Tracey's house rhythm section. The McNair band played there, from time to time, and also appeared a little further north at the Marquee, which was at that time on the corner of Oxford Street and Poland Street. Although Alexis Korner's Blues Incorporated was the resident band for much of 1962, in its policy for booking the groups that appeared opposite Alexis, the Marquee played host to musicians across the stylistic spectrum from the free improvisation of Joe Harriott and Shake Keane, via the urbane post bop of John Dankworth, to the Kansas City swing of Humphrey Lyttelton's band, or the New Orleans-meets-rhythm'n'blues of Chris Barber. As well as playing there with McNair, Ian also worked there as a freelance with various other groups.

Not far away was the Flamingo, on Wardour Street, where manager Sam Kruger presented a cross section of contemporary British jazz and blues. A little further off still was Studio 51 in Great Newport Street where Tony Kinsey's modernists alternated with the New Orleans purism of Ken Colyer, and finally there was the 100 Club on Oxford Street, which included mainstream and swing sessions amid its regular diet of Trad by the likes of Acker Bilk, Terry Lightfoot and Alex Welsh. Because of its vast size, this club occasionally played host to visiting American soloists, of a rather different kind from those who appeared at Ronnie's, including the fiery Chicagoan cornetist Wild Bill Davison, who toured the UK with Alex Welsh that October.

Some of the major British jazz personalities of the 1960s had yet to arrive in London when Ian first got there in 1962. John Stevens and Trevor Watts, for example, were still doing their national service in an RAF band, and would not start playing regularly in the city until the following year. Mike Westbrook, however, first appeared in the capital just a few weeks after Ian, having decided to move from his West Country jazz workshop in Plymouth, and form his own band. John Surman came with him, enrolling at the London College of Music during September. Meanwhile, the other major new talent from the West of England, Keith Tippett, was still at the heart of the Bristol jazz scene in 1962 and did not come East for another four years.

Nevertheless, what was already on offer in London made a huge impression on Ian. 'The Flamingo was full of American servicemen in big coats and homburg hats,' he laughs. 'There were black and white, pimps and prostitutes, dope pushers, all of human life in those audiences. Later, I'd walk through that part of Soho with Don Rendell, and he'd be muttering, "Sodom and Gomorrah! Sodom and Gomorrah!" under his breath. The music at the Flamingo went from midnight to five in the morning, and there were some tremendous bands that played there. The one I most remember was Georgie Fame, who'd put together the Blue Flames that summer, after they'd all been working with Billy Fury. John McLaughlin was in the band on guitar, they had a great drummer called Red Reece, and a guy called Mick Eve who was a fine tenor saxophonist. Georgie was really under the influence of Mose Allison at that time, and he was a lovely singer with great time. But for me the star was McLaughlin. He was at the top of his form, and playing fantastically.

He was steeped in the blues, but he had also absorbed all sorts of other kinds of jazz. He was truly phenomenal, and I used to go down there sometimes, just to hear him. As he played, there'd be all these homburg hats, silhouetted by the lights, jiving away.

'But the Marquee club was equally great, and it was a beacon for the blues. One of the guys who played opposite us in Alexis Korner's band when I worked there with Harold was their bassist, Jack Bruce, shortly before he started creating with Ginger Baker. So I felt really at the centre of things, at the heart of it all. Everything that was going on in music at the time seemed to be there.'[9]

At the same time, Ian's personal life took a turn for the better. During his period in Newcastle with the EmCee Five he had become involved with a King's College student called Margaret Bell. She was reading for a general language degree, including French, Greek and Roman culture, but shared Ian's interests in jazz, particularly the latest Miles Davis recordings, Coltrane's current discs, and the singing of Billie Holiday and Joe Williams. She had first become his girlfriend after meeting him at the Downbeat. At this point, Ian moved from his mother's house to a flat in a shabby area of Newcastle, which he shared with the artist, Scott Dobson. 'He was an abstract expressionist artist,' explains Ian. 'He was a really entertaining rogue, who'd do about six action paintings at once. He'd hired a big studio in Newcastle, which I lived in illegally for a time. There'd be canvasses all over the floor and he'd go with a bucket of paint and slop it on in various ways. But I had a room in the place.'[10]

In the months that followed, Margaret would frequently come back there with him after the gig, and she later went with Ian on the EmCee Five trip to Italy, along with other band wives and girlfriends.

In the autumn of 1961, however, Ian and Margaret split up, when she left him for a painter. At the time, this had upset Ian considerably, and he had become depressed, walking the streets hoping to catch a glimpse of Margaret, until he eventually took up with another girl. But at his leaving party in Newcastle, when he was about to leave for London, Margaret reappeared. Both of them realised what they felt about each other, and agreed to start over again, save for the complication that Margaret was taking off to study abroad for a few months, and Ian was moving South, with no fixed address.

Ian had been in Harold McNair's band for a couple of months when a postcard arrived addressed to him c/o Ronnie Scott's club. It was from Margaret, saying she was about to come to the end of her short stay in France, where she had been lodging with a French family since July, studying and working on her conversation skills. She told Ian the flight on which she would be returning to London, and suggested he might meet her.

He duly turned up, and whisked her back to the flat he shared with McNair. 'Harold wasn't there when we got back,' Ian remembers. 'I rudely took her clothes off and we made love. She burst into tears and I asked her to marry me. She said "Absolutely, yes!".'[11]

Soon afterwards. McNair returned home. At this point he was good friends with Rex Harrison's actor son Noel, who had a flat nearby, and McNair frequently stayed there. This was a good arrangement whenever girlfriends were involved, as Ian and McNair had their beds in the same room. For some reason, on this occasion, McNair refused to go out again, saying loudly, 'This is my house!'

So eventually he slept in the same room as Ian and Margaret, despite the passionate noises emanating from their bed. In the morning, McNair took Ian aside and said, 'Don't ever do that to me again!' To which Ian retorted that it served him bloody well right for deciding to stay. However, this was the turning point in Ian's relationship with McNair, and he knew he had to leave the band as soon as possible. He also moved out of the flat, finding a much better apartment near Regent's Park, which he shared with bassist Jeff Clyne. His old friend from Newcastle, Johnny Butts, lived in the same building, which had a good view over the green expanses of the park.

'We thought it was very expensive,' Ian recalled, 'because it was six pounds a week, between the two of us. Three pounds a week for a flat was very highly priced in those days, but this more than made up for it, because it was such a pleasant flat.'[12] Although Margaret was now Ian's fiancée, she had to return to her studies in Newcastle, but during her final academic year, she became a frequent visitor to London during weekends and vacations.

So, as 1962 drew to a close, Ian had found a new place to live, and his only problem was to find a new musical setting in which to work. Before long, however, the solution arrived in the person of saxophonist Don Rendell.

6 shades of blue – the rendell-carr quintet

When the Don Rendell-Ian Carr Quintet was first formed in late 1962, it is unlikely that any of its members envisaged that the group would last almost seven years with very few personnel changes, finally breaking up in the autumn of 1969. It is even less likely that they expected to win over that most curmudgeonly jazz critic of the *Daily Telegraph*, the poet Philip Larkin, whose reviews of the band, despite his love of such traditionalists as Eddie Condon and Henry 'Red' Allen, gradually grew warmer over the years, in due course praising Carr's 'astonishingly adroit' trumpet playing, and awarding Rendell the accolade of 'best British tenor'.[1] Indeed, ultimately it was the reactionary columns of the *Telegraph* that praised the band as 'musicians whose abilities as composers and interpreters is second to none, either in Britain or abroad'.[2] During its seven year life, the quintet established itself as a ceaselessly innovative and inventive group, winning numerous *Melody Maker* awards, and creating a distinctive and distinguished collective voice that nodded in the direction of, but remained independent from, what was going on in North America.

The genesis of the band was the long-established small group that Don Rendell had fronted in London since making his debut as a leader in 1955 with the album *Meet Don Rendell* for Tempo Jazz. That same year had also seen what he still regards as one of the highlights of his career, when he was chosen to play in the backing band for Billie Holiday's last visit to Britain. Don had previously been a member of the Johnny Dankworth Seven, and of Ted Heath's Orchestra, and his subtle blend of Lester Young's whimsicality with more forceful bebop inflections had also led him to become a temporary member of both the touring Stan Kenton and Woody Herman orchestras, in which Don more than held his own amid such tough American section-mates as Lenny Niehaus, Bill Perkins and Lucky Thompson. The personnel and size of his own group evolved over time, and the direct antecedent of the

Rendell-Carr band was Don's 'New Jazz Quintet' of 1961, which made the album *Roarin'* for Jazzland. Since then, Don has often adopted the soubriquet 'Roaring Band' for his groups.

Don's own playing had increasingly come under the sway of John Coltrane as the 1950s progressed, nevertheless his New Jazz Quintet on that 1961 disc had one even more significant influence, Charles Mingus, in terms both of his arranging and compositional style. This directly shaped the voicings of Don and his frontline partner, altoist Graham Bond, on such Gospel-influenced tunes as *Manumission*. Their joint playing of the head arrangement on this tune recalls Mingus's two-saxophone line-ups for the period, and their trading of fours is exhilarating. Don's own solo is a marvellous example of his ability to compel attention towards his playing, something that I experienced at first hand in the late 1980s, playing alongside Don myself when he deputised in the resident big band at the Ritz Hotel in London, where he often caused the dancers in the Palm Court to forget about their footwork, and gather round the bandstand to listen to him. Don's power to draw people in to his playing, no matter how complex, was at its most developed in the 1960s, and it seems to me to have had a lot to do with the stimulation he gained from playing new music that frequently abandoned the period's abiding conventions of the popular song form of 16 or 32 bars. Consequently, the idea of intelligent, well-shaped original compositions forming the major part of Don's repertoire was one that was to continue after Bond's departure, which occurred more or less simultaneously with that of pianist John Burch, and forced Don to recruit a largely new line-up. In place of a two-reed frontline, Don now brought in Ian Carr on trumpet and flugelhorn.

'Graham rang me up one day and said he was going to have his own band, singing and playing the organ,' recalled Don. 'I've never tried to hold on to any musician against his will so if a guy rings me and says what Graham said, I could only reply by saying, "Cheerio, no hard feelings!" Ian came in because Tony Archer, the bass player, suggested I get in touch with this very good trumpet player he'd worked with at the Flamingo Club in Wardour Street. Tony arranged for me to meet Ian, and he came in the band.'[3] Ian's personality, background and style were a great contrast to Don's own, but they were to develop into extremely sympathetic musical partners and co-leaders of the group.

As it turned out, the new Rendell-Carr line-up was somewhat thwarted in early January 1963, within a few weeks of its formation. 'Illness hits the jazz boys,' thundered the *Melody Maker* headline, going on to report that 'Ian Carr, trumpeter with the Don Rendell Quintet, was rushed into hospital on Saturday with acute appendicitis. He had an immediate operation at the Royal Free Hospital, Hampstead. Ian, named as one of the new stars for 1963 by the *MM*, is likely to be off work for at least a month.' What the report did not say was that, despite the operation, Ian's appendicitis had developed into peritonitis, and he was much more seriously ill than was first thought. During his subsequent convalescence, tenorist Stan Robinson deputised on the band's gigs at London's Marquee Club.[4] Nevertheless, the doctor's predictions were more or less accurate, all was soon back on track, and *Downbeat* reported in its February 1963 edition that 'Don Rendell's New Quintet consists of Rendell, tenor and soprano saxophones; Ian Carr, trumpet and flugelhorn; Johnny Mealing, piano; Tony Archer, bass; Trevor Tomkins, drums.'[5]

The new band was an immediate contrast for Ian to the group led by Harold McNair, which he had left to join Don. 'We had more work than Harold,' he reflected, 'and more idea of how to run a group.'[6] Nevertheless it took time for the band to make a recording that was heard by the public. Its first attempt, made in January 1964 for the American producer Hank Russell, lay unissued for many years until Tony Williams at the independent Spotlite label finally released it, and it shows the line-up in transition, with Dave Green having joined on bass, and Mealing, who was soon to move on to a long and successful career as a pianist and arranger, still in the piano chair. In repertoire terms, standards such as *I've Never Been In Love Before* mingle with originals, pointing the way towards the quintet's later discs which entirely consist of non-standard material.

Because that January 1964 session didn't see the light of day at the time, it was *Shades of Blue*, cut the following October, and the earliest of the five albums the group was to make for Columbia, via Denis Preston's production company Record Supervision, which became the first disc by the band to be issued. It also gave the group its title, as the band had hitherto played under Don's name. Renaming it was an act of generosity on Don's part in return for Ian's success in securing the record date.

'Ian and the EmCee Five had previously recorded with Denis Preston for the Lansdowne series,' said Don. 'And Ian arranged this recording session for us. I thought that was really good, because you need that kind of prestige. You need recordings, and I couldn't get one, but Ian did. He got this record session set up and it worked out really nicely...So I said to Ian, 'Let's call it the Rendell-Carr Quintet.'[7]

The new album immediately confirmed the idea in the public mind that the Quintet was devoted to playing newly-written numbers, mainly by members of the group themselves. Rendell remembers that 'in 1965 we'd suddenly found we could go a whole concert without using a standard,'⁸ and this became the band's hallmark, even causing angry exchanges when a BBC Jazz Club producer urged them to 'throw in a few American standards,' and they refused. Interestingly, Ian had approached Preston to see if he would record the band precisely because the producer had expressed his enthusiasm for the way the EmCee Five was devoted to playing original material.

The two pieces on *Shades of Blue* by outsiders are the title track by Neil Ardley, and *Sailin'* by Ian's brother, Mike. At the time, Ardley was the director of the New Jazz Orchestra, a large semi-pro band that met once a week in South London. Ian had joined it in 1963, to improve his sight-reading, when the band was being led by its previous director, Clive Burrows. Ian played alongside fellow-trumpeters Bob Leaper, Mike Phillipson and Tony Dudley, plus, occasionally, Kenny Wheeler. Indeed, Ian recorded a solo flugelhorn version of *I Remember Clifford*, on a still-to-be-released session for Burrows in January 1964, just days apart from the original recordings by the Rendell-Carr group, which, as I mentioned, also remained unissued at the time.

During early 1964, Burrows gave up leading the band and it became self-governing for a period, until Neil Ardley was brought into the frame by the writer Lionel Grigson, who was an occasional member of the line-up on piano. After graduating from Bristol as a scientist, Ardley combined a career as a science author for children with his musical activities, and he'd met Grigson through their mutual literary connections. At the time, Ardley was a composer in search of an orchestra, and although he played 'arranger's piano', his main instrument was always the ensemble. As a result he was the natural successor to Burrows, and during the next few years he built the New Jazz Orchestra into an impressive force in London's contemporary music scene.

Neil was, and remained until his death in 2004, interested in composing jazz pieces that employed unusual scales, and in 1961, inspired by the Miles Davis Quintet and its use of modal jazz, he first drafted out an early version of *Shades of Blue* using a simple modal scale, built on only the white notes of the piano. Over time, he gradually worked towards the final form of the piece, finishing it in 1964, when it was given its title by Don Rendell. Originally the intention was to call it *The Blue Guitarist*, after a long poem by Wallace Stevens, later illustrated by David Hockney, but inspired by the famous painting of Picasso's 'blue period'.⁹

Ian was to record the piece again a few months later, as his solo feature on the New Jazz Orchestra album *Western Reunion*, and some

The New Jazz Orchestra recording in London, 1965. (Ian Carr)

aspects of the performances are similar, including the use of pauses. Nevertheless, the Rendell-Carr Quintet version is the first time Ardley's tune was recorded, and as *Jazz Journal* said then, marks his 'first flowering as a composer'.[10] Mike Carr's piece from the album – a 12-bar blues in 6/8 time with some substitute chord changes – was inspired by an afternoon in a dinghy on Regent's Park boating lake.[11]

The feeling of the entire album *Shades of Blue* is summed up by its title: 'What Don and I aimed at,' said Ian, 'was to play the blues, either in form or feeling. We wanted to get as much interplay as we could between the instruments, and to make the approach as free as possible...we start off with the chords, and then make occasional forays into the no-man's-land beyond them.'[12] Although the Miles Davis quintets and sextets with John Coltrane of a few years earlier shaped part of the band's approach, there's no doubt that with this album, from the 20-bar bossa nova theme of *Latin Blue* to the lyrical moodiness of Colin Purbrook's *Blue Mosque,* the band brought a fresh and original sound to British jazz.

Colin Purbrook, who only remained with the Quintet for this one album, was a significant factor in this. He was a hugely talented and inventive pianist, who died tragically in 1999 after a long and bravely fought battle with cancer, aged just sixty-two. For much of his life, Colin also had his personal demons to fight, including a lengthy struggle with

The Rendell-Carr Quintet: (l to r) Ian, Trevor Tomkins, Dave Green, Mike Garrick, Don Rendell. (Ian Carr)

alcoholism, but in the mid-60s he was a sought-after freelance. Because he was also a multi-instrumentalist, playing double bass with bands as varied as Sandy Brown's jazzmen and Dudley Moore's trio, not to mention being Tony Coe's long-term pianist, he did not stay long in the line-up of the Rendell-Carr group.

Colin's replacement on piano was Michael Garrick, then, as now, a ceaselessly inventive composer and educator, and also a bandleader, who cut three albums under his own name with Ian Carr on trumpet in the eighteen months leading up to the making of the Rendell-Carr group's next album, *Dusk Fire* in March 1966.

Garrick's compositional skill brought new ideas to the quintet, and with his arrival the band coalesced into its final and permanent form. It was beginning to get critical attention as well, with Don Rendell placed 5th among the tenorists in the 1964 *Melody Maker* poll, and Ian ranking 4th as a 'new star' in the following year's table, behind Ernest Ranglin, Roy Budd and Shake Keane. Whereas some critics had dismissed *Shades of Blue* as being somewhat cerebral and restrained, there could be no such perception of the band on its second major album, *Dusk Fire*.[13] The outstanding track, *Tan Samfu* (named after a 'samfu' costume brought back from the Far East by Rendell's friend Gerry Tan), provokes both co-leaders into rousing, aggressive solos, and Garrick into a sparky, two-fisted chorus, underpinned by some forceful drumming from Tomkins and strong bass playing, building on Green's opening ostinato. The piece was selected by producer Denis Preston for his *Jazz Explosion* budget-priced sampler of new British jazz, which brought the band's sound to a larger-than-ever audience.

Dusk Fire is, in many respects, the first fully mature disc the band made, its qualities being admirably summed up by a contemporary description of the group by Martin C. King, who wrote:

> '[Don] had increasing command over a number of instruments, and he could evoke a variety of moods by switching among tenor, soprano, clarinet, flute and alto flute during an evening. Contrasting with Rendell's warm passion were Carr's fine trumpet work — generally cooler, a little distant and slightly austere — and Garrick's piano, often delicate and introspective, but capable of a crashing two-fisted assurance when this was called for. Mention must be made too of Green and Tomkins, who successfully gave impetus to the band's playing without dominating. All these factors combined to form a unit which was greater than the sum of its parts.'[14]

Track by track, *Dusk Fire* exemplifies King's points. The fiery *Tan Samfu* contrasts with the gentle flute, muted trumpet and restrained drumming of the opening number *Ruth*, and the equally laid-back opening of *Jubal* with its paring of tenor and flugelhorn, which leads to one of Rendell's most poised solos. *Spooks* epitomises everything that was original about the band, from the pairing of clarinet and trumpet on the fragmented figures of the opening against Garrick's treble trills, to the collective improvisation that follows, proving that the same instrumentation as a conventional Dixieland line-up can also sound convincingly contemporary. The second side of the original LP builds to a climax, from the opening *Prayer* which accurately catches the feel of Garrick's devotional works from the period, via the spontaneous dash of *Hot Rod* (a Carr theme inspired by the custom-built automobile of Ian's friend Gerald Laing,) which was worked out more or less on the spot by the band-members, to the more structured feel of the title track, which Garrick subsequently re-scored for big band. Every track on *Dusk Fire* was a first take. Although a couple of pieces were recorded in more than one version, none of the retakes and no edits were used on the issued disc. The band was equally capable of this level of consistency on its regular gigs.

The album also gives us an insight into the compositional methods of the group, which were not unlike those of a Mingus jazz workshop, or — as Ian himself would experience much later in life — the collective development of George Russell's bands. The odd spontaneous creation such as *Hot Rod* apart, most of the group's original repertoire underwent a lengthy period of being worked over in rehearsal, tested on gigs and constantly refined. It has remained an aspect of Ian's work that he still does this, taking pieces from one area of his past and reinterpreting them, altering them and revising them for whatever current context he is working in. His discography shows plenty of examples of pieces such as *Hey Day* that have undergone multiple incarnations.

Ian said at the time *Dusk Fire* was recorded, that: 'We usually start with a complete score...maybe even down to having bass parts written in. But very often this gets pulled to pieces at rehearsal and completely reorganised.' A good example is *Spooks*, which began life as a sketch for a piece in 12/8 by Ian. 'I worked out a bassline at the piano, taking in three chords mainly' recalled Don. 'I produced this at a get-together we had at Ian's place. We just went from there, adding other lines on top.'[15]

In Don's memory, it was usually Ian who made the running in setting up their joint compositions. 'He wanted to write,' Don recalls, 'so together we wrote things. Which was interesting because we didn't have a harmony of personalities. We never had an immediate, lasting desire to be together all the while. If I was together with anyone in that band, I suppose it was Dave Green, who was particularly my friend, but as time goes on you sort these relationships out in a group. Ian wanted to write, and as the time for the next album came up, he was saying, "What are we going to do on it?" And he would instigate a joint composition. I think we probably wrote at least a third of the band's overall repertoire as joint things, partly his idea and partly mine, and the contrast of our personalities led to a contrast in the music. You don't get fire and vitality if things are too smooth, so it's good to have some friction. And between me and Ian there was friction.'[16]

Even so, this close writing partnership between the bandleaders, coupled with Garrick's equally committed output of new compositions, plus an unusually high level of intensity on the bandstand or in the studio, did not entirely account for the band's maturity and consistent rate of development. The confidence and sense of collective personality in *Dusk Fire* came at least in part from Ian's own rapid development on both a personal and professional level, which made him a co-leader as weighty and musically mature as Don Rendell had already been when Ian originally joined the line-up.

During the first full year of the band's life, in June 1963, Ian had married Margaret Bell. At this point, she was still in her final year as a student, and could only come down to London to stay with him during her vacations, until she had finished her degree. She finally moved to London permanently in September 1964, a few weeks before the band recorded *Shades of Blue*. It is her face that appears on the album cover,

Ian's wedding to his first wife, Margaret Bell.
(Newcastle Chronicle/Ian Carr)

and the relationship with her brought both passion and stability into Ian's life in equal measure.

In the days when Margaret was still travelling down to London for holidays and weekends, Ian had left the flat he had shared with Jeff Clyne, and since recovering from his illness had been living in the East End Georgian enclave of Fournier Street in Spitalfields, in the shade of Hawksmoor's great church, and virtually opposite the famous market.

Gerald Laing had introduced him to the area, having rented number 12, in the most celebrated terrace of eighteenth century facades, amid what had once been Huguenot workshops and dwellings. 'It was extremely beautiful,' Laing remembers, 'but my first encounter with it was more prosaic as the place was infested with fleas, and we had to get the local council in to eradicate them. Actually later my house passed through several generations of St. Martin's artists. In due course it ended up with Gilbert and George, I think, but in my day it was less up-market, right in the middle of the banana importers and East End tailors.'[17]

Ian's own flat was at number 9, an even less salubrious address on the opposite side of the road, but one that was nonetheless covered by numerous preservation orders, which meant that no detail of the building's structure or appearance could be altered in any way. To complicate matters further, his lodgings were in a building designated a workshop, and so technically no-one was allowed to live there permanently. Ian's two attic rooms had little more than a gas ring and a sink, and in a reference to *Down and Out In Paris and London,* Don Rendell described it, tactfully, as 'Orwellian'.[18] But despite the squalor, the place was cheap, and although it was in what was then one of the roughest sections of the East End, it was conveniently close to the City of London.

Being an illegal sub-tenant, however, meant that Ian lived in an even greater state of constant anxiety than normal. His fears came to a head one night when Trevor Tomkins had driven him back from a gig. Trevor and his girlfriend came upstairs for a cup of Nescafé, and were relaxing in the small hours of the morning, when despite being four floors up, there came a knock on the window.

'I pulled back the curtain and opened the window,' remembers Ian, 'and there was a police sergeant outside. "Excuse me, sir," he says, "very sorry to disturb you, but have you seen a man go by?" I told him we hadn't but that we had heard a bit of a thump on the roof. "Oh, what a pity," says the policeman, "I was chasing a thief over the roof, and I thought he'd gone right by here. Sorry for the intrusion." And he disappeared, climbing back up on to the roof to look for the thief. Trevor was amazed, until he looked out of the window and saw there was a tiny little walkway behind the parapet of the Georgian facade, just before the angle of the roof started to rise. Of course it was a sheer drop on the other side of the parapet.'[19]

Too intent on his quarry for the sergeant to question what Ian was doing there, the incident led to no further developments with the police. But it added to Ian's unease, and to further complicate matters, Ian and Margaret acquired a large dog — an Alsatian/Collie crossbred bitch —

The rooftop view from Ian's Spitalfields flat,
where the police chased a burglar. (Ian Carr)

who required considerable amounts of exercise. This was not too problematic until the dog went on heat, at which point every neighbourhood stray homed in on her. During one of these periods, Ian took the dog out with him when he went to post a letter. Armed with a walking stick to beat off the unwelcome attentions of the area's male canine population, he set off past the market for the postbox, when one particularly persistent little dog took no notice of Ian's attempts to deter it. Eventually, he tried a well-aimed kick, and immediately a huge man appeared from behind a fruit and vegetable stall in the market.

Ian remembers the incident only too well. 'He rushed up to me and said, "Are you you trying to kick my dog?" And so I said, "Yes, because it's trying to interfere with mine." He picked his up and stalked off, but just as I reached the postbox on the other side of the road, he obviously thought the threat was over and let his dog go. It dashed across and made a beeline for the rear-end of mine. So I lashed out with my foot and caught it fair and square. It retreated, yelping. At that moment, the whole street froze. A woman pointed at me and shouted, "Spiteful beast!" And the man rushed over to me again and started threatening me, saying, "You kicked my dog, do you want me to kick yours?" although as mine was Alsatian-sized, I think he was unlikely to follow through with the threat. Things were getting a bit nasty when two policemen strolled round the corner. One took him by the arm, and the other took me by the arm, and they listened to our various accounts of what had happened. Finally, my policeman took me aside, and said, in a quiet voice, "Look, if you want to kick a dog don't do it in front of the general public." That's all he sad, he let me go, and that was the end of it. But I always got a prickly feeling every time I walked through that bloody vegetable market after that!'[20]

As a result, Ian soon decided to move away, and shortly after Margaret had moved to London for good, the couple found a new flat in Belsize Park at England's Lane, NW3. Coincidentally, Gerald Laing, depressed that his recent work had been excluded from a contemporary exhibition at the nearby Whitechapel gallery, also made the decision to leave Spitalfields. His luck took a turn for the better however, when the art dealer Richard Feigen came over from New York and bought up a vast stock of his work to display in the United States. Gerald ended up moving to America for some years, where his work swiftly became much appreciated and sought after.

His marriage and move to Belsize Park stabilised Ian's personal life, despite the prevailing feeling that he was working hard for little reward, and there is no doubt that the period between *Shades of Blue* and *Dusk Fire* offered him substantial opportunity to grow as a musician.

The Rendell-Carr Quintet did work regularly in London and beyond, but it was still necessary for Ian to take as much other freelance work as he could get to keep hand to mouth. As well as big band sessions, he also played regularly with John Stevens' experimental groups at the Little Theatre Club, jamming with the likes of John McLaughlin and Jeff Clyne in what briefly became a fairly consistent quartet.

In early 1965, Ian recorded with the piano *wunderkind* Roy Budd, playing Harry South's big band arrangements on the disc *Birth of the Budd*. Soon afterwards there was more big band work, with blues singer and guitarist Alexis Korner, who had recently decided to take a break from touring to spend more time at home with his three young children.

Margaret Carr and the dog that caused the incident in
Spitalfields market. (Ian Carr)

Alexis, who never did things by halves, probably spent just as little time
with his family as he had done before, because he promptly became the
media reporter for the *Today* programme on the BBC Home Service, and
had his own weekly spot, 'Korner's Corner' on the television magazine
programme *Roundabout*. Approached by Rediffusion to become music
director on its more pop orientated programmes for the ITV network,
Alexis took on running the resident band on a new pop show which ran
until August 1965 called *Gadzooks! It's All Happening.*[21] Ian was
recruited to join the trumpet section, and during his time on the show
backed Sonny and Cher, Tom Jones and Lulu. However, he was forced
to leave the band several months before its run ended because his sight
reading was still not good enough instantly to read complex new charts
for every show.

Clearly this was something that now needed urgent attention, and in addition to woodshedding with the New Jazz Orchestra, Ian went back to Kenny Wheeler to help him read his way through a selection of charts. As 1965 went on, his reading improved dramatically.

Following the New Jazz Orchestra sessions of March 1965, there were several recordings and concerts with Michael Garrick's sextet, a group which the pianist continued to run independently from the Rendell-Carr Quintet, although increasingly the personnel of the two bands overlapped. Since his studies in English at London University, Garrick had been heavily involved with the poetry and jazz movement, and for some time he had worked with the writer Jeremy Robson in putting on concerts of music and verse. He had also been the pianist for the revolutionary Jamaican alto saxophonist Joe Harriott, who was one of the pioneers of free jazz in Britain, and who was now a regular sideman in Garrick's own band.

Ian took the place of the charismatic Caribbean trumpeter Shake Keane in Garrick's line-up, often improvising freely with Harriott to lines read aloud by poets, just as Keane had done. Keane had decided to move to Germany for personal reasons, but before he went, he and Ian did a BBC broadcast together with just two trumpets and rhythm. Keane's nickname came from his fondness for Shakespeare, and it was fortunate that in Ian, Garrick found a musician equally sensitive to the power of the English language, and as moved by the poetic muse.

There was, however, nothing narcissistic, prissy, or withdrawn about the playing of Garrick's bands. They reacted as gritty contemporary improvisers to the equally contemporary writing of the poets, and to the depth of Garrick's own increasingly confident compositions. His May 1965 album *Promises* features Ian alongside Harriott and Tony Coe, and the playing here is at times blisteringly ferocious, as it is on *Shiva*, a track by a similar line-up released by Garrick on his posthumous tribute to Harriott, *Genius*. There are examples of Ian's spontaneous reaction to poetry on discs by Robson and John Smith, both made in 1965, and he plays too on Garrick's *Jazz Nativity*, one of the pianist's earliest recordings of a liturgucal piece, on the January 1966 album *Black Marigolds*.

By this time, Garrick, whose love for using the church organ in jazz was first put on disc with the eminent organist Simon Preston in May 1965, was beginning to produce linked pieces of writing which in due course would form the basis of his larger scale devotional works, mostly written for children's choirs as a consequence of the enthusiasm of the Hampshire local authority music officer Victor Fox. Ian was subsequently to play a prominent role in two of the largest of these, *Jazz*

Praises, recorded in St Paul's Cathedral in 1968, and the premiere of *Mr Smith's Apocalypse,* which began life as a Farnham Festival commission under the title *Requiem for Martin Luther King* in 1969.

Michael Garrick himself paid tribute to the strength of Ian's contributions at his own 70th birthday concert at the Queen Elizabeth Hall in London in May 2003. He opened with a movement from *Jazz Praises,* called *Behold a Pale Horse,* and when I asked him why, he said: 'Because of Ian Carr's flugelhorn solo from the original concert. I listened to it quite recently, and thought, "I wonder how it would sound if I took down Ian's solo from the record and orchestrated it?" Consequently I did just that, and it worked, although I never told Ian about it. Then, not long before the concert, I happened to see Ian and I told him if he came to the concert he'd have a surprise. He came along, and there was his solo, played by the whole orchestra, which proves better than anything that jazz improvisation is real composition. You hear it, notate it, orchestrate it, and there you are – a demonstration that the soloist produced a lovely piece of music on the spot. And I wanted to do this for Ian in gratitude for all the music we've made together.'[22]

In the summer of 1965, there had been another quite unexpected musical adventure for Ian, which both harked back to his Novocastrian days and looked forward to his future with Nucleus. The manager on the EmCee Five's trip to Italy in 1961 had been Mike Jeffreys, who was now managing the Animals. The band's lead singer, Eric Burdon, of course, knew Ian from Newcastle days, and so when the idea came up that the Animals would form a special big band for a one-off performance at the Richmond Jazz and Blues Festival, it was Ian who got the call from Eric.

'We had a meeting and they said they wanted three trumpets, three tenor saxophones and a baritone,' he remembers. 'So I got Kenny Wheeler, a very good lead player called Greg Bowen, and me. And I put together a sax section [Al Gay, Stan Robinson, Dick Morrissey, and Paul Carroll on baritone]. Kenny took down some of Ray Charles's arrangements from records, and we added some original arrangements of Kenny's on a few other numbers that the Animals particularly wanted to do. By this time my sight reading had improved enough for me to do the arrangements, and we got together and had a rehearsal. It was a big, rough band. But it was very, very exciting. Gerald Laing had come back on a short visit from America, and he was driving a hot rod, with no bonnet and a big silver engine, huge rear tyres and small front ones. There wasn't another one like it in the UK at the time, and I don't think it was even road-legal, but he drove me out to Richmond, which was sensational! Eric was all over it with his camera, and soon everyone was taking photographs.

'A night or two later, we were out in it in London, and stopped at some traffic lights when a car stopped right beside us. The window wound down and it was Patrick McNee from *The Avengers*. "How much d'you want for it?" he asked. "Not for sale!" shouted Gerald, and drove off.

'Richmond was great, not a polished show, but wildly exciting, and part of the set was broadcast. We maybe did one or two other gigs and then it was over. I began thinking some of the more amazing aspects of it were normal, like Margaret and me going to Ronnie Scott's with Eric and the Animals, and looking over to see Ursula Andress at the next table. Being right in the middle of the whole scene, we didn't really think how extraordinary it all was.'[23]

It is a tribute to the hard work that Ian put in on his reading that he not only read his way through the Animals arrangements, but was asked to join Harry South's Big Band for a recording session the following January, in which he held his own alongside Greg Bowen, Hank Shaw and Les Condon, all among London's first-call trumpeters of the time.

In retrospect it is slightly unusual that Ian didn't draw his Quintet colleagues into the Animals line-up, because it was generally the case that as a way of keeping the band together, each member would try to wangle the others into other freelance work that came up. The way, for example, in which Garrick brought his Rendell-Carr colleagues into his own groups was typical of the way that they looked out for one another professionally. In this early period, the Quintet was a band that clearly enjoyed working together, whenever the possibility presented itself. The sense that it was growing musically was shared by all its members. Dave Green, for example, recalls: 'I became a much better musician than when I joined the band. I got so much help and encouragement from Ian and Don. They really gave me a musical grounding because up to that point I was an entirely self-taught musician. I didn't go to a music academy or anything like that, although I did have serious lessons later on. If it hadn't been for Don and Ian, I'd never have got to the point where I was playing with Sonny Rollins and other players of his calibre. We were a respected band, and after I'd been playing with it for a couple of years, I started to get those kind of offers for the first time.'[24]

All the activity that went on between the first two Rendell-Carr albums had brought a huge range of additional experience to bear on Ian's playing, and much the same range of diverse influences (including an abortive period of work with Herbie Hancock on the soundtrack to the Antonioni film *Blow Up*) continued in the eleven months between *Dusk Fire* and its successor, *Phase III*, made in February 1967. Most importantly, the summer of 1966 found the band playing a regular weekly session at the Flamingo club in London's West End, opposite Georgie Fame. The gigs ran from midnight to 5am, and John McLaughlin was a regular in Fame's line-up. Undoubtedly this residency helped stabilise the band and give its work a focus that shaped the run-up to its next disc.

Language and puns were always important factors in the imaginative world of the Quintet, and for this third Columbia album, again issued as part of Denis Preston's Lansdowne series, they chose a title that superficially summed up where the group had arrived at musically. The record represented the 'third phase' in the band's development as a creative unit, and its growing confidence in forging an original style which blended the invention of its members with sources that ranged right across the jazz tradition. As Ian said at the time, 'I think we're now beginning to use the whole language of jazz'.[25]

But back in 1967, 'Phase III' was also a tariff of the London Electricity Board, and to those who heard the name in those days, it immediately implied late night heat, as well as the accumulation and release of energy, all vital components in what, with its third successive win in the *Melody Maker* band poll, had become one of the most popular groups on the national modern jazz club scene. The album itself came third in the subsequent *MM* poll for LP of the year.

'The Quintet features a strongly musical approach to jazz, which also displays considerable ingenuity,' ran the flier for one of the band's regular concerts on the university circuit, in this case a midnight session at Bangor opposite the more overtly experimental Howard Riley and Evan Parker, and most similar contemporary reviews stress the band's unusual blend of innovation and musicality, which are very much in evidence on the disc.[26]

The punning, erudite echoes go further on this album than the clever double meaning of the *Phase III* title. 'This collection,' wrote Philip Larkin, in his *Daily Telegraph* jazz column, 'suggests that their eclecticism is literary as well as musical, extending as it does to "Crazy Jane" (Yeats) and "Neiges d'Antan" (Villon) for titles, and Coltrane and the chevaliers of free form as stylistic influences'.[27] He might have added that the band's literary world encompassed more than Europe, stretching as far as India for the inspiration behind Michael Garrick's *Black Marigolds*, a phrase drawn from the poetry of the Brahman writer Chauras, composed as he lay in a prison cell, condemned to death for having fallen in love with the daughter of the King of Kanchinpur.

Garrick had actually recorded the piece before, on his 1966 album of the same name. But although the majority of that disc featured the members of the Rendell-Carr Quintet, plus additional saxophonists Joe

Harriott and Tony Coe, the first recording of *Black Marigolds* was just by the trio of Garrick with Trevor Tomkins and Dave Green. This new session gave Garrick the chance to re-record his composition with the full band, and it is notable for Don Rendell's soprano playing, and also for Trevor Tomkins's use of hand-drums. Using a source that digs deep into human emotions – because Chauras compares his vision of a wedding feast with the King's daughter to the collapse of his dream, finding only 'black marigolds and a silence' – produced a depth of feeling in the band's playing that few other British jazz groups have managed, either in the 1960s or since.

The other two pieces with literary associations by Ian both concern the transience of love and female beauty, and come from a turbulent time in his relationship with Margaret, as she had given birth to a stillborn child early in 1966. The tragic experience brought them 'very close,' as Ian put it, and this overt strain of romantic love imagery surfaced in his music soon afterwards. Both these compositions had also been recorded earlier than the Quintet versions, by an experimental free jazz quartet made up of Little Theatre Club alumni, in which Ian was joined, in June 1966, by Trevor Watts on alto, Jeff Clyne, bass, and John Stevens, drums. However, as was often the case at the time, these tracks were not issued immediately, so that the versions of *Crazy Jane* and *Les Neiges d'Antan* by the Rendell-Carr Quintet were actually released first.

The former takes its title from a character in the late poems of W. B. Yeats, and is the central figure in a cycle the poet called 'Words for music perhaps'. She is generally portrayed by Yeats as an old woman, a soothsayer, who conceals wisdom beneath her erratic actions, and her overall theme is that not only is true love hard to recognise, but it is a brief thing that flourishes and then withers with age, 'a skein unwound between the dark and dawn'. Ian composed the piece with a highly eccentric head arrangement, leading to several choruses of blues.

'It was way out, so different,' he laughs. 'Michael Garrick helped me work out what the head actually was so that we could play it with the Quintet. The structure is a disorientated eight-bar theme, with two bars in 6/4, one in 5/4, another in 6/4, three in 4/4 and a final one in 2/4. There was no cant, no pretentiousness in Yeats's character Crazy Jane, and I wanted a piece that was similarly direct.'[28]

The sentiments of the 15th century poet François Villon are remarkably complementary to those of Yeats, and the stanza that inspired Ian's composition *Les Neiges d'Antan* reads as follows:

'Tell me where, or in what country
Is Flora, the beautiful Roman,
Or Archipiada, or Thaïs

Who looked like her,
Or Echo speaking when one called
Across rivers or pools,
And whose beauty was more than human,
But where are the snows of yesteryear?'

There's a haunting ambivalence in Carr's composition, a duality of key between D flat and B flat minor, which eventually resolves into A major, and this is because Ian originally conceived it without explicit harmonies. 'All I wrote was a melody line and a bassline,' says Ian, 'so it's a free ballad.'[29]

The other main ballad on the album, *Bath Sheba* (a title not without echoes of Thomas Hardy) is far more conventional in form, and finds Ian's flugelhorn counterbalancing Don's flute. Some astute listeners might notice a difference between the sound of Don's flute sound here and on the previous album *Dusk Fire*. This is because he was using a different instrument, an old French wooden flute that he felt had a better tone than the more commonplace metal version he had previously used. Finally *On!* takes the 32-bar popular song form, but frees up the A section, using the bridge, or middle eight B section as a harmonic anchor. Don's solo, taking note of the historical roots of the rest of the album, contains deliberate echoes of Lester Young.

'What we're doing here comes from a pretty deep level of everybody's consciousness,' Ian told Charles Fox at the time. 'It seems to me the music is more intense than anything we've put on record before.'[30]

Charles Fox was one of the most perceptive of British jazz critics of the period. A seasoned broadcaster with an impressive knowledge of the music's history, he introduced *Jazz Today* on the BBC Third Programme, the network which subsequently became Radio 3. His industry and schoolboy-like enthusiasm were channelled into literally hundreds of LP liner-notes, as well as reviews for the *New Statesman* and the *Guardian*, and it is a matter of regret that he only found the time to write three books, all of them short, but all of them indicating immense promise, were he to have essayed a longer work. He was also the co-author of numerous record guides, displaying a balanced critical judgement and a sense of taste that informed his enthusiasm for the newest sounds in jazz. His consistent support for the Rendell-Carr Quintet was therefore important in itself, but he also encouraged Ian to start writing and broadcasting about jazz.

At one point, in the mid-60s Charles planned to write a book with Ian on contemporary jazz, but this did not come off, although it probably sowed some of the seeds for Ian's first book, *Music Outside*, eventually published in 1973. More immediately, however, Charles introduced Ian to Teddy Warwick, the BBC's main jazz producer of the time, and this led to Ian presenting four half-hour talks on jazz, the first of which was on his beloved Miles Davis. In due course he met another producer, Geoffrey Haydon, who shot a black and white documentary about the Quintet during the spring of 1967, which included some footage of Ian's famous dog from the Spitalfields incident. The band was also to be the subject of another BBC film documentary, made in colour the following year by the director Mike Dibb, who went on to become a close friend and colleague of Ian's.

But well before the 1968 film by Mike Dibb was made, tragedy had entered Ian's life on a major scale. Early in 1967, Margaret found she was pregnant again, with the baby due in midsummer. Although the band had been doing well, Ian was anxious that he was short of money, so he decided to accept an offer to play and teach at the annual Barry Jazz Summer School in South Wales, despite the fact that it more or less coincided with the baby's due date. As it was, he was at the hospital for the birth by caesarean of his daughter Selina, on July 29, but rushed straight back to Barry to teach the next night. He rang daily, and mother and baby seemed to be doing well, until Margaret said to him a few nights later that she was frightened.

'The next day, I got a phone call from the hospital, and they said, "Mr Carr, your wife's collapsed." I asked if it was serious, and they told me it was very serious indeed. I just said, "Okay," and put the phone back. I rushed home to London, and when I got to the ward where she'd been she wasn't there. I was shown into a room to wait for the doctor. He was a very young man, and all he could say to me was, "We did everything we could." I just burst into tears, but when I calmed down, he told me that despite her taking anticoagulants, a clot of blood had worked its way from her leg to her heart, and killed her. He told me how they'd tried everything, but nothing was possible. "We've tidied her up now, and you can come and see her," he said. She was looking very beautiful, very pale, but she looked very, very cold. I stayed in there a bit, and gave her a kiss, but it was a weird experience. Although I'd seen death before, it was a very strange experience.'[31]

The suddenness and shock of Margaret's death had a huge impact on Ian's life. The immediate effects were, perhaps, not obvious, but the unexpected removal of what had in many ways been his muse during the most creative period of the Rendell-Carr group was to create a probing restlessness, a sense of things not being resolved, and a burning urgency to achieve before it was too late. On top of this, Ian now had a baby daughter. Selina was looked after by Margaret's mother in the North-East as soon as she was strong enough to leave hospital.

Reflecting later in his diary, Ian recognised that Margaret's death was by far the most significant among many changes that were affecting him at the time:

> '1967. August. A long, hot summer. It was the height of rock and roll, because rock really arrived that summer. It came of age. Jazz was at its lowest ebb in the United States. Coltrane died in July, just before Margaret. It was the end of an era. A weird turning point.'[32]

In the immediate aftermath, he could think of little to do apart from returning to the routine of his everyday life. He went home from the hospital. That evening, Trevor Tomkins, who happened to be in London because he wasn't teaching at the summer school as usual, came to the door.

'I decided I'd go round, whether he wanted it or not,' Trevor recalled. 'I arrived on the doorstep and said, "Ian, I'm very sorry. I'm here because I want to be here and to see you. You can tell me to piss off if you want, but I think I'll just come in anyway. I want to talk. If you want me to shut up, just tell me. But I'll just be around." As it turned out, we did start talking, it all came out, and there were lots of tears and much confusion. We drank a bottle and a half or two bottles of scotch between us. Not deliberately to get drunk...in fact we both stayed completely sober. That was a lesson to me about how strong emotion is. Far stronger than alcohol!'[33]

With the funeral arranged for the following week, Ian went back to Barry. 'I didn't know what to do with myself, and the Quintet was booked to do a concert there. Everyone else was going, so I went too. I was too upset to teach, but I went, did the concert with the group, and came away again.'[34]

Such a swift return to normal life, however, meant that much of the emotion of Margaret's death remained bottled up. Friends gathered round, and both Margaret's and Ian's mothers came South for the funeral. Ian even had a brief affair with the matron in charge of the ward where Margaret had died, but after one or two other brief flings he soon found that he had become impotent. He finally consulted a doctor who urged him to let his grief out.

'Tears were streaming into my beard as I drove home,' Ian says. 'I had permission to weep, and it stopped me pulling girls like that. But before I saw the doctor I was in desparate straits, I didn't know what to do. The baby kept me sane. While she was still in the hospital I had to feed her with a bottle at two, three or four o'clock in the morning. If the baby had died as well I think I'd have gone completely crazy. As it was, I channelled my emotions into a poem, a lament about death. In it the penis is a dagger. Through it men give life, but it also stabs, and I had the feeling of it as a death weapon. It brought life out, but it had killed Margaret. I had that feeling very strongly, which was terrible, and it took a long time to go away.'[35]

Ian's life gradually came back into some semblance of order. It improved dramatically following a concert that October when he took Sandy Major, the woman who was to become his second wife, to hear Miles Davis playing in London. He had first met her while Margaret was still alive, through his friend George Foster, then at London University, and who had promoted the Quintet. Ian's relationship with Sandy did not take off until the following spring, but he always dates the start of their getting to know one another to the moment when, with George Foster's help, he offered her a spare ticket to the Miles Davis concert. From April 1968 onwards, she provided some much-needed stability in his life.

Ian's main therapy in any time of stress was music, and in 1968 he threw himself into his profession with an energy and enthusiasm that exceeded anything he had achieved before. Something the Rendell-Carr Quintet had not done up to this point was to record an album in the atmosphere of a live session, which was, after all, the setting in which its substantial number of fans had got to know the group. This was rectified in March, with *Live!* when for one night Denis Preston's studio was transformed into what Ian described at the time as 'the rumbustious atmosphere of a typical jazz club'.[36]

Although the order of tracks played at the session was slightly different from that on the eventual album, Michael Garrick's *On Track* was the opening number played, to a crowd of about forty guests, including such friends as George Foster, who were squeezed into the studio. Its measured opening soon gives way to an opportunity for everyone to loosen up. There's a fiery solo from Ian, suitably rewarded by the crowd, before Don's passionate soprano takes its turn, and then Trevor Tomkins ushers back the introductory theme.

One of the most unusual things about the Rendell-Carr band in the late 60s continued to be Don's use of clarinet, at a time when (with the exception of Tony Coe) other British modern jazz musicians largely ignored the instrument. It provides the perfect timbre opposite Ian's muted trumpet for Don's ballad *Vignette*, which accurately catches the quintet's ability to leave wide open spaces in its playing of slower pieces. The voice shouting 'Bravo' over the applause is that of the actor Warren Mitchell, a studio guest whose passionate enthusiasm for the contemporary jazz at the time was sharply at odds with his television persona as the bigoted and conservative Alf Garnett.

To those who know Ian Carr's work from his later recordings with Nucleus, there's a foretaste of some of the feeling of that band in what he called 'our Rock'n'Roll dance', a number called *Pavane,* which consists of a Carr melody over a bassline, piano part and rhythmic pattern mapped out by Trevor Tomkins. The way the piano drops back at the start of Don's solo was a regular Rendell-Carr device, and part of the distinctive sound of the band. *Nimjam* has its origins in the Northeast, as it was written by Newcastle saxophonist Jeff Hedley, and had been featured in the band's club sets for some time. Garrick's subtle and moving piece *Voices* has its origins in his work with the Poetry and Jazz movement, and was (in common with *On Track*) written as a setting for verses by Jeremy Robson. And to round everything off, keeping the idea of words and music alive, *You've Said It* was dreamed up by Don and Ian as a 'conversation piece' – a series of dialogues between different elements of the band that emphasise the extraordinarily close-knit understanding that underpinned everything the quintet recorded.

It's clear from these pieces the degree to which Ian had thrown himself into his music, and he was playing with more fire and daring than at any previous time in his career, having also recently been featured as a soloist on disc with Stan Tracey's Big Brass in a disc of Ellington material, *We Love You Madly* for which he produced a flugelhorn solo on *I'm Beginning To See the Light* that stands out against the power of Tracey's scoring. Nevertheless, almost everything he did musically now become an intense search for growth, change and new interest. Privately, and before long publicly, he was fretting that the rich vein of inventiveness that had characterised the Quintet for most of its seven year life was all but played out.

A major factor in Ian's unease arose as a direct consequence of two collaborative discs that the Quintet made at producer Denis Preston's suggestion, during 1968. One, *Integration* featured the highly original electric guitar playing of the Indian-born Amancio D'Silva, and the second, *Afro Jazz* gave centre stage to the assorted percussion and talking drums of Guy Warren of Ghana. Both these newcomers brought new ideas and energy to the quintet, and Ian – who also spent a fortnight in the summer of 1968 playing in Spain alongside the legendary figure of American tenorist Don Byas, free of the Quintet's home-grown repertoire and jamming on standards – thrived on the liveliness and novelty of such outside stimulus. This was further fuelled by his invitation to be a guest on D'Silva's next album, *Hum Dono*, which featured Joe Harriott.

Some of Ian's unrest is readily apparent in the Quintet's next album, from April 1969, *Change-Is*. 'By all accounts,' wrote critic Mark Gardner in the Christmas 1969 edition of *Jazz Journal*, 'this is the last LP in the Rendell/Carr partnership, which has produced much good music and several durable albums'. He goes on to enumerate the finer points of the disc, and to end his piece both on a note of regret and hope for the future: 'One of the best British groups of the 1960s bows out extremely gracefully with the aptly titled Rendell piece, *Mirage*. Rendell's solo is a peach. In the 70s, one hopes that Rendell and Carr apart will be as artistically productive as Rendell and Carr together were.'[37]

Certainly the 1970s were to become a fertile period for Ian who went on to found Nucleus. Don Rendell, however, did not achieve quite such a high profile during the following decade, but in his new quartet with Trevor Tomkins and fellow tenorist Stan Robinson (who made his recording debut on *Change-Is*), Don nevertheless continued to play extremely distinctive jazz, beginning with his new group's appearance on Neil Ardley's *Greek Variations* album in November 1969.

With the benefit of hindsight, it is possible to see the conflicting pressures that were brought to bear on the Rendell-Carr group, and why it was perhaps inevitable that the band would break up at the end of the decade, as the swingin' sixties metamorphosed into the more confusing seventies. Signs were apparent at their by now annual poll-winners' concert for *Melody Maker* in April 1969 at the Royal Festival Hall, where their fifteen minute set struck the critics as aloof and uninvolved.[38] What had been a uniquely productive coming together of complementary talents now began to chafe. Don was still producing the kind of exciting post-bop playing that grew naturally out of his highly personal blend of his principal influences Lester Young and John Coltrane, and his composing was focussed on suitable vehicles for his impressive improvisatory powers on flute, clarinet, soprano and tenor sax. Don himself thinks that an even greater contribution to the break-up was that his desire to live and work in and around London became incompatible with Ian's desire for bigger and better things for the band, which inevitably involved travel and days, even weeks, away from home. 'My wife and I had become keen Bible students as Jehovah's Witnesses,' Don says. 'I started to appreciate something really important to me that meant more than music. That was my family. We had our daughter Sally nearly at school age and I wanted to be home more. I didn't want to be always charging round the world on tour.'[39]

Meanwhile, both in this quintet and in his own groups, Michael Garrick was working on ever-larger canvases, producing vast works in which fellow members of the quintet frequently found themselves playing alongside children's choirs, sophisticated vocalists and the cream of England's experimental poets. The very month after the second of the sessions for *Change-Is*, Rendell, Carr and Garrick took part in Garrick's hour-long *Jazz Cantata for Martin Luther King*, a piece which was eventually commercially recorded as *Mr Smith's Apocalypse*; and in June the Rendell-Carr group, plus Art Themen, played at London's Queen Elizabeth Hall, under Garrick's leadership, recording three more of his recent compositions.

But it seems that the catalyst in the final break-up of the band was Guy Warren. He was a remarkable, warm-hearted individual, who liked to be known by his friends as 'Shanaba'. The Ghanaian percussionist also cut a highly distinctive figure visually, and even today, Ian hasn't forgotten the impression Guy made when they first met at Denis Preston's office. He recalls: "'There's someone here I want you to meet," Denis told me on the phone. So I went down to Holland Park, and there was this fellow in full regalia. He was wearing a leopard skin over his coat, and he had a totally shaven head, but you didn't realise that at first because he was wearing a pith helmet with thongs hanging down off it to keep away the flies, and dark glasses. And when it came to playing, he used all kinds of traditional percussion instruments, African xylophones and things, as well as the usual drums. His behaviour could be completely wild – I remember him lying on the floor in all his robes, playing a little bamboo flute and beating time in the air with his feet, which were shod in beautiful moccasins. He might shout across to Dave Green "She's only sixteen, so take it slowly!" before suddenly blowing a whistle and shouting "Police coming!"'[40]

After playing together on the *Afro Jazz* album, Ian and Guy Warren became friendly, and Ian felt energised by what he described as the mixture of 'African rhythms plus jazz improvisation and a jazz beat'. In a tide of enthusiasm, Ian not only recorded a lengthy but unissued version of Ravel's *Bolero* with Guy Warren and Don Rendell, but he encouraged Guy to become a member of the Rendell-Carr group. Unfortunately his enthusiasm was not shared by the other four members of the band. 'There was some contention over the presence of Guy in the group,' he remembers, 'and it was left to me to tell him.'[41]

Hindsight also allows us to view the tensions in the band with rather more diplomacy and discretion than was felt at the time. Trevor Tomkins, for example, has an album which Warren dedicated to him as 'Little Brother T', and he recalls that at a personal level the two percussionists got on well. But whereas Trevor is a perfectionist about tuning his kit and creating tremendous rhythmic subtlety, Warren was the opposite, hitting hard, aiming at high drama, and often going, as

Trevor put it, 'way over the top'. This very basic difference didn't exactly help matters.

Dave Green expressed it more explicitly. 'The band developed very well over the course of its life, and you can hear that on the albums. It was getting quite loose and free, and ironically, by bringing in Guy Warren, it took a retrograde step, musically. That's because his whole specialisation is African drumming, and playing with him you had to work within that context. It seemed to me the band wasn't breathing enough, in terms of its rhythm.'[42] Add to this the fact that Warren's somewhat touchy character meant that he spent several weeks off speaking terms with Don Rendell after some remarks that passed during a gig in York, and all the elements were in place for the gradual disintegration of the band to occur.

Nevertheless, the quintet was as busy as ever during the first half of 1969, and *Change-Is* catches it in fine form. As well as gigs around London, the quintet (with or without Warren) played several university campuses, and it made its final broadcast for BBC Radio 1's *Jazz Workshop* on Wednesday 9th July.

Rather than looking further at the negative ingredients that saw the eventual break up of this fine band, *Change-Is* gives the opportunity to focus on the positive, and in particular on several ideas that would be further developed by Ian during the following decade. Firstly comes the idea of making the entire album in a seamless sequence, with the numbers on each side drifting into one another by means of improvised bridge passages. This would be a key ingredient in the Nucleus albums of the 70s, trying to capture on disc the way the band played a live set. Secondly comes the idea of expanding the line-up with guests, something Ian was also to do with Nucleus for his *Solar Plexus* suite in December 1970, and again on *Labyrinth* in March 1973. In particular, Ian liked the idea of using two basses, and on *Elastic Dream* with Dave Green and Jeff Clyne, he hints at the way Jeff and Roy Babbington would later work together on *Solar Plexus*. Finally that track and *Boy, Dog and Carrot* give us the chance to test Dave Green's assertions about Guy Warren's effect on the band's rhythm. At the time maybe it all seemed a bit less free than the band's usual intuitive understanding, but many years later all that is forgotten, and we can only regret that this marvellous British group did not survive to make more such glorious music.

7 elastic rock – the formation of nucleus

Deciding what direction to take when he left the Rendell-Carr group was Ian's main concern when he came home from teaching on the regular Barry Summer School in August 1969, still feeling angry over Guy Warren's relationship with the band. His home life had stabilised, Selina having moved in with Ian and Sandy in October 1968, after being looked after first by Margaret's mother, and then by Ian's sister Judith, but his professional life was far from stable. By now he was sure that the rich vein of invention that had led to the five Rendell-Carr albums, not to mention the related projects with Michael Garrick, Amancio D'Silva and Guy Warren, was a spent force. Yet there were several possible directions in which he could develop his own career.

The latter part of 1969 was a difficult time to be facing such decisions. British jazz was then at one of its most active phases in history, with creative forces like Mike Westbrook, John Surman and John Stevens forcing the pace of development with a string of new ideas and large-scale projects that pushed in several new directions. In particular it seemed that at long last the very distinctive vein of free jazz that had developed in Britain in the late 1960s was beginning to get major attention. That very September, the London arm of CBS announced the launch of a series of discs it called Contemporary British Jazz, and at the bargain price of 25 shillings and elevenpence each (approximately £1.30), its Realm label issued sessions recorded the previous January by Tony Oxley, Frank Ricotti, Howard Riley and Ray Russell. Notable among the personnel were guitarist Chris Spedding with Ricotti, and bassist Jeff Clyne with Oxley.

Equally prominent was the extravagantly marketed series of new jazz on the Marmalade label, of which the centrepiece was John McLaughlin's *Extrapolation* which featured Surman and Oxley, but which also included sessions by John Stevens' Spontaneous Music Ensemble and – bizarrely – Chris Barber, whose *Battersea Rain Dance* eschewed his New Orleans roots, and included a lively collaboration with organist Brian Auger and some spirited covers of Mingus material. All this activity prompted some action from Polydor, who finally made the decision to release the *Springboard* quartet disc that Ian had recorded back in 1966 with John Stevens, Trevor Watts and Jeff Clyne.

The critic Barry McRae, reviewing *Springboard*, was extremely enthusiastic, pointing out that whereas the recent Rendell-Carr output had been 'rather specialised', the quartet disc contained 'music more meaningful than their present output and more closely aligned to the idealistic ardour of the embryo British free movement.'[1] On the crest of such positive writing, and with the torrent of activity going on in London, Ian could easily have opted to take the free jazz route, but he felt that if he were to go in this direction he would want it to be part of a wider scenario, and not an end in itself.

Consequently, having ruled out the kind of small group free form music that John Stevens was still presenting regularly at the Little Theatre Club in Garrick Yard, just off St. Martin's Lane, and deciding not to return to the post-bop style he had played with the EmCee Five and then developed with Don Rendell, Ian set out to jot down everything he liked most about music, and which he wanted to retain in his next venture. High on the list were boogie woogie, blues and worksongs, and equally important were the rock-inflected modal vamps that Ian had played in his collaborations with the Animals. There was, he thought, a huge opportunity for a soloist to explore complete freedom in playing over a single chord for long periods. Consequently, although he was also attracted to the Indian scales being explored by Michael Garrick and Joe Harriott, it was the experience with the Animals that won out.

'I thought I should really go for the rock thing: the roots of the music, but with electronics,' he recalled. 'Many Rendell-Carr gigs had been ruined by bad pianos, so I thought I would go for an electric piano. Some time before, I'd met Karl Jenkins when I was a competition judge for new pieces, and his writing impressed me. He played electric piano as well as oboe and baritone, so I approached him. Then there was John Marshall, who had depped occasionally for Trevor Tomkins, and had also worked regularly in Mike Garrick's sextet. At one point in the earlier sixties, John's timing had been a bit erratic, either racing, or slowing down, but after he went on a three month European tour with a black American soul band, his time became rock steady, and his playing was absolutely fantastic.'[2]

Although he had been a double bassist up to this point, Jeff Clyne had recently begun to play electric bass, and he knew both Ian and Karl, so he was also drawn into the fold. The original choice of reed player was the versatile Australian, Ray Warleigh, who was frequently to be heard with Ronnie Scott's band, as well as with Humphrey Lyttelton and John Warren. However, his very versatility was a disadvantage, as Ian feared that Ray would not have the commitment to put Nucleus first if a lucrative alternative offer came up – a sentiment that was proved right when Alexis Korner proposed a tour, and Ray left before the new band had played in public. His replacement was the New Zealander, Brian Smith. The final piece of the jigsaw was guitarist Chris Spedding, who joined after a couple of alternatives had been tried.

To start with, the new band's repertoire was drawn from pieces by Karl, Ian and Brian, but in mid-October, before it had had an opportunity to play together much, five of its members, with the exception of Karl Jenkins, appeared an an album largely written by Neil Ardley called *Greek Variations*. The main soloists on the first side of the disc were Ian and Don Rendell, playing with a fourteen-piece band (including strings) directed by Ardley, in a six-movement suite built around a Greek folk melody that doubled as the call-sign of Greek Radio. In characteristic Ardley style, the compositions themselves were constructed from a number of theoretical starting-points, such as inverting the melody, or playing it backwards, and the twelve-tone scale was prominent. Yet, however highbrow the writing techniques were, the results were hailed immediately as 'unselfconscious swinging jazz with plenty of satisfyingly melodic invention from the soloists.'[3]

More importantly from Ian's point of view, side two of the disc was shared between his new group and that of Don Rendell, who had split front line duties with saxophonist Stan Robinson, retained Trevor Tomkins as drummer, and added Neville Whitehead on bass.

Ian's contributions (written by him, rather than Ardley) could be described as 'Nucleus minus one', but the seeds of his new band's style were already obvious, with a pugnacious version of *Persephone's Jive* that was to be re-recorded by the full Nucleus line-up the following year.

The preparations for the new band were then put on hold, as Ian was selected by the BBC to be Britain's representative in the European Broadcasting Union Big Band, a multi-national institution that met each year, and was made up of star musicians from the member states. Ian's solo on *I Got Rhythm* attracted attention, not least from the large number of radio producers in attendance, several of whom, as it rather fortuitously turned out, were to be judges at the following summer's Montreux festival competition for new bands.

Soon after Ian's return to London, Pete King of the Ronnie Scott club approached him about the prospect of managing the new band, and with King's help, Ian not only established the band as a regular attraction at Scott's club, but was able to annul his record contract with Denis Preston, in favour of a new deal negotiated for him by King with the emergent Vertigo label, which if nothing else, offered vastly more studio time – a very necessary ingredient for a predominantly electronic group.

Playing frequently in the club, and being booked into numerous other UK venues by King meant there was plenty of work for Nucleus, as Carr's new sextet came to be called, not least because it was established as a co-operative, rather than being a group led under Ian's own name. It played frequently enough for its collective identity to develop very rapidly, for the band to test its limits and to arrive at a definitive style. The band's first full year, 1970, was to be one of extraordinary productivity. Its first album, *Elastic Rock*, was recorded in January 1970, and the follow up, *We'll Talk About It Later*, was made in September, following a prizewinning performance in June at the Montreux Jazz Festival, which led in turn to appearances in the United States, both at the Newport Jazz Festival and at New York's Village Gate.

One of the first live reviews of Nucleus, by Pete Gamble, dates from a session played well before the Montreux success in the spring of 1970, and because it concerned a couple of deputising musicians in the line-up, highlighted the degree to which the band needed to retain its regular personnel. Summing up the evening at London's Phoenix jazz club as 'one of the better attempts to fuse jazz with rock', the article otherwise did the band few favours, by going on to observe that Art Themen, sitting in for Brian Smith, lacked the gravity to be an effective counterbalance to Ian, and that the band's other temporary guest, keyboardist John Taylor, a highly regarded player, was too tentative to replace Karl Jenkins convincingly. 'With the high standards of musicianship set by the trumpeter, the band needed a second authoritative soloist which they obviously lacked,' he wrote. 'Chris Spedding's front-line excursions were nothing short of disastrous; however his bottleneck work was thankfully down to a minimum.' There was, nevertheless, praise not just for Ian but for the interaction between Jeff Clyne and John Marshall.[4]

This review, and similar comments from elsewhere, ended up having a beneficial effect on the group, since it made Ian determined to keep his regular line-up together, and to demand sufficient loyalty from his musicians to put Nucleus first. Ironically, the only exception he made at the time was for Brian Smith, who received frequent invitations to moonlight, but who eventually became the longest-serving member of the original personnel. Smith agreed to put Nucleus first after Ian initially fired him, but then invited him to rejoin for the band's trip to Montreux.

At Ronnie's for a fortnight beforehand, and for a concert at the festival itself, Nucleus worked with the American scat singer Leon Thomas, a man most famous for bringing the glottal yodelling of African pygmy music into jazz. Thomas had just launched his debut album under his own name, *Spirits Known and Unknown*, and in promoting it, and himself, in Europe, he established a relaxed collaboration with Nucleus. Each night at the club, they played a set of their own material before he joined them for a sequence of his songs, which the band accompanied. However, for the band, the main excitement of the Montreux trip was the contest. Pete King made arrangements to ship out their gear, and drove down himself in his Jaguar.

Ian himself still maintains that competitions don't mean a lot to him, but in this case it was his fellow band members who urged him to take part in Switzerland. In those days, the Montreux Festival was in its infancy, having only been founded three years before in 1966, but then as now, Claude Nobs, the director, realised the publicity value of including a competitive element in the programme. In conjunction with the EBU (European Broadcasting Union), he invited bands from all over the world to take part in an contest to find the best newcomers, to be judged by those same radio producers that Ian had impressed with his playing in the EBU big band. As well as Nucleus, the contestants included a German ensemble with Ian's future collaborators, Wolfgang Dauner, Ack Van Rooyen and Eberhard Weber, and a Swiss band led by George Gruntz.

Ian had decided that as the band was going to compete, then it would go for broke. One important element of the competition was that each group had to perform within a 20-minute slot, with marks deducted for over- or under-running. To make the most of their segment, Ian enlisted the help of BBC producer Ray Harvey, who offered advice on devising and playing a varied 20-minute set, and discussed devising a series of signals to ensure a prompt finish. Whereas Grunz over-ran, and Dauner's band played a single long, modal number, Nucleus applied Ian's concept, first tried on the *Change Is* album and refined on *Elastic Rock,* of playing pieces that slid easily from one to another, to form a seamless sequence.

'We must have done *Elastic Rock* and *Torrid Zone*,' he recalls, 'and other things from the albums, all slotted together in a continuous set. We ended with *Persephone's Jive*, which was really explosive with its series of eleven-eight bars at the end, with a massive "Pow!" to finish. We got an incredible round of applause from the audience which was just about all made up of musicians, because it was dynamite, and also because what we were doing was so new.'[5]

Nucleus won by a considerable margin over Dauner's band, but this led a number of die-hard German jazz fans in the crowd to boo loudly

Nucleus win the band contest at Montreux, 1970 (l to r) Chris Spedding, guitar; John Marshall, drums; Karl Jenkins, piano; Ian; Jeff Clyne, bass; Brian Smith, soprano. (Harry M. Monty/Ian Carr)

when Nucleus came on stage later in the evening with Leon Thomas. Stung by this, Ian responded with a forceful solo on Thomas's first song, which Jeff Clyne remembers as winning over this hostile element in the audience. The band's triumph in the competition was announced on the BBC radio news, and when Ian got home, despite the emotional distance between them, he received a telephone call of congratulation from his father.

The immediate result of winning was that the band had to up sticks and set off for the United States within a matter of days. For most of the members this was an exciting prospect, but for Jeff Clyne and his wife, who had booked a package holiday together, it was something of a disaster.

'My wife was pregnant, expecting my first daughter,' he remembered. 'We'd booked a holiday abroad to get away for a few days before the baby arrived, and we weren't due back until the day the guys were supposed to fly to the States. I was making frantic phone calls to Pete King, saying, "Look, I'm stuck here, and I can't get back until such-and-such a date, because everything's booked!" Eventually he said, "Fine, we'll leave a day later." But I'll never forget the last minute dash to get out to the airport the day after we got back from holiday. And then I got stopped by the U.S. Customs, and I missed the connecting flight to

Rhode Island. But I got there in the end, and the whole experience was great – the band was very good by that time.'[6]

Newport proved to be an unforgettable experience, especially for Ian, who arrived in time for the festival's extravagant Louis Armstrong 70th birthday concert, which not only featured an appearance from the great man himself, but guest spots from Wild Bill Davison, Dizzy Gillespie, Bobby Hackett, Ray Nance, Joe Newman and Jimmy Owens.[7] The vast crowd was stilled into silence later on the rainy Friday evening by the magnificent Mahalia Jackson, singing *Just A Closer Walk With Thee*, as a dedication to Armstrong.

Nucleus did not go on until the Sunday afternoon, and on the Saturday, between bursts of inclement weather, they were able to hear a trumpet workshop with Dizzy Gillespie on top form, and Joe Newman, followed by a set from Elvin Jones. There were also nods in the direction of fusion, with some unexpected musical pairings, including Steve Swallow taking melodic bass solos with Chico Hamilton, and Gary Burton welcoming Keith Jarrett into his line-up on electric piano and soprano sax. The evening finished with a tumultuous set from Tony Williams' Lifetime.

Nucleus went on stage to open the proceedings on what turned out to be bright, sunny Sunday afternoon. It was so hot that Ian left his trumpet at the side of the stage while he went off to find a Coca-Cola, only to return and find it had been knocked over, and a valve was damaged. As a result, brimming with anger, he played the entire set on flugelhorn. But this was no bad thing, the music took off, and the band played, as one reviewer put it, 'a well integrated and inventive set...heavily electronic in the jazz rock idiom.'[8]

To many seasoned jazz listeners in the United States, this idiom was still unfamiliar, and challengingly new. By the time the band arrived in New York for its booking at the Village Gate, people in the crowd had begun shouting out, 'What do you call this music?'.

Ian and Karl found themselves explaining to eager fans the principle of unusual time signatures (there is, for example, a bar of nineteen-sixteen in *1916*). One listener who was unfazed by it all was Rahsaan Roland Kirk, an old acquaintance from the Rendell-Carr group's days at Ronnie Scott's, who came down to check out what Ian was up to. 'We'd been working at Ronnie Scott's opposite his band,' John Marshall recalls. 'He was aware of what we were doing, and around the same time he began calling his group the Roland Kirk Vibration Society. Suddenly it was fashionable to give your band a name.'[9]

Back in Britain, flush from this international success, Nucleus became the only UK act to appear in a prestigious week of concerts at the

Hammersmith Odeon, called Jazz Expo '70, appearing on October 26th in support of Elvin Jones and Albert Mangelsdorff, amid an overall bill that featured Ray Charles, Oscar Peterson, the MJQ, Earl Hines, Dave Brubeck and Gerry Mulligan. For the most part, live British appearances by Nucleus were every bit as successful as the band's triumphant overseas festival shows, bringing former Rendell-Carr fans along on the strengths of Ian's playing, and adding newer listeners, who were likely to have been introduced to fusion through the sounds of Jon Hiseman's groups or the Keef Hartley Big Band with Henry Lowther.

From the outset, the band took on a visual image that owed more to the pop world than to the suits and ties of modern jazz. In David Redfern's photographic report from Newport for the August 1970 edition of *Jazz Monthly*, his backstage picture shows Nucleus in tee-shirts and vests, Chris Spedding sporting a headband, and everyone's long hair flopping down to their ubiquitous dark glasses, making a stark contrast to the elegant suits of Louis Armstrong and Buddy Rich. Only Gary Burton's flowing locks and hand-designed waistcoat shared the new look. Furthermore, the design of the band's albums for the Vertigo label could hardly be more different from the staid conservatism of the Rendell-Carr discs for Columbia. There were startling, fiery cover designs, and the disc labels themselves had an op art pattern of concentric stripes, that wound endlessly inwards towards the central hole as the record was playing, like an animated Bridget Riley painting.

At this point, Nucleus was still one of the first bands anywhere in the world to explore the territory where jazz met rock, and it was living proof that in jazz, just as in the pop world of the Beatles and the Rolling Stones, Britain was pioneering the way forward for music. The group had been formed, and was already playing regular week-long stints at Ronnie Scott's, well before the British release of Miles Davis's album *In a Silent Way*, although that album did make an immediate impact once it appeared. More significantly, the members of Nucleus did not hear *Bitches Brew* until their visit to the USA in 1970.

'The only other comparable band that existed in 1969, when we began,' recalls Ian, 'was Tony Williams' Lifetime, which included our friends and former colleagues from Britain, John McLaughlin and Jack Bruce. We went to hear them when they made a rare UK appearance at a club in Hampstead at the end of 1969, and they were incredibly loud, but we liked what they were doing. Fundamentally they had a very different approach from ours, with some very highly arranged things that featured Larry Young's organ blending with the guitar, as well as intricate passages where Tony doubled the melody on the drums.'[10]

Nucleus took a rather different route. To be sure there were also some intricate and highly arranged passages, but these were generally for the horns, and Ian's preoccupation was more about playing long seamless sets where numbers and ideas flowed into another, often exploring a small body of source material in various contrasting ways, than it was about the dazzling power and virtuoso display of Lifetime. There are excellent examples of this on the band's third and fourth albums, because both the entire *Solar Plexus* suite and *Suspension* from *Belladonna* demonstrate what Ian calls 'making maximum use of minimum material'.

A little later in the band's life, Ian gave a revealing interview about exactly where he thought Nucleus stood, *vis-à-vis* the more extreme displays that were becoming commonplace in the rock world. In a characteristically forthright set of comments, he said, 'A lot of it is extremely pretentious and the techniques are often pathetic...I am not so interested in the kind of music that is played by Chicago or Blood, Sweat and Tears. If I want to listen to really basic music that is vital as well, I would go to Howlin' Wolf with his electric Chicago rhythm section. I like Sly and the Family Stone because they have a fantastic feel.'[11] He went on to look back appreciatively on his earlier work with Eric Burdon and to suggest that he would eventually like to collaborate with the Who, 'if it was a mutual give and take operation', thereby suggesting exactly the kind of two-way dialogue with the UK rock scene that Miles was to explore on the American side of the Atlantic by progressively adding more collaborators from the funk and rock worlds to his recording line-ups.

The essentially minimalist strategy that lay behind much of the musical development of Nucleus in the early 1970s was also eloquently spelt out. 'I could never do without the ostinato bass rhythms,' said Ian. 'I always want, at some point, to have them in – the sheer rhythmic guts of the music. It requires incredible imagination to think up a really good, original and vital riff which is only really a melodic and rhythmic fragment. But to get a good one is very hard without it sounding trite, corny or too pretentious...What we do in Nucleus is simply to have one note which is a root and over that note we can play literally anything. That is the kind of freedom we are interested in. Not total freedom where you don't even have a root, but we have one note and over it we have complete harmonic choice. We are interested in building up tension and in the release of it.'

Ian went on to observe how totally free music, of the kind he had played only a short time earlier with John Stevens, no longer held any interest for him as it lacked drama, and he was determined to keep a sense of drama – of tension and release – in Nucleus's sound. Almost the only compromise in the direction of free jazz that Ian allowed himself in 1970 was an appearance in November with Keith Tippett's 45-piece Centipede, an anarchic ensemble playing an eponymous new work by Keith in a fundraising concert for the Jazz Centre Society at London's Lyceum Theatre. Between Nucleus gigs he still occasionally worked as a session player, including an album with Blossom Dearie that she recorded with a large band of London musicians, and he also made sporadic appearances with his former Rendell-Carr colleagues in Mike Garrick's *Jazz Praises*, which continued to be performed around the country. He had also recorded with Garrick for the *Heart is a Lotus* album within days of the first Nucleus studio sessions, but essentially Ian's new band, and its jazz-rock direction became his all-consuming obsession.

In retrospect it is ironic that Ian worked quite so frequently with Garrick, as the pianist was an outspoken opponent of electronics, even going so far as to say it wasn't 'real music'.

'We were having so much pressure from other jazz musicians,' Ian recalled. 'They are a very conservative lot and they have very puritanical ideas about what you should be doing. If it's pleasant, for example, it must be wrong, because only pain is good. Several of our former colleagues denigrated what we were doing, and referred to it all the time as "pop music". The idea that we'd "sold out" was ridiculous, because it was actually the poorest time of my life!'[12]

Unwittingly, Nucleus found itself in the middle of a debate between 'purist' jazz fans and more open-minded listeners that soon became every bit as ferocious as the turf wars of the 40s between beboppers and 'mouldy figs', or the early 1960s Beaulieu riots between Acker Bilk's 'trad' followers and the suited modernists loyal to John Dankworth. The debate was heated up by Digby Fairweather, writing in *Jazz Journal* about 'The Problem of Pop', in which he observed 'creativity and popularity are usually wary bedfellows.'[13] His conclusion that 'jazz and pop have their courses to run and they do not intertwine' was one adopted by many writers, and it took a firm stance from critics like John Fordham in *Time Out* and Richard Williams in *Melody Maker* to rebut this pessimistic conservatism. Interestingly, even the normally sympathetic Barry McRae was initially hostile to the band, slamming *Elastic Rock* in a review that labelled the album 'a disappointment', satisfying neither the listener's taste for 'the creativity of jazz, not the explosive energy of the best in heavy pop.'[14] Yet even McRae was forced to admire Ian's 'shapely solo' on *Torrid Zone*, his empathy with Smith on *Twisted*, and John Marshall's 'exemplary' drumming. At least

McRae's arguments were based on a critical premise, which was that the rhythmic basis of the band was unworkable. 'A jazz solo is no more successful with a rock rhythm section than it was with West Indian, Bossa Nova or Indian styles. It seems futile to reject the rhythmic tradition, so brilliantly extended in recent years by men like Elvin Jones or Milford Graves, for the predictable pulse of rock with all its superficial vitality.'[15]

Thirty-odd years later, after the hugely successful impact of fusion on almost all areas of jazz, it seems strange how hostile normally perceptive critics were, but in the event, it was the more percipient reviewer for *Music Now* who caught the turn of the tide, and wrote of *Elastic Rock* that 'this wealth of talent fused together has produced an exceptional album'.[16] His enthusiasm was justified, and in August the band received the welcome news that the first pressing of *Elastic Rock* had sold out – a total of 5,000 copies.[17]

As Nucleus was getting up and running, Ian was not its major composer, that role falling to Karl Jenkins, who not only wrote the title track for *Elastic Rock*, but many of its other best-known pieces, including *1916 (the Battle of Boogaloo)*, *Torrid Zone*, *Stonescape*, and *We'll Talk About it Later*, the title track of its second disc. In reality, many of these pieces were worked out together by Karl and Ian at Ian's flat, and at the time the two were very close collaborators, a dark shadow only entering their relationship once the band was truly established. Ian believes that within their partnership, he was the one most responsible for the overall sound of the early band, even if he wrote a minority of its repertoire. In fact, with all the band members contributing to its library, only five of the twenty compositions on the first two Nucleus albums were actually by Ian, which seems at first glance a dramatic contrast to the level of input he had contributed to the Rendell-Carr Quintet during the previous decade. However, this did not worry him unduly, because from late 1969 he had been hard at work composing *Solar Plexus*, with the idea that an enlarged version of Nucleus would record an entire disc of his own music before 1970 was out, thereby completing this year of remarkable creativity with a third exceptional album. The work was given its first performance at Notre Dame Hall, just off Leicester Square, on 12 September 1970, only a week or so before the six-piece band recorded *We'll Talk About It Later*. It was not until ten days before Christmas that the extended ensemble playing *Solar Plexus* was finally captured on disc, and there was also a BBC television ballet based on the music, rounding off this extraordinary year.

'There was a guy at the Arts Council called Keith Winter,' recalls Ian. 'He was a brilliant man with a double first in music and physics, who had introduced the principle of awarding grants to jazz composers with an award to Graham Collier in 1967. I rang him up, and not only did he know all about me, but he encouraged me to apply. In the end I was given a grant to write a piece for double quintet, and the first thing I did was to go out and spend £20 or so on a cheap electric keyboard. Everything I'd written up to that time, I'd just worked out in my head without recourse to a piano, but now I had something to compose with, and that speeded up the process.'[18]

Maybe it was that keyboard which inspired the electric piano opening of the movement of *Solar Plexus* called *Spirit Level*, but the two part writing in the calm prelude to this section is just one of a series of highly effective tonal effects that Ian brought to the album. Others include the contrast between the austere neoclassicism of Karl Jenkins and Jeff Clyne at the beginning of *Bedrock Deadlock* and the bass clarinet of Tony Roberts and Ron Matthewson's bass guitar on *Spirit Level*, or there's the tone-bending synth introduction to *Elements I*, which momentarily hints that it'll turn into *Telstar* by the Tornadoes, before the sinister series of falling glissandi ushered in by Jeff Clyne's bowed bass.

Above all, two elements stand out about *Solar Plexus*, the equally brilliant but widely differing solos of its three trumpeters, Kenny Wheeler, Harry Beckett and Ian himself, and the exuberant confidence of John Marshall's drumming. Kenny Wheeler's clear upper register on *Changing Times* gets to the essence of his wide-open singing style, while Harry Beckett's joyous lyricism on *Spirit Level* contrasts with the choppy phrasing, occasional plaintive cries and subtle use of electronics in Ian's own *Snakehips' Dream* solo. Ian's enthusiasm for his fellow trumpeters came across in a magazine interview he did a few months later, in which he told Tony Hopkins how much he admired Wheeler and Beckett's work (together with that of Henry Lowther and Marc Charig). These UK-based players seemed to him, he suggested, to have the qualities he most admired in Miles, where 'every note counts and [he] really tries to live it all the way'. Comparing Miles to the technically astonishing Maynard Ferguson, who was then living in Britain and leading an Anglo-American big band, Ian dismissed Ferguson as 'twice or six times the craftsman and only a quarter the artist'. What he looked for in his fellow trumpeters was the degree to which 'you are really saying something with your whole being'.[19]

As for John Marshall, as Ian commented more recently, 'it's like an essay on how to play drums for this kind of music. He's got incredible strength, he's very powerful, yet he has equally incredible sensitivity. He's got a very good ear, and I think his drumming is marvellous on those early Nucleus records.'[20]

The live premiere of *Solar Plexus* was every bit as rewarding as the album. 'No rock bassist has ever played with the technical brilliance or melodic ingenuity of Jeff Clyne, and no rock drummer could match the complexity of the magnificent Marshall's fiercely swinging rhythmic patterns,' wrote Ron Brown, in a piece about the Notre Dame Hall concert which, although it criticised the PA balance, praised the 'wonderfully meaty...joyous swinging' of the enlarged ensemble, 'with ballad-like statements from the soloists floating in a sea of organ-like comments from the synthesizer, alternat[ing] with punchy up-tempo sections relying heavily on the blues and the good old big band bash tradition'.[21]

A BBC radio session from March 1971 marks the final recorded appearance of the original line-up of Nucleus. It was made for the Transcription Service, who packaged programmes for overseas listeners, and it was logical that the band would include a version of *Elastic Rock*, which had become one of its most well-known pieces, in order to introduce its sound to an even bigger international audience than it already had. This version has the tight feel of a regular working band, but nevertheless features a very open solo from Spedding. On the whole, press critics were hard on Spedding as a soloist during his time in the group, but they miss the point that what Ian was looking for from him was the textural quality of his playing. Ian once described the guitarist's sound to me as 'like sandpaper on your face', and his playing for the BBC session has that same trenchant feel. Ian's own solo on *Snakehips' Dream* (the closing movement of *Solar Plexus* scaled down for the regular line-up) is magnificent, but it is the opening piece, *Song For A Bearded Lady*, a Karl Jenkins composition in a different arrangement from the version on *We'll Talk About It Later*, that is the best BBC offering. A free-form introduction prepares for Ian's trumpet to bring in the familiar head arrangement, ushering in the band's characteristic rhythm. The tempo is a fraction slower than the original recording, which gives the ensembles a more relaxed feel, although there's no lack of tension or passion in Ian's own opening solo.

Chris Spedding left soon afterwards to be replaced by Ray Russell, and Jeff Clyne also departed, with Roy Babbington joining in his place. The band was heard regularly around London, mainly in the new jazz venues at the Country Club (off Haverstock Hill,) or at the Phoenix in Cavendish Square, and it ventured out of town as well, appearing in June at the late night inaugural concert of the summer season at the Stables in Wavendon – the recently launched 'All Music' venue at John Dankworth and Cleo Laine's Buckinghamshire home. There were college gigs, too, such as a set opposite Mike Osborn's experimental trio at Leeds University. As a result of a group of German listeners having heard the London premiere of *Solar Plexus*, the band also worked quite often in Germany. Nevertheless, it was eighteen months after *Solar Plexus* before the band returned to the commercial recording studios, to make *Belladonna* in July 1972.

By this time there had been huge further changes in personnel. Critical success had not always translated into commercial rewards, and touring close to the economic margins meant that Ian became ill, with pneumonia and a spot on the lung which had to be kept under observation for some time afterwards. Despite his earlier pronouncements, he freelanced on discs by John Stevens and Keith Tippett, as well as trying to keep Nucleus together. Internal tensions and more tempting offers from elsewhere eventually broke up the original line-up, from which Ian had continued to expect an equivalent degree of commitment to his own, and by mid-1972, only Brian Smith remained from the founding members. Ironically, Smith had been absent from the *Melody Maker* pollwinners' concert during March, which featured an unusual transitional line-up, with tenorist Alan Skidmore playing in his place, Karl Jenkins, Roy Babbington, and John Marshall, from the regular band, plus New Zealander Dave McRae on keyboards.[22]

Ian had by then parted company from Ronnie Scott's management business, partly because of difficulties over getting advances against touring expenses and accurate settlements when the band came off the road, and partly because the club's management had turned down an offer of $5000 for American rights in *Elastic Rock*. By holding out for a more lucrative offer that never came, this ensured that the group remained relatively unknown in the United States, despite their success at Newport. The good distribution of the UK issue in Europe explains why the band became much better known on the continent, although at the time, British journalists who knew and liked the band always appeared mildly perplexed by its huge success in Germany and the low countries, compared to its profile in Britain or the USA. A typical press piece from that year makes the point that: 'Immensely popular on the Continent, Carr and his band have yet to break through in a big way in Britain.'[23]

The new 1972 line-up of the group, with Jon Hiseman acting as its record producer, offered Ian the prospect of changing this perception, not least because it was just as exploratory and innovative as the original version, but also because he now took a more central role in the band's development himself.

His experiences of 1971-2 had led to a permanent falling-out with Karl Jenkins who went back to work at Ronnie Scott's after the parting of the ways. Furthermore the band's record contract which Ian had negotiated via the Scott office as a collective partnership with the original members who were no longer in the group, took considerable unravelling. As a result, Ian put ideas of Nucleus being a co-operative band behind him, and he became the sole leader, so that it is his name alone which appears on the original sleeve and label of *Belladonna*. Perhaps because the album was something of a personal release for him after the tensions of the preceding months, he also believes that *Suspension* is one of the most magical moments of his entire career in the studios – a single take on the basis of minimum preparation that came as close to perfection as it is possible to be. The piece takes its name from the flattened ninth, the D flat, that hovers above the tonal centre of C throughout the number. Other numbers on the disc also live up to their names, *Summer Rain* sounding like just that, and *Mayday* building on a throbbing pulse borrowed from Isaac Hayes. None of the early Nucleus albums exemplify Ian's concept of tension and release as well as this, and in particular Ian sees the title track itself, an ensemble effort with no formal solos, as demonstrating both his musical concepts and his new-found role as leader: 'My role is that of a ringmaster, or perhaps a ringleader. I bring in or initiate things, the ensemble responds to them, and the whole thing builds, very naturally and in such a groove!'[24]

At the same time as becoming sole leader of the band, Ian attended to his own role as a player. For a start, following the damage to his Conn Victor trumpet at Newport, he now adopted a new instrument, the Selmer 99. 'I was put on to one of them by Henry Lowther,' he said at the time. 'It costs around £140, but it's just as good as one costing £300 to £400. It blows like a Rolls-Royce.'[25]

In the same interview, he observed that he was now tending to use the trumpet more frequently than his old Couesnon flugelhorn, an instrument he had bought during his EmCee Five days for £33. In the jazz rock context of Nucleus, he preferred the greater attack offered by the trumpet, but he also harboured ambitions to follow his idol Miles Davis, and begin to use electronics more widely, for which the trumpet was ideally suited. 'I want to get into the electric side of things,' he said, 'using wah-wah, reverb and loop echo. I'm not one of those people who believes in the pure tone of an instrument because to my mind there's no such thing. For a start, what one person might consider pure is totally opposed to the idea of someone else. In fact I don't believe in purity at all, be it sexually or musically!'[26]

Belladonna was a success, and as 1973 dawned, the new line-up of Nucleus had become a fixture on the British jazz scene. The group was

Roy Babbington, bass. (Ian Carr)

regularly winning polls in *Melody Maker* with what was still generally seen at the time as a highly innovative blend of jazz and rock music. Public perceptions of Nucleus, fuelled by the enthusiastic reception of its discs and tours to Italy and Finland, might not entirely have kept pace with the ups and downs of the band's day-to-day life, and not all those to whom it played were aware of the almost complete change of personnel that had taken place. However a period of relative stability followed, and an enlarged version of the line-up that recorded *Labyrinth* in the spring of 1973 drew on the core of musicians who had made

Belladonna, nine months earlier. Brian Smith, Dave MacRae, Roy Babbington, Clive Thacker, regular 'guest' pianist Gordon Beck, and Ian himself were now at the stage where they understood one another musically extremely well, whether on tour, in clubs or in the studio, so they formed a perfect launch pad for a similar kind of expansion of the line-up to that with which Ian had first experimented in *Solar Plexus*.

With the backing and encouragement of the Park Lane Group, headed by the supportive figure of John Woolf, *Labyrinth* got its first performance at the Queen Elizabeth Hall in London on 12 March 1973, the piece running for almost an hour. The recording was made the same month, before the core of the band flew off to appear at the Bergamo Festival in Italy. The piece received further live performances during the year, including a setpiece concert for Merseyside Arts at the Liverpool Playhouse in November, at which the augmented line-up played *Labyrinth,* and the regular Nucleus group played selections from *Belladonna* and *Roots*.

Looking back today, Ian is characteristically self-deprecating about what was, by any standards, an ambitious project. '*Labyrinth* suffered from my own musical ignorance,' he says. 'I just didn't have the know-how to make it more complete, and I was at the very limits of my knowledge in writing it.'[27] Yet in many ways it is a pivotal recording in his career, drawing together his skills at creating an extended piece of work with his intention that Nucleus sets should shift almost seamlessly from one piece to the next. At one level, it looks back at the related compositions that he and Neil Ardley wrote for the 1969 album *Greek Variations* (which also took thematic ideas from classical literature), but it takes several steps forward into the stylistic territory Carr had explored with Nucleus in the intervening years. Later, Ian was to write other extended works, many of them accomplished, through-composed suites, but few of them have the mixture of compositional integrity and palpable excitement that he achieved in *Labyrinth*.

It is full of great moments, from the eerie shadowing of trumpet and voice in the *Origins* section to the magnificent solos by Tony Coe (on bass clarinet) and Kenny Wheeler that follow, and capped by Dave MacRae's uninhibited, powerful playing on *Exultation*, ably supported by Tony Levin's thrashing drums, plus Trevor Tomkins' percussion, and – as the piece unfolds – the additional drums of Clive Thacker. Yet the disc has more to it than some interesting themes and fine solo blowing, notably the reflective contributions of Gordon Beck and Norma Winstone to *Ariadne*.

The main reason for this is that Ian's use of literary and mythical inspiration led him to conceive clear-cut dramatic roles for his instrumentalists. The tale of how Theseus slew the monstrous Minotaur – half man, half bull, and confined to the labyrinth made by Daedalus, where it devoured the yearly tribute of seven youths and seven maidens – is stirring stuff. Carr envisioned Kenny Wheeler's trumpet as representing the heroic element of the tale, Coe's clarinet as the embodiment of tragedy, and Winstone's voice as the human element, both in overall generic terms, and in the specific portrayal of Ariadne, the daughter of Minos, who assists Theseus and is then abandoned by him on Naxos. Below this, other layers of imagination were operating. Carr wanted to include the bass clarinet, as he admired Miles Davis's use of the instrument in *Bitches' Brew*, but in his mind it assumed a tragic symbolism, linked with the sinister cowled monk in Eisenstein's film *Peter the Great*, who surveys the German troops before they go into battle against the Russians. In the same way, he saw the two pianos having a role akin to that of the Greek chorus, prompting crowd reactions and spurring them into insurrection. Also drawn into the mix were bassline figures borrowed from bluesman Howlin' Wolf's song *Evil*, which Ian transformed into the underlying pattern for *Exultation* and his later version of the piece, *Gone With the Weed*. The lyrics sung by Norma Winstone were by Ian's wife, Sandy.

However he might feel about *Labyrinth* now, Ian was sufficiently proud of it at the time to send a copy to Gil Evans, in the hope he could interest the great arranger in working with British musicians – something that came to pass a number of years later.

The idea of using ideas drawn from the world of literature, and particularly those areas of writing about which he was passionate, was a key theme in Ian's thinking. He told an interviewer at the time: 'We realise that we will never appeal to teenyboppers. But there are more and more literate people, and there is an audience for the kind of thing we are doing with Nucleus. It is quite a substantial one, and with an little bit of preaching and a little more exposure, it could become very substantial indeed.'[28]

There are literary associations, too, in *Roots*, the album by the regular Nucleus line-up that followed, although one might not think so from the original cover art, which featured a green robot and barbed wire cat's cradle. In April 1973, the director Sam Wanamaker had asked Graham Collier to organise a Shakespeare's birthday concert, and for it Ian had written a piece called *Ban Ban Caliban*. It was composed as a three-part number for Collier's ten-piece band, and was quite clearly the hit of the evening, following a set of standards by Annie Ross (whose plan to sing John Dankworth's settings of Shakespeare was thwarted by the slowness of the mail from the United States, where John was temporarily based).

Other pieces on the bill were Collier's own *Rosemary For Remembrance*, Mike Westbrook's *Happy Birthday William Shakespeare*, and Mike Gibbs's haunting *For Lady Mac*. 'The most immediately enjoyable piece,' ran one review, 'was Ian Carr's *Ban Ban Caliban*, in essence a rocking blues with a long, delicious build-up, conducted by the composer and featuring a solo from Harry Beckett that consituted a moment of jazz truth. Bill, earthy fellow that he was, would have dug it.'[29]

Following this success, Ian decided to use the final section in a new arrangement for the Nucleus line-up on his next album. It was an exploration, he felt, of his literary roots, because Shakespeare was every bit as significant to him as Greek tragedy. This burgeoned, as he recalls, into the concept for the entire album, (some of the music from which had a new lease of life during 2002, when it was sampled by DJs Richard E. and Mr. Christy, otherwise known as Solar Apple Quarktette, on their disc *Kali Yuga* on the Further Out label.)

'*Labyrinth* had been all by me, composition-wise,' recalls Ian. 'But I wanted to use the other guys in the band as writers. So I suggested to them we do an album called *Roots*, which would delve back into our childhood roots, or any kind of roots that meant something to us in our lives. The title track is all about my childhood in that remote country cottage during the war, whereas *Images* is a very gentle song, comparable to *Ariadne* on *Labyrinth*, which was beautifully sung by Joy Yates, Dave MacRae's wife. Dave himself wrote a marvellous celebration of his roots in the Southern hemisphere, while Brian chose to celebrate two places in his native New Zealand, as well as his birth sign. Everything was to do with where we came from as people and overall, the album is our collective roots in music.'[30]

Right up until the time of *Roots*, which was recorded in November 1973, Ian's consistent front-line partner in Nucleus had been Brian Smith. As I mentioned earlier, he is a New Zealander, and he first arrived in Britain in 1964, working with Alexis Korner, Mike Westbrook and Graham Collier, before joining Nucleus. Before the start of 1974, when he took off for an international tour in Maynard Ferguson's big band, Smith always returned to the Nucleus fold after going off for a while to pursue other projects, but on this occasion he took his longest leave of absence. He was to come back again in 1976, for the recording and tour of Neil Ardley's *Kaleidoscope of Rainbows*, but he was absent from the line-up for a large part of 1974 and 1975, returning to the Southern hemisphere and also working with his fellow-New Zealander and ex-Nucleus colleague Dave MacRae in the band Pacific Eardrum. Smith's replacement in Nucleus was another antipodean, Bob Bertles, from

Dave McRae, keyboards. (Ian Carr)

Australia, an extremely versatile reed player who admirably took on the role of counterbalancing Ian's trumpet and flugelhorn. Subsequently, he also returned to his native country, but Bertles was a very creative addition to the British jazz scene during his time in the Northern Hemisphere, and he was also a prolific composer, this aspect of his work being reflected by *Rat's Bag* on the 1975 album *Snakehips etc.*

Alongside Bertles came another new arrival on keyboard. He was twenty-five year old Geoff Castle, already a veteran of NYJO and the Graham Collier Sextet. By the time Castle and Bertles joined, the hugely experienced drummer Bryan Spring had been in the band for some months, having previously worked with Stan Tracey, Frank Ricotti and Tubby Hayes. At the start of 1974 he toured in Germany with Nucleus, and he remained in the line-up for the band's next album, *Under the Sun*, cut in March of that year. Spring was replaced in due course by Roger Sellers, a New Zealander recommended by Brian Smith, and who subsequently remained with the band for a considerable time.

For *Under The Sun*, Jocelyn Pitchen and Roger Sutton stayed on from the 1973 line-up that had recorded *Roots*, but 1974 also marked the arrival of Ken Shaw, who eventually replaced Pitchen, and continued to record with Nucleus into 1976.

Having traced the rather fluid personnel history of Nucleus in 1974-5, the music on the band's next two albums shows how it was continuing to evolve. *Under The Sun*, as its name suggests, is largely to do with themes that reflect the outdoors, starting with the street parade-influenced *In Procession*. Ian's suggested title for Bryan Spring's composition *The Addison Trip* was 'The Rites of Spring', but Bryan chose to avoid the pun and opt for his own more obscure title. Once again, Carr was seeking connectivity between the titles included on the disc, and the strong melody of *Pastoral Graffiti* leads into the somewhat fragmentary *New Life*, with Bryan Spring at his most energetic, and a characteristically effects-laden guitar solo from Pitchen.

Gordon Beck was not a regular member of the touring version of Nucleus at the time, but as he had done on *Labyrinth*, he came in for the studio sessions on *Under The Sun*. His assertive playing on *Sarsparilla* contrasts with the brief fragment of Geoff Castle's delicate accompaniment on the forty-four second prologue to this piece, and ranks as one of Gordon's finest solos from the period. *Feast Alfresco* is one of the long, snaky themes that Nucleus specialised in, and harks back to the sound of the band's first album. Perhaps the most unexpected critical comment Ian has ever received was inspired by the album's closing track, the slow sensuous *Rites of Man*, with its endlessly repeated ostinato pattern. He was sitting on a bus in Germany, when he was recognised by a man and his wife sitting nearby. The man came over and said, confidentially, 'Mr. Carr, I want to thank you for that wonderful piece, *Rites of Man*. It's done wonders for our marriage!'[31]

It was over a year after *Roots* was recorded that the band returned to the studios for its next album. From its very un-politically correct cover to the sensuous content of the music itself, *Snakehips etc.*, cut in April

1975, was an album on which Ian 'wanted to do something outrageous', and the thinking behind it came from a line by the American poet e.e.cummings. Famous for his unorthodox use of English and his avoidance of upper case letters, there is a line in one of cummings's First World War poems about being in a trench 'dreaming of your old etc.' and Ian took the double entendre of this line as the theme for the entire album.

There's a literary connection, too, with *Hey Day*, the track that closes the album. It was written by Ian as one movement of his *Will's Birthday Suite* for a another performance celebrating Shakespeare's birthday in Southwark Cathedral – this time his 410th, in April 1974. As was the case the previous spring, several other composers were involved, and on this occasion there was music by Neil Ardley, Mike Gibbs and Stan Tracey. Originally performed by a band including Kenny Wheeler and Tony Coe, the concert recording of which was issued on an album called *Will Power*, the version of *Hey Day* on *Snakehips etc.* marks the number's arrival in the Nucleus recorded repertoire. The piece was often played on live concerts, and the earliest studio recorded version contrasts with the later live one on *In Flagrante Delicto*, which the group recorded in 1977.

This period of the 1970s was a time when Ian was touring constantly with Nucleus, at home and abroad, and, as he says, 'taking the music to the people'. He gave himself an ulcer from worry about taking the group out on the road, more often than not without a financial advance to cover the costs until the money came in for the first gigs of a tour. Statistically, in terms of the number of concerts played, Nucleus continued to be far busier on the Continent than in Britain, in particular undertaking tours of Germany organised by the band's agent there, Vera Brandeis. Despite Ian's own health problems, the regular touring brought a growth in confidence and further consolidation of the band's individual sound. Attendees at live gigs remember the group getting progressively louder during the period, to the extent that Roger Sellers began to set his drums further back on stage so he was to some degree isolated from the volume of the PA stacks, which by now had begun to resemble those of band like Yes, which Ian had found awesomely loud when the original line-up of Nucleus played support to them in the early 1970s.

8 united jazz and rock, and the long dark

Nucleus continued to tour throughout 1975 on a very similar pattern to before, but by the end of the following year, after what had been a six-year period of unswerving loyalty to his own group, Ian finally embarked on playing live concerts with another band, cementing a new long term association with the United Jazz and Rock Ensemble that was to last for the next twenty-eight years. However, because the UJRE was a collective of bandleaders and major soloists from all over Europe, it only met for a few weeks each year, leaving all its members free to continue with their own various commitments. As a consequence, Nucleus continued more or less uninterrupted.

Nevertheless, by this time Ian himself was experiencing an underlying sense that all this work, constant travelling and regular production of albums was a blind alley. Although it would be difficult, if not impossible, to sense this from the brash self-confidence of his recordings, he felt little inner certainty that his playing was any good, or that he was any great shakes as a composer. So the backdrop to his entire output from 1975-8 was a slow-burning fuse of 'unhappiness, despair, confusion and weariness,' feelings he finally came to terms with in his outstanding album *Out of the Long Dark*, made in December 1978, whose very title recognises Ian's inner torments. As Tom Callaghan says in his notes to the recent reissue, 'few artists in British jazz have fused deeply considered thought and deeply felt emotion as productively as Ian Carr,' and he goes on to hail this album as a 'milestone in his musical, emotional and intellectual growth.'[1]

In 1975, however, these personal problems were still hidden well below the surface, and to the public at large, Nucleus remained as prolific and creative as it had been throughout its first five years. Even its regular changes of personnel had done little to damage the band's sense of collective identity, or its overall sound. Indeed, it is one of Ian's most impressive achievements that despite undergoing two or three almost complete cast changes during the 1970s, the band continued to sound like itself.

Alleycat, the next Nucleus album to appear, dates from December 1975, and it is by the same line-up that had recorded *Snakehips Etc* the previous April, with the Australian saxophonist Bob Bertles still replacing the absent Brian Smith in the front line. Bertles had been a member of the rhythm and blues band Max Merritt and the Meteors, and he brought with him an extrovert style that is at its best on this album, particularly during the passionate interchanges with Ian's trumpet on the track entitled *Splat*. Although this is a studio recording, it has all the intensity of a live gig, with the rhythm section building up a considerable head of steam, and the front line horns trading phrases and interlocking with one another like the collective improvisers of early jazz.

That degree of mutual interdependence on *Splat* is evident throughout the entire *Alleycat* album, from the melancholy beauty of *You Can't Be Sure*, with Ian's Harmon-muted trumpet weaving in and out of Ken Shaw's guitar figures, to the straightahead walking bass and bebop-inflected drumming of *Nosegay*, backing up one of Geoff Castle's most fluent solos. The rhythm section plays outstandingly well throughout this disc, from the heavy percussion layers under the guitar on *Phaideaux Corner* to the contrasts between openness and complexity on the title track. Indeed, *Alleycat* itself also sees Ian's most exciting solo on the album, building gradually from an uncluttered backdrop and a mellow start via double-time drum figures to a fast-moving torrent of ideas, with some double tracking at the most dramatic moments, before everything is pared away again towards the reprise of the head arrangement.

Then, in the months following *Alleycat*, came another of those periodical projects in which Nucleus was enlarged to incorporate extra players, most of them already long-established among Ian's colleagues. The piece was Neil Ardley's extended composition *Kaleidoscope of Rainbows,* and during the spring of 1976, the expanded band took part in both a tour and recording.

Shortly before Ian and Neil's earlier collaborations on the second New Jazz Orchestra album *Dejeuner sur l'herbe* in 1968, and the following year on *Greek Variations,* Neil had written a much larger-scale piece (not involving Ian, but with Don Rendell among the sax section for its June 1967 recording) called *A Symphony of Amaranths*, which had won him considerable praise. It had been the first in a sequence of long pieces that developed his distinctive compositional method.

Looking back, Ardley believed that it was his experience with the New Jazz Orchestra that had provided him with the necessary knowledge to undertake these extended compositions. 'It was,' he recalled, 'a tremendous proving ground for all of us. As the players learned to read music and play well together, I learned – eventually – how to arrange music. The idea was not to repeat one's mistakes. I remember Gil Evans saying he'd never had any formal training, he'd just learned by practice, and it was much the same for me, having read sciences at university. It takes a long time, but you can form an original style that way.'[2]

His new work, *Kaleidoscope of Rainbows*, was to be his biggest and most ambitious, and for the rest of his life, Neil considered it his best. It grew out of a commission, for his own orchestra and a cello duo, of a piece that for reasons which will become obvious, was originally to be titled *Biformal from Bali*. 'It took me three years to do,' he recalled. 'I first wrote it for a conventional big band line-up as a Camden Festival commission in 1974, but as soon as we began to rehearse it I felt the sound of those forces was wrong for the music. With Ian's help, I began to rewrite it, and I think I got it right the second time round. Sometimes I find I have to do a thing two or three times to find the best way of doing it. After hearing it with the big band at Camden, I asked Ian if we could try it with Nucleus, but add a few extra players, and that's what we did, bringing in Barbara Thompson, Tony Coe and Paul Buckmaster, plus one or two others, to make a total of thirteen players, plus me as director, and it came out right.'[3]

The additional musicians who took part in some, but not all, of the sessions, were the young saxophonist Stan Sulzmann and the mercurial pianist John Taylor, both of whom added to the depth of experience that Neil, Ian and their colleagues brought together for the recording. The piece consists of seven movements – each a 'rainbow' – plus a prologue, and it is built on two five-note Balinese scales, a pelog (from Indonesia) and a slendro (a pentatonic scale quite widely used in Eastern music). In much the same way as the *Greek Variations* had used various formal devices to manipulate the simplest source materials into something altogether larger and more complex, the various 'rainbows' achieve similar results, through adjustment of rhythm, tone colour, or the way in which the scales interrelate. The piece brilliantly demonstrated Ardley's ability to create complex explorations of very simple and specific source material. I once asked him to describe this process in his work, starting with *Greek Variations*.

'In that case,' he explained, 'I was using a Greek folk tune that was itself built on a minor scale, which I manipulated in various ways. I had previously written another big piece, *A Symphony of Amaranths*, which was, incidentally, the first jazz album to get an Arts Council grant. It was dedicated to Duke Ellington and Gil Evans, and so I used their initials

D-E and G-E, (as well as the contrasting phrase A-C-G-B, to acknowledge the Arts Council of Great Britain,) which I built up into a big piece. I suppose it proves I have always been fascinated with this idea of taking little scales or motifs and expanding them to produce large works that mix both composed and improvised music.

'But the trigger for *Kaleidoscope of Rainbows* was Denis Preston who produced *A Symphony of Amaranths*. After we'd recorded it, he gave me an LP, saying, "I think you might like this." It was a collection of Balinese music, and I thought it was wonderful. But at first I couldn't work out how it fitted together, musically speaking. So I went along to Westminster Music Library and got out several books on the music of Bali, until I'd figured out the five note Balinese scales, and then I took it from there.'[4]

The results, as the critic Max Harrison has pointed out, 'do not seem Balinese, the ensemble could hardly sound less like a gamelan, and there is no trace of "ethnic exploitation"'.[5] *Kaleidoscope of Rainbows* is both a logical extension of Ardley's compositional method and an entirely convincing addition to the musical language that Nucleus had already established, in just the same way as Ian's own previous works for enlarged line-ups, *Solar Plexus* and *Labyrinth*, had built on the band's basic sound. Certainly, Barbara Thompson's soprano solo in *Rainbow 4* and Tony Coe's clarinet in the following movement suggest that the Balinese five-note scales fell easily under their fingers and added to their natural improvisatory vocabulary. Ian himself, with his spare, Davis-influenced sound, alternating spacious, relaxed phrasing with passionate flurries of notes, was at the heart of the disc and the live concerts.

Neil himself remembered the effect of Barbara's solo on *Rainbow 4*, while it was being recorded. 'I think it's just about the best solo anyone ever played for me,' he said. 'It was overdubbed late at night and at the mixing desk in the booth were Martin, our recording engineer; Paul Buckmaster, who produced the album; and me. Barbara was playing alone in the studio, and Paul leaned across and whispered to me, "Look at my arm". All the hairs on his arm, were standing on end. It was simply spine-tingling what she was doing.'[6]

In addition to framing some exceptional solo playing, the discipline of making the album in tandem with going on tour with the rewritten piece was also beneficial. The first version of the suite was nearly twice as long as the eventual recording, as it had originally been intended to make an entire concert in its own right. During the rewriting and recording process, Neil wisely realised that it would be better to form the second half of a live concert, prefaced by other material. 'It wasn't quite an evening in two halves, as I originally wrote it, but it came close,' he reflected. 'A lot of it turned out to be, shall we say, musical dead wood, so all that had to be pruned away, to make a piece of one album's length. I just kept all the good stuff!'[7]

Kaleidoscope of Rainbows, well-received at the time, went on to be re-explored on several occasions in the years that followed, notably by Ian and Neil on record with the electronic band Zyklus in 1991, plus a subsequent Radio 3 broadcast, and later by an expanded version of Nucleus, including Thompson and Coe, for a brief UK tour in the spring of 1999. The final performances of the piece under Ardley's direction took place in April 2002, with a short sequence of events including a concert at London's Purcell Room. For that edition of the band, violinist Billy Thompson, a regular colleague of Barbara Thompson and Jon Hiseman, joined the line-up.

Hearing the Wavendon concert from the 1999 reunion tour, in the old Stables, I wrote at the time that my main fear of resurrecting the piece after a quarter of a century was that a little Balinese background would go a long way. However, this proved unfounded, and the work had worn extremely well. Reviewing it, I noted that 'the textures of the woodwind writing, notably for alto flute, clarinet, bass clarinet and soprano sax, were glorious in themselves, [and that] after some gritty tenor from Art Themen, all the original fire of the piece was rekindled...as Coe's quicksilver clarinet and Thompson's forthright alto coaxed the rhythm section into one final and ecstatic climax'.[8]

After the original *Kaleidoscope* tour in the spring of 1976, Nucleus returned to its normal line-up, but by this time Ian had become a regular participant in a studio group in Germany, which, at the very start of 1977, was to make its first live appearances as the United Jazz and Rock Ensemble. Ian had first joined the band for a series of videotaping sessions during the previous eighteen months, alongside his long-term friend and colleague from the New Jazz Orchestra, Jon Hiseman (who was also the producer of *Alleycat*), plus other old friends, including Hiseman's wife, Barbara Thompson, who had been so strongly featured in *Kaleidoscope of Rainbows*. As Ian explains, the UJRE had initially been put together for a television series in Germany: 'Werner Schretzmeier, the television producer, wanted to have a group to play for a young audience on Sundays. He wanted to unite jazz, rock, and politics all in one big soup. So he invited people who were already doing music that crossed over between jazz and rock, for a series of studio sessions.'[9]

Finding the right combination of musicians might well have been a tricky job for Schretzmeier's musical director Wolfgang Dauner, had it not been for some long established friendships. In many ways Dauner's career had been parallel to Ian's, in that during the 1960s he had played first bebop with Joki Freund and then free jazz with his trio of bassist Eberhard Weber and drummer Fred Braceful. Then as a sideline to his main job of leading the Radio Jazz Group in Stuttgart, he formed Et Cetera in 1970, which was one of the first jazz rock groups in Germany. When Dauner began looking for musicians for the television band, Weber, who was by then already one of Europe's leading bass virtuosi, was an obvious choice, and so too were Dauner's occasional duo partners, the expatriate American saxophonist Charlie Mariano and the innovative German trombonist Albert Mangelsdorff.

Jon Hiseman traces the origins of the international component of the band, which started life as the Elf-1/2-Ensemble, back to the beginnings of his own friendship with Dauner in 1971.

'That year,' he says, 'Colosseum did a concert in Heidelberg. The equipment for Wolfgang Dauner's band Knirsch broke down, so I told my roadies to help them have a good show, lend them whatever equipment they needed, so that they could play an effective set before we came on, as top of the bill. After all a good show is a good show, and we all benefit if it goes well. Wolfgang, who is a brilliant German pianist, never forgot that, so that four years later when he was asked to provide the music for the television show, he asked me to come over to Stuttgart and do the first shows with him. It was a youth-orientated political talk show, except that every item was interspersed with a piece of jazz music, played live by us, lasting four to five minutes. The idea was to go to Stuttgart with this band and play in the studio for a week, putting enough material in the can to keep the show going for the next three months. So, from some time around the middle of 1975 onwards, regular as clockwork, we'd go over every three months to record more material to keep the show on the road. After we'd been doing this for a while, Wolfgang asked me one day, "You don't happen to know a saxophone player who doubles on flute do you?" So I rowed Barbara, my wife, in, and gradually other friends and colleagues became part of it. Before long the band had Eberhard Weber on bass, Volker Kriegel on guitar, Ian Carr and Kenny Wheeler on trumpets, Charlie Mariano alongside Barbara on reeds, plus another trumpeter Ack Van Rooyen from Holland. It was a fantastic line-up.'[10]

Ian enjoyed making new music in such stellar company, but he had another reason for wanting to take the gig, which is that the regular recording sessions in Germany were very well-paid, and he was beginning to want to flex his muscles as a writer. To write any book takes time and money, and Ian had little of both in his touring schedule with Nucleus. 'The first week's recording with the UJRE was so well-paid,' he confirmed, 'that it paid for me to go to New York for three weeks to do first-hand research on Miles Davis, on whom I was planning to write a book. Not only that, but there was money to spare. So this was exceptionally well-paid work for the time.'[11]

Fiscal rewards notwithstanding, such was the band's success that its television audience started clamouring for the band to appear in concert, so at the very start of 1977 it played a limited number of live dates, those on the 7th and 9th of January being combined into the phenomenally successful album *Live in Schützenhaus*.

'It may have sold more by now,' says Ian, 'but at the time it sold 60,000 copies, which was a really big sale for a jazz record. I have a soft spot for it, but actually most members of the band don't like it – or at any rate, they don't play it to their friends. There's also surviving live footage of the concert recording, which we were shown on the 20th anniversary of the group, and if nothing else, it's an amazing historical document! Like it or not, the album floated Mood, the record company set up by members of the band, and because of its success they became able to record other people.'[12]

'More than that,' recalled Hiseman, 'in due course it became the biggest-selling jazz album in Germany, ever.'[13]

Mood was set up by a co-operative of Dauner, Kriegel, Mangelsdorff, and Von Rooyen, plus their producer Schretzmeier, and although its main output has been the regular albums issued throughout the late '70s, the '80s and '90s by the UJRE itself, it has also played host to a number of independent projects by the various bandmembers, including some later Nucleus output.

The original UJRE Schützenhaus album included a powerful version of Ian's *Hey Day*, revived from its earlier outings in his *Will's Birthday Suite* and on the *Snakehips etc.* disc of three years earlier. The big, fat, sound of the UJRE contrasts interestingly with the two earlier recordings of the piece, and this version is dominated by a powerful solo from Ian himself, using some electronics, and rippling through the trumpet registers to blow forcefully at the very top of his range, before the massed brass and reeds come in behind him with a reprise of the main theme to take the number out, propelled by some incisive, yet uninhibited drumming from Hiseman. Other highlights of the album include Volker Kriegel's composition *Hypnotic Pignose*. This begins with his effects-laden guitar playing, and after some ensemble and front line solo section, opens up for a further long solo by Kriegel, echoing the powerful long solo lines of John McLaughlin's playing, and supported by some blistering basslines from Weber. Kriegel's playing here is a conscious step into more rock-orientated territory than some of his more gentle efforts with the Dave Pike Set from the late '60s, the band in which he'd come to international attention. Overall, the UJRE's first recording had a unity of form and purpose about it that became less apparent as time went on.

'It was called a band of bandleaders,' recalls Hiseman, 'because each person contributed music to the repertoire. Actually for me, this made it more difficult to play with, because the variations in style each composer brought with them meant that I was constantly wearing different musical hats. Nevertheless, essentially it was a jazz-rock band, although over the next twenty-eight years, the jazz part grew and grew, until more recently I was the only rock part left! On some of those gigs, with everyone else playing jazz, I found my role extremely difficult, to try and preserve the sound of the band. But we all smiled at each other, we all got along brilliantly, and even if it wasn't particularly original, or influential, as a successful jazz-rock group with a long track record, it's without equal.'[14]

Ian, too, recalls with affection the early success of the band's tours: 'It was not uncommon for 1,000 people to be turned away from one of our concerts. I think the band was good for a couple of years, although it had a bit of a slump towards the end of the decade. Then Kenny Wheeler joined in late '79, and it came up again in the eighties, to a very high musical level. And it kept going well into the 21st century.'[15]

Nucleus was due to tour in Germany immediately after the UJRE came off the road from its initial sequence of live dates in January 1977, and so Ian decided to stay out in Stuttgart, to be joined by his own band en route to the first gigs. The intention was to record one of the concerts midway through the tour as the band's next album, as there had hitherto been no live Nucleus session on record. By this time Roger Sutton had left the line-up, and a replacement had been booked for the German tour, but with twenty-four hours to go before the band set off, the new bassist pulled out. Ian was still on the road and uncontactable, so his long-term friend and roadie Alf Dodd had to sort things out.

'I'm stuck here in London,' Dodd recalled, 'and Ian's in Germany. So I phone around to the other guys and ask "Do you know any good bass players?" Finally I called Roger Sellers, and he said, "Yes, there's this New Zealander called Billy Kristian that's just come over, why not give him a ring?" So I called him out of the blue and said, "Can you leave with us tomorrow for Germany?" and he says, "Yes!" He knew Roger and Bob Bertles, who had both started their careers in Australia, and so he was happy to come. For the first three or four concerts, he just took it quite gently, listening to what was going on. Then, the night before *In Flagrante Delicto* was recorded in Düren, we played the Quartier Latin club in Berlin. Suddenly Billy let go and played this absolutely amazing solo, and everyone stood up and cheered. It put us in the right frame of mind for the concert the next night, which was being recorded, and he played another brilliant solo on the album.'[16]

In Flagrante Delicto also marks the band's transition from the Vertigo label, with which it had begun recording in 1970, to the American Capitol company. However this was almost an accident, and certainly something that Ian, who was by now beginning to fall into the depression he suffered in the mid-70s, almost jeopardised because of his mental state, and the desire not to go on making records on a treadmill basis.

'At the time we made *In Flagrante Delicto*,' he told me, 'I had just been kicked out by my original record company, with whom we'd been for better or worse since Nucleus began. Inside, I was feeling a worse emptiness than when I left the Rendell-Carr group. I think this was because I'd been a bandleader for too long without enough creative input. You're so busy with organisational things, you don't keep learning as much as other musicians when you are a bandleader, unless you're very clever or very careful.

'I'd probably done too many albums in too short a time. After all, I'd been contracted to do two albums a year which was really too much. When I got out from the Vertigo contract, I told my manager, David Apps, that I didn't want him to try and get me anything else. I stopped thinking about recording, and turned back to music. Among other things, I practised a lot on keyboards.

'But unbeknownst to me, in America, John Dixon at Capitol Records had every record I ever made. When he read in the trade press that I'd left Phonogram (who owned Vertigo), he sent a message to EMI in London saying "Ian Carr is free − sign him up!"

'At the time, I needed some money, and so I had put together the Nucleus group for the German tour. We started in Hamburg and the first night there was nobody in the club. In fact there were more of us in the band, than there were in the audience. Even the barmaid was trying to cheer me up, saying, "Come on, Ian, don't worry! It's not that bad!"

'Then that same night, after the gig, David Apps rang to tell me that the next evening two guys who'd just signed the Sex Pistols were coming over from EMI to sign me up.

'I said "Oh no!"

'He said, "Ian, there's money involved."

'The next night it was the same. Not too many people in the club and not a very sparky performance, but I saw two guys come in during the middle of the first set. When the interval came, they beckoned me over, and said, "Oh, that was great! What was the time signature of that last one?"

'I said, "It was in five-four."

'"But you don't have a guitar. Why not?"

'I said, "I haven't heard a player I like very much, and anyway I'm playing second keyboard and I think that works very well with our keyboard player, Geoff Castle."

'Before that they'd said, "The bass player moves very well!"

'When they made that remark about the guitar, I thought for a moment, and then I said, "Look, you're really nice guys and you've come a long way, but I couldn't possibly have anything to do with you."

'Nobody had ever said anything like that to them.

'"Why not?" they asked.

'I couldn't explain it. Later that evening David Apps rang up and asked what in heaven's name had I done that for?

'I said, "They wanted me to be something I'm not and I'm through with all that."

'He agreed. But what he didn't know was that when they went back and told EMI that I wasn't interested, John Dixon immediately said, "I thought so! Never mind, we'll sign him direct."

'Which they did, so I had an American record contract and with it, American levels of money.'[17]

Consequently, by the time the band got to the Düren concert, Ian had been signed to the parent company in America, helped along by Capitol's head of A and R, the expatriate Englishman Rupert Perry, rather than to the British arm of EMI. When the album came out, Nucleus was firmly under the wing of Dixon, who forged a long and creative friendship with Ian in the years that followed, which was to prove a decisive factor in pulling Ian out of his depression.

On its first live album, *In Flagrante Delicto*, the band quickly hit its natural groove to great effect. It is impossible to tell from the recorded results that the band had only arrived at the theatre after its long drive about 30 minutes before the start of the concert, and that the indomitable Dodd was still setting up the gear until seconds before curtain-up.

'Don't think of it as a recording,' whispered Ian to his musicians as they went on, 'just think of it as an ordinary gig!'

The way the musicians worked together on that 'ordinary gig', and the sense of tension and release that ebbs and flows through the longer numbers on the disc, helped by the interaction with the audience, captures much of the adrenaline of late 70s Nucleus. Yet beneath the fun and good-hearted enjoyment of the gig, there is, as Tom Callaghan has pointed out, a sense of the underlying sterility that Ian was beginning to find in the band's music, and which had fuelled his bleak moods. It is something which even the effervescent feelgood funk of this public workout in Düren cannot quite dispel.[18]

So, aside from the factors Ian himself quoted, what lay at the heart of this disquiet? Why didn't the invigorating effect of adding new musicians of Kristian's creative level help him to feel more positively about the band?

Keyboard player Geoff Castle believes it was to do with the general state of the music scene in England at the time, and the relentless hard work that went into the long continental tours and festival appearances necessary for the band to survive.

'The band was definitely doing a lot more work in Europe than it was in Britain,' he recalls. 'I think England went through a bit of a bad patch, jazz-wise during the mid-to-late 70s. It just seemed like everybody lost interest in jazz. Our tours were excellent, musically, and very enjoyable to do, but they were usually done on a very small scale and a small budget. We'd be travelling round in our VW minibus, Ian would be driving, with the rest of us sitting in the back. It'd be minus 20 degrees outside, and we'd be freezing, and saying to Ian, "Are you sure you can't get the heater going?" And he'd turn his head and shout back over his shoulder, "It is going!"'[19]

Alf Dodd, who drove the van of equipment – originally a converted ambulance – as Ian drove the minibus, agrees. 'It was a big worry for Ian, because the management wasn't always very good.'[20] Dodd can relate dozens of anecdotes about his time with the band, all of which tend to be amusing, but most of which demonstrate the kind of stress that leading the band on stage, writing much of the music, driving it to gigs and organising its personnel had put on Ian throughout the 1970s.

There was the gig in Modena for which guitarist Allan Holdsworth accidentally double booked himself and didn't turn up. There was a trip to Finland on which the band's temporary (and very well-known) bassist managed to get so inebriated before a headline festival gig that he was unable to play more than a few notes, all of them wrong. There was the tour of Italy where an irritated hotelier refused Ian a drink after driving through the night after a gig because the rest of the band were making too much noise.

There were lighter moments, including the night when Ian and Dodd returned a set of unusually-shaped PA speakers that they had borrowed from a band called Crematorium to the 100 Club on Oxford Street, and caused a furore by apparently carrying several coffins out of an ambulance, across the pavement and into the club. On another

Ian and the first VW band bus he bought for Nucleus. (Ian Carr)

memorable occasion, Dodd used the blue light on top of his old ambulance to cut a swathe through London traffic en route for Dover, in order to make a tight ferry deadline for a single night's gig in Paris. And not long afterwards, Bryan Spring was too slow in getting off another ferry in Scandinavia and watched in disbelief as the gates swung shut while he was still on board, and he was whisked away, leaving the band en route to Molde with drums but no drummer. At the end of a subsequent Italian tour, during a period of severe exchange control, all the band's money had to be stuffed into the PA stacks, and driven to Germany, where the cabinets were taken apart and the money recovered.

Such light-hearted stories are only part of the picture. More typical was the moment when, coming back to the UK from Ostend, rough weather separated Ian's minibus and Alf's van. After driving across the low countries during the night, the musicians set off en route for an Oxford May Ball on an early afternoon ferry, but a sleepless Alf Dodd was on a crossing two hours behind, and after struggling around London in those chaotic pre-M25 days, only arrived amid the dreaming spires at 3am, just before the band was due onstage, following Status Quo. The Oxford organisers looked around for the pantechnicon of equipment that usually accompanied such a band, and were amazed when Alf said it was all in his van. 'I guess when you're as good as Nucleus, you don't need all that much equipment,' said the students, as they helped lug in the gear – which may have been a fine compliment to the band's musicianship, but it didn't reduce the pressure on a leader who had spent the evening wondering whether Nucleus would be able to go on stage at all.

Shadowed by the police through the outskirts of Aachen late on another night, to help him concentrate as he navigated through the unfamiliar town, Dodd reached out for one of the wrapped glucose sweets Ian kept by the dashboard. But unknown to him, one of the band had left a tab of amphetamines in the same place, and Dodd popped it into his mouth. He was only able to explain why he had suddenly roared into town the wrong way down a one-way street by holding up a piece of paper with the band's hotel address on it, and explaining loudly but simply to the officers who flagged him down that he was completely lost. The police car eventually led him through the streets to the band's digs, and a tragedy was averted. It took Dodd several days to come down from his high.

On another occasion they weren't so lucky. Dodd turned left across some tramlines in Hanover and was pulled over by the police. Ian, who had had a couple of drinks after the concert, was following, and when he saw what was happening, jumped out of his minibus and walked over to offer his opinions. Dodd was stone cold sober and gave a negative breathalyzer, but Ian, who was promptly tested as well, gave a positive result. He was whisked off to the Police station, and it took all of Alf Dodd's diplomatic skills to point out that when the discussion began, Ian had not been driving but walking, and the police had no proof of who had been driving the second vehicle. Eventually they were released, but Dodd recalls sitting anxiously in the Police station, beneath

Nucleus, France, mid-70s: (l to r) Bob Bertles, Roger Sutton, Bryan Spring, Geoff Castle, Ian, and the French tour manager. (Ian Carr)

huge posters of the Bader-Meinhoff gang, who had used fake American ID to carry out their early 1970s terrorist attacks in Germany. As he waited for the police decision about Ian's possible imprisonment, he reflected on the similarity of appearance between the terrorists and the scruffy-looking jazz musicians in the band's line-up.

'All those tours were a huge amount of work for Ian,' Dodd confirmed. 'It wasn't just the driving and the playing, but often things would get cancelled as well. The busiest period was after we met Vera Brandeis. In the early days, with Ronnie Scott's managing the band, we didn't do too much. But later we spent about four years touring on the continent, doing festivals, most of them very good, and working almost constantly. We didn't do much work at home, and I think Ian kind of gave up on the English scene. We did occasional gigs at the 100 Club, the Phoenix in Cavendish Square, the Torrington, and clubs like that, and in the early days, we played lots of universities, which were probably about 70 percent of the work for jazz in those days, but as the 1970s wore on, and punk began, that all seemed to stop.

'Being forced to find most of our work abroad was tough on Ian. I don't know how he ever lived through it, because it must have been a terrible worry for him, and that's how he ended up with an ulcer. He had great strength of character during that time in the mid-70s, and lots of energy, fuelled by a belief in what he was doing. He fought really hard for the band, and couldn't have done any more than he did. At the same time, he was fighting hard to get some recognition for jazz on the media. It was all pop and rock in the music press and on radio or television. There was no comparison between the way we were treated on the continent and the way we were treated in England. Over there you were treated like artists, but in Britain jazz musicians didn't get any respect.'[21]

Ian's fight for recognition for jazz as a whole had also, somewhat earlier in the band's life, led him into writing a full-scale book, *Music Outside: Contemporary Jazz In Britain*. Although during the Rendell-Carr period he had done a number of radio talks, mainly at the instigation of the critic Charles Fox, this book was his first serious attempt at writing since his attempts to be a poet during his time on the bum, apart from a few pieces of journalism intended to fire up the Newcastle community's enthusiasm during the era of the EmCee Five. With a brightly coloured cover, deliberately related to the colourful pop-art of the *Roots* album by Nucleus, and by the same designer, Keith Davis, this 180-page survey of Ian's colleagues in cutting-edge British jazz appeared in 1973, issued by his old friend John Latimer Smith's publishing firm, Latimer New Dimensions. There is a chapter on Nucleus, but the book as a whole places Ian and the band firmly in a context that also embraced Mike Gibbs, Jon Hiseman, Chris McGregor, Evan Parker, John Stevens, Trevor Watts, and Mike Westbrook.

The incentive for the book had come from the pianist Stan Tracey, who was working so little that his local job centre had recommended he retrain as a postman or something similar. 'He rang me up,' remembered Ian, 'and said he was calling a meeting of all the contemporary players in British jazz at a church in South London. "There's nothing on the BBC," Stan told me, "nothing in the media, no help, no publicity. We've got to do something." So on a warm summer's day, I went down to this church, and it was full. I looked around and all the guys were there. John Marshall said, "If a bomb fell on this building now, the entire flower of British jazz would be destroyed...and nobody would notice!" There was a howl of laughter.'[22]

At a vote of the musicians present, following a proposal from John Surman, Ian was put in charge of public relations for the jazz community as a whole. Along with a select group of other players, including Gordon Beck and Sandy Brown, he had a meeting with Howard Newby, then the head of music at the BBC's Third Programme, to see if there was the possibility of more space for jazz on the network, as there was on its European counterparts in France and Germany. The frequent trips abroad by Nucleus had given Ian plenty of opportunities to hear the kind of programming in which public funding was often used to commission large-scale jazz works, alongside classical pieces. But Newby was not to be moved, even though Ian had presented several successful talks for the station, and the overall levels of jazz on the Third Programme remained roughly the same as they had been.[23]

Around the same time as the musicians' meeting at the church, Ian had a conversation about its aims with John Latimer Smith, who had been a fellow-officer during his National Service, and with whom Ian had remained friendly, not least because of John's enthusiasms for both jazz and literature. Smith immediately suggested that Ian should write a book for his firm Latimer New Directions, extending his scope beyond the circle of musicians who had been agitating for change, and taking on the more ambitious task of surveying the whole burgeoning contemporary jazz scene in Britain.

'God, this is the way to promote these people,' Ian thought to himself. 'If you do journalism, it's here today and gone tomorrow, but if you do it in a book, it's here for ever, available in a library even after it's gone out of print.'[24]

The book succeeds admirably in presenting a portrait of the British contemporary jazz of the early 1970s, and together with Roger Cotterrell's *Jazz Now: The Jazz Centre Society Guide*, published three years later in 1976, the book became something of a bible for promoters and clubs all over the country. It was also used by the Arts Council as background for assessing grants for new jazz projects.

Ian's intention was to present a survey of the overall scene in his introduction, and then for his portrait chapters to focus on 'leaders or composers who drew people together, and who stood for something'.[25] Although by that time Ian's own tastes had moved away from abstract free jazz, he was scrupulously fair in his coverage of it, especially as it had been such a major element of his own playing background in the mid-60s. In retrospect he believes the chapter on Evan Parker contains some of his best writing.

The book also employed a method of research that was to become central to Ian's later books on Miles Davis and Keith Jarrett, namely to incorporate lengthy (and preferably informally-conducted) conversations with the players themselves. 'I decided to do in-depth interviews,' recalls Ian, 'usually in people's homes or at my house. I wanted somewhere where we would not be hurried, and we would really get to the heart of the matter with each individual person.'

At first glance, Jon Hiseman might look a slightly less obvious choice for inclusion in the book than the others. He wasn't a composer such as Gibbs and Westbrook, nor an instrumental innovator in the manner of Parker, Watts or Stevens. He was, however, a great mover and shaker in the world of 70s jazz, and above all he had been very important to Ian.

'I asked him a few years later, in 1979, when he was helping me again over something, why he'd gone out of his way several times to help me and the band,' recalled Ian. 'He told me that when he'd been nineteen, I was nice to him. Which I suppose may be some kind of lesson.'[26]

The original intention had been to call the book *Music Underground*, but Ian felt that jazz was still very much a music that was 'outside' the establishment, and it was this, rather than a deliberate attempt to use the free jazz terminology of 'playing outside' the conventions of form and harmony, that gave the book its final title. The book was launched with a certain amount of hoopla at the ICA (Institute for Contemporary Arts) in Carlton House Terrace, and several of Ian's contacts at the Arts Council, such as its head of music John Cruft, a well-known classical bassist and doyen of one of Britain's most high profile musical families, were in attendance, along with most of the subjects of the book. As the copious alcoholic refreshment began to exert its influence, wine was thrown at the pictures on display in the ICA gallery and a couple of other attendees resrted to fisticuffs. Ambulances were called as both of them ended up in a heap on the floor.

Ian apologised profusely to John Cruft, who was rather enjoying what he regarded as 'the Bohemian spirit'.

The book did very well in jazz circles, and served as an introduction to a whole generation of players who had not been seriously covered in print before. Sales in Europe, in particular, ensured that the work of these musicians came to be better known in countries where they would play and be appreciated, perhaps more than in their home nation. In terms of Ian's career as a writer, it launched him as a serious documenter of the jazz world, and someone who could handle writing at book length. Over the years that followed, despite illness and depression, the germ of an idea for Ian's comprehensive Miles Davis biography was to transform into reality.

Yet the very reason why *Music Outside* had been a necessary project to push what was going on in British jazz into the media spotlight graphically illustrates one of the underlying causes of Ian's depression in early 1977. To be a prophet without honour in one's own land is a tough and stressful occupation, and however well Nucleus was received abroad, the band still found working at home an uphill struggle.

There were additional stresses on Ian as well, because of his continuing doubts over his self-worth, despite the fact that he now been married again for some years to Sandy Major, whom he describes as 'an absolutely gorgeous woman, with jet-black hair, who was very spirited.'[27] Sandy worked in publishing, providing much-needed security for the family, at a time when Ian himself could not always be sure where the next pay cheque was coming from.

However, Ian came out of his depression as a consequence of putting his head down and grafting his way through it with sheer hard work. That he did so successfully, and ended up creating one of his finest albums in November 1978 is tribute to the support of Sandy, of his old friend Gerald Laing, and his new colleague John Dixon.

Dixon trod a fine line in what he described as the 'macho, male dominated rock'n'roll culture'[28] of 1970s Capitol between commissioning commercially certain ventures, and pursuing his own vision, which at different times brought both Kate Bush and Ian Carr to the label. Despite Bush's success in most of EMI's world markets, Dixon was never able to establish the same degree of market penetration for her in the United States, although this was not for the want of trying. He was a man who did everything he could to support his artists, given that all major decisions came out of the Tower in Los Angeles, and he was always prepared to act as a powerful advocate for his ideas in that setting.

He first met Ian face to face in the summer of 1977, when the two of them travelled together to the Edinburgh Festival. By then, *In Flagrante Delicto* had come out, and, just as it would have done for a mainstream rock act, Capitol arranged numerous promotional activities for Ian. 'This was part of promoting him as an artist,' recalled Dixon. 'We had set up several radio and press interviews for Ian, and I wanted to meet the staff of the EMI office in Edinburgh, so we had a common purpose in making the trip.'[29]

At the Festival, Gerald Laing was holding an exhibition of his bronze sculptures, for which he had asked Ian to write accompanying music, in particular for a set of portraits of Laing's second wife. As a result, Ian had created a tape, using electronic keyboards, of ideas inspired by four of the works, and this music was being played at the show to those who went to view the sculptures. 'I was totally inspired when I wrote those,' recalls Ian. 'I wrote the structure for each piece first. Then I played this onto tape, and improvised the melodies over the top. They came out fantastically well.'[30]

During their trip to Scotland, Ian and John Dixon cemented a firm friendship. Dixon was cajoled into trying haggis, without having first had it explained to him what this Scottish delicacy is made of. He took his discomfiture very well. A day or two later, Ian recalls him pulling a similar face when he read the over-intellectualised notes that were handed out to visitors to Laing's exhibition. 'They were unbelievably arid,' remembers Ian, 'without ever saying anything much.'[31] Finding out that both of them shared a hatred of pomposity and cant moved the friendship along well, and before long they were discussing the plans for the next album.

Strictly speaking, this ought not to have been produced by Dixon at all, because he had just been moved from his A and R job in Los Angeles to take over international marketing for Capitol in London. His job was to co-ordinate the work of all the Capitol label managers in Europe, monitor sales figures, co-ordinate artist tours, and make sure everyone on the ground knew what the marketing priorities were back at the parent division. Rupert Perry had promised him that he would remain as close to A and R in London as he had been in the United States, but his day-to-day marketing work made this virtually impossible. When he eventually decided to honour his promise to Ian and produce the next Nucleus album, he took the week off from his normal job to do so. Immediately Perry came on the phone: 'Dixon, what are you doing at Abbey Road studios?'

Despite initially being irked that Dixon had not cleared it with him in advance, Perry gave the project his blessing, and so *Out of the Long Dark* came into being.

It was recorded in November 1978, by which time Ian had decided to build the album round the four pieces he had written for Gerald Laing's show, *Sassy, The Human Condition, Black Ballad*, and the title track, while adding further new music in a similar vein. Some of this stemmed from a visit to Scotland that Ian had made with his family in May of that year. It was a hot Bank Holiday week, and they stayed with Sandy's mother, before meeting up with Gerald Laing for a seaside picnic on the beach.

'I went to see his sculpture again,' Ian says, 'which was a preparatory stage for this big event of recording the album. On the way home from Scotland, we stopped off at the cottage where my family had lived from 1940-45. It was derelict by this time, amid dry stone walls, with no electricity or running water, a well that was about to go dry for the summer as it usually did, and a stone privy. I took a lot of photographs of this tumbledown cottage in the middle of nowhere, surrounded by a fantastic landscape. The whole year seemed to be about knitting together

A 1970s visit to Morey Cottage, where Ian lived during the War, now derelict and with Selina skipping through the gate. (Ian Carr)

old memories and new friends. I think all of that went into the album. That is what the music was about, because at one level or another, all art and all music comes from memories. When you go back and examine the feelings you had as a child, or revisit old places and old friends, you remember those feelings with incredible intensity, and this comes out in your art.

'But there was another thing that happened too, at the time we finally came to make the album. Liam Frankel, the three-year old son of my friend Frances Astor, had been killed in a car accident a week before we were due to go into the studio. I didn't know about it until Frances rang me up and asked me to be in charge of the music at the memorial service for the dead child. The funeral actually took place during the week we were recording, and I missed one of the sessions because I was so wiped out by the emotional experience of the funeral. A piece of music came to me, which was a trumpet elegy. I was asked to sit at the back of the church, and during the sermon the vicar gave me a sign and I came forward into the aisle and played. The trumpet sounded fantastic in the church, but I felt all these people's grief descending on me as I played. It was part of the whole experience that went into making the record, and I think that gave the music another dimension.'[32]

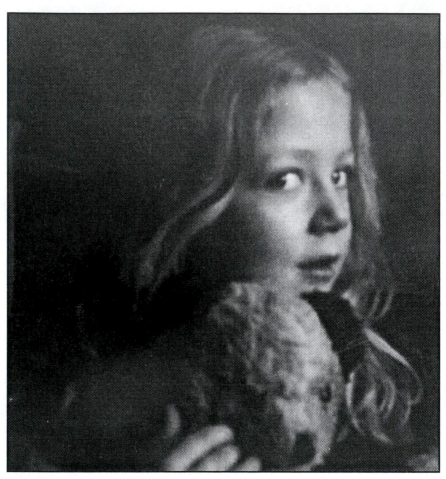

Ian's daughter, Selina (Ian Carr)

The way in which the recordings were made also contributed to the powerful atmosphere of the disc. Dixon ensured the studio lights were turned down low, creating an atmosphere not unlike one of the clubs in which Nucleus habitually played. 'Out of the Long Dark was the most expensive recording I've ever done,' Ian says. 'We had forty-two hours of studio time, and John Dixon helped with the sound, which he was good at. He worked on the way the drums appeared in the title track, which he did very well. He paid for everybody's drinks, beer and everything, and generally made us feel like a million dollars. In the next studio to ours, Paul McCartney was doing one of his albums, and my daughter was lurking in the corridor trying to say hello to him.

'Our album turned out to be a really good one, because I felt really inspired with my compositions. Doing it, I came out of my terrible depression, through sheer hard work. The four pieces inspired by Gerald

Laing's sculptures started it all off, and then other things just came to me. They were all good pieces, and so it was a really rich album.'[33]

Of the new material composed as a follow-up to the set of pieces inspired by Laing's sculpture, *Lady Bountiful* was written for Sandy, and *Selina* has an obvious dedicatee. The first includes some brilliantly inspired playing by Brian Smith who had returned to the Nucleus fold, while the second has a gospellish feel, set in motion by Geoff Castle's piano against a riff which quotes liberally from Miles Davis's *All Blues*. But the centrepiece of the album, and its most original music is the title track. Starting with a snarling bass note from Billy Kristian, it moves into some lyrical if free phrasing from Ian and Brian Smith, before the bassline picks up.

'It's about the moment a sperm penetrates the egg,' explains Ian, 'and I thought what it must do is start in chaos, or almost chaos, free, slowly and out of time, and then move slowly into rhythm and time. It should be improvised, but slowly get more and more controlled all the way through. The structure starts on one chord, then a few more chords come, and then more and more until there are chords changing every two beats. There's a long melody for the flute, and then a countermelody, which is unusual, as the main theme comes round again.'[34]

With the release of the album, it was clear that Ian had found a new depth in his composing, his artistic block had been overcome, and he was bringing new vigour to the band. Ironically, and partly because Capitol then decided not to exercise its option on a third Nucleus album, it also marked the point at which the band gradually ceased to work even as much as it had done before, and beyond which Ian would begin to turn more fully to teaching and writing, as well as fighting the unexpected onset of illness.

9 old heartland

Ian's unease with the rate of production demanded by his Vertigo contract, which had led to his regular string of albums during the early years of Nucleus, was replaced by a different kind of unease as the time came to see if there would be a sequel to *Out of the Long Dark*. Ultimately, the band suffered from being a very small fish in the large pool of a major label, and an American major label at that. Capitol, after providing ample funds for the first two discs, finally decided against making a further album with the band, and this had the effect of lessening demand for the group's live appearances. John Dixon was in no position to help, as he left the record company in 1980. After staying on for a short time in England, he returned to the United States to present radio programmes.

'My only regret is that sales-wise we didn't go on to a third album,' he recalled. 'Unfortunately if you work on the sales level of Nucleus, and I think *Out of the Long Dark* probably did somewhere between 15,000 and 20,000 units in the States, you don't get up to that 30 to 40 to 50,000 unit level, or whatever it needed at the time, for Capitol to say "Let's go for the next one". For a lot of groups who were musically distinctive but failed to break through to a wider market, Capitol was a two-album label. Within the company, fusion was lumped in with R and B marketing-wise, and it was a big disappointment to me that this album didn't do better. It surely deserved to, for this was quality music. But another factor that influenced Capitol was that radio was changing then. It was much harder to get jazz like this on to the airwaves, as compared to the more funk-rock-type Black American jazz. European fusion wasn't a big part of national radio programming in the States at the time, because the system had changed and was becoming much more centralised. That's not to say that on some specialised stations [Nucleus] didn't get a lot of play, and some people were really very thrilled about it.

'Another factor was that during my last years with the company I was living in England and all the decisions were being made in the Tower in Los Angeles. There always must be one person in the company who will follow through and care about the artist and make sure the rest of the company feels the same way. And part of Nucleus's problem was that they now had the stigma of me not being there, at the centre of things, but in England.'[1]

Fortunately, as a consequence of Ian's ongoing relationship with the UJRE, at the beginning of the decade Nucleus did get to make one album for the German Mood label, *Awakening*, which – although it did not receive the distribution and marketing that Capitol had brought to the last two albums – gives us the opportunity to hear that the band was still developing, not least in the rhythm section where the powerful and charismatic bass playing of Chucho Murchan produced a refreshingly loose feel. However, rather than remaining constantly at work, mainly on the Continent, as had been the case over the previous few years, Ian now got the band together only for tours, occasional UK gigs and for broadcasts.

More significantly for Ian's future career, he also began doing workshops, working with up-and-coming young players. The first of these came about as a consequence of the interest of the television producer Dennis Marks, who was at that time making films for the BBC. He followed Nucleus on a 1979 British tour on which there were several educational events, and then proposed that later in the year, when the band returned from a lengthy stint in Germany, he put together a workshop that would be shadowed from start to finish for television.

'He suggested we recruit a selection of the brightest young players, and go to the West Country to do the filming,'recalls Ian. 'So we sought out a number of players. Some of them, who are famous on the scene now, such as Guy Barker, actually asked to be included, and, after auditions, we all went off and worked on a difficult piece of mine called *Midnight Oil*. It made a very interesting programme, and when it was shown in 1980, somebody at the Guildhall School of Music in London saw it. They asked me to go there and do some workshops, and these began in 1981.

'At the same time, because the band worked so little in the UK, I wasn't doing much between tours, so I thought I might go and do some jazz at the Interaction Weekend Arts Workshops for young people in Camden. It seemed to me this was something I could actually do in England. So I went to see Ed Berman who ran it, pointed out I was living round the corner in Kentish Town, and along with his dance and theatre classes I might be able to do jazz workshops. He said, "OK, do it!" They gave me some money to set it up, and although I started with only about two or three students, it very soon turned into a beginners', intermediate and advanced class. I mainly taught the intermediate and advanced level, and we arranged things so that I could put a dep in to keep things going while I was away on tour.'[2]

The Guildhall association has lasted for almost twenty-five years so far, and Interaction is still going strong, although Ian himself no longer teaches there regularly. Over the years, his Interaction students have included many of the rising stars of British jazz, such as Jason Rebello, Julian Joseph, the Mondesir brothers, Nikki Yeoh, and Zöe Rahmann.

Ian sees one of his main functions as giving young players confidence, and that with this confidence comes the ability to explore and grow as a musician. He would sometimes display a short fuse of temper during his rehearsals, and occasionally students were offended, but for the most part he communicated his passion for the music. Other long-term colleagues like Trevor Tomkins, Nic France and Geoff Castle would come in and work alongside the students as well. Although Ian's class sometimes averaged as many as fifteen musicians, they seldom worked in a big band format as the young players on the television workshop had done. Instead, they played in a series of small bands, and one benefit of this was that for the surprisingly large number of students who wanted to try their hand at composing, there was plenty of opportunity to hear their new music being played.

'One year I had nine composers in the group,' he remembers. 'In some respects that was quite hard for me, but I am pleased to have been instrumental in getting Julian Joseph and Nikki Yeoh to write some of their first compositions.'[3]

There was also practical hands-on experience for all students, firstly of different time-signatures. For young players whose instrumental tuition or school musical education had usually consisted of pieces with two, three or four beats to the bar, Ian began to introduce the more complex metres that had been part of his musical world since the early days of Nucleus and *Snakehips' Dream,* with its loping five-four rhythm. Some students didn't find the asymmetrical rhythms all that easy, and so there was plenty of group work, clapping and singing in five, seven and nine, as well as efforts to write down the more complex patterns.

'Ian was great for teaching us about music through repertoire we wouldn't normally play,' remembers Julian Joseph. 'He would introduce us to *Stella By Starlight, Blue Bossa,* and those kinds of tunes – simple tunes, but still things you had to get your head around if you weren't familiar with that kind of harmony, or harmonic movement. Ian would write out things for a piano player or horn player to do and see how well we'd tackle playing the changes...He would give us things [he would] do with the United Jazz and Rock Ensemble, and things he would do with Nucleus. We had all these challenges playing pieces in different time signatures.'[4]

Joseph's contemporaries included drummer Rober Fordjour, bassist Paul Hunt, and flautist Philip Bent. With drummer Mark Mondesir, and a non-participant in the Workshop, who nevertheless absorbed its influence, Courtney Pine, this coterie of musicians formed a rehearsal band that was eventually the launch pad for all their careers.

It is significant that Interchange students' practical experience also took in rehearsing, something Ian had experienced himself with bands from the EmCee Five days onwards.

'Students in my workshops learned how to rehearse,' he says. 'Always with a new piece, I'd get the rhythm section to run it down first, and have all the horns listen, so that everyone knows all about the piece. This goes for most of the rehearsal bands I've played in and all my own bands. Not least because when you are rehearsing you have to know what's wrong. I found this workshop experience incredibly good for my ear...for me teaching is learning.'[5]

But if teaching was one kind of learning experience for Ian, the start of the 1980s was also the framework for another, because it was the moment that he came of age as a writer. Some years earlier, in the wake of *Music Outside*, the publisher of that volume, John Latimer Smith, had given him the initial advance for a book on Miles Davis. This money, and the proceeds of UJRE concerts and tours had financed much of the research, so that when Latimer Smith's firm was no longer able to proceed with the publication, Ian did not abandon his years of work, but paid back the advance, and then moved to Quartet books, who became the home of what became his acclaimed 1982 biography of Miles. The experience of writing this was no less a learning experience than teaching the young musicians of Camden Town.

'Real writing is a process of discovery,' he maintains. 'You may start off, as I did with the Miles Davis book, thinking, "I know more than anybody about this." But once I began I made so many discoveries. It was very exciting. And some were things I could transfer to my own life. You could learn from it, in terms of what to do with your own career.

'I was staggered by the revelations I found doing the book. It became a much richer experience than I ever dreamed of because of that. Most of my discoveries were in areas that had hardly, if at all, been written about by other people. For example nobody had identified the importance of his film music for Louis Malle in terms of his future work. I was the first person to make that connection, thinking, "Christ! He's using methods here that everyone thinks he started using later." That was a shock. And then there's a session he did with Charlie Parker in 1946, which I describe partially in terms of the non-Western elements in the way Parker approached his music. In Miles's own book, his ghost writer, Quincy Troupe, uses exactly those words, "non-Western", and a lot of people have used it since. I've seen critics using language that I used to describe Miles that had never been used that way before my book was written, like creating and releasing tension, or making music breathe.'[6]

To me, the most remarkable element of Ian's life of Miles is its highly personal tone. Although it is written in standard English prose, it is far from dispassionate, and fairly bubbles with Ian's own enthusiasms and interests, becoming as true a mirror of his distinctive personal accent and individual take on the world as much of his own music. Indeed, the Davis influence is a huge element in Ian's own playing, and has been since his earliest days as a professional, no doubt inspired by his discovery of the *Walkin'* session during his time in Nice. So it is no surprise that Ian's personal mantras, from the use of tension and release to the importance of physical fitness in keeping illness at bay, suffuse the text. His impatience with the BBC and its coverage of jazz – despite his own long-term involvement with the organisation as a talks and radio documentary presenter – boils over in his anger at the fact the corporation failed to interview Miles or record his latterday European or British appearances. 'Old snobberies and ignorances die hard in Britain,' he writes, blaming Reithian values for the omission.[7]

But in this parallel to the proselytising stance of *Music Outside*, we glimpse the real passion of Ian himself, and this is what makes his writing spring to life on the page throughout the book. His love of Miles, but also his own critical values, shine through every paragraph. 'If you don't feel passionately about something,' he has observed, 'then you'll never have the energy to go through with it. That's why I can only write books about what I feel really strongly about. Because then you get the energy. That's why I couldn't write half a book about Gil Evans, which his wife wanted me to do, from 1960 to his death, because I'm more interested in his whole life...I wouldn't have the energy to do that.

'When I'm writing a book, I never criticise myself when I'm writing a first draft. I just write out everything that comes to me in each chapter, even if I know it's rubbish. I write the whole thing out, and then when I'm finished, I go back. I wrote the whole Miles Davis book out three times. When you go back, [you leave] no spare words, every word must count, every word must mean something, and it all must be in the right order. If you start doing that from the beginning, you lose the flow, the dynamism, and everything.'[8]

The Miles Davis book, orginally published as 'A Critical Biography' garnered exceptional reviews, including a full page in the *New York*

Times Book Review. Here in Britain, my colleague on *The Times*, Clive Davis, accurately described it as 'the standard work' in a retrospective article that confirms the book to have been 'a labour of love', and in the same piece, Ian compares his modest financial rewards with those of his old friend Norman Sherry for his lifelong study of Graham Greene.[9] This original edition of the book, notwithstanding the limitations caused by its subject still being alive and creating at his usual prolific rate, hence threatening to date the material instantly, still ranks as one of the best jazz biographies in the literature, and this is because in it, Ian successfully mixes his passionate enthusiasms with the keen insights of a working musician who was playing at the very highest level. The 1998 reissue, with a newly written survey of Miles's final years and several fresh interviews, deservedly acquired the tag 'definitive' in its title. Yet despite the promotional round that went with the book, which established Ian in the public mind as an author, leading to several more broadcasts and reviews, and ultimately another book on Keith Jarrett, he still regarded himself very much as first and foremost a professional musician, not a writer.

Although Nucleus by now only did occasional UK tours, it did – as I have mentioned – appear on sporadic radio broadcasts. These include a memorable BBC session for *Jazz Today*, the weekly Radio 3 modern jazz programme presented by Charles Fox, which took place in October 1982. It is important in the annals of Nucleus because this particular version of the band never recorded commercially. The broadcast was also the occasion for Ian's only known recording of his piece *The Pretty Redhead*. The number was inspired by a poem of the same title by the French writer Guillaume Apollonaire, which Ian found greatly inspirational.

'I didn't think much of the number at the time,' he says, 'but listening back now I can't see what the problem was – I'm very pleased with it. The poem that inspired it was written at the end of Apollonaire's life, and facing death, the poet lays himself bare. He talks of "the long quarrel of tradition and imagination" and goes on to describe "new fires, colours never seen, a thousand phantasms", and these are some of the images I was trying to capture in music. The "redhead" is the sun.'[10]

Surrounding it are *Easy Does It Now* and *For Miles and Miles*, two pieces that became part of the band's established repertoire, which also exist in live versions from a Stuttgart concert, recorded three years later. However these BBC recordings match the concert versions for intensity and fire, and mark the point when, after Geoff Castle's departure, the band no longer had a specialist keyboard player, and instead featured Mark Wood on guitar as the only chordal instrument.

This radio session is also the saxophonist Tim Whitehead's only recording with Nucleus, although he had first replaced Brian Smith on a tour in 1977 and came into the band permanently in 1982 when Brian returned to his native New Zealand. Up until that time, the early 80s rhythm section had continued to feature Chucho Murchan on bass and Nic France on drums (as on the *Awakening* disc), but when they decided to go to Spain to play a gig for Mark Wood,[11] instead of accompanying Ian on a short visit to Italy where he was to receive an award, Ian fired them, and brought in the band's original drummer John Marshall plus bassist Joe Hubbard. (The BBC session is also Hubbard's only recording with the group.)

Tim Whitehead was not happy about Ian's decision to fire the others, and shortly after this recording, he also left, to be replaced by Phil Todd, who is still in the line-up over twenty years later. Tim's departure more or less coincided with an entirely unexpected development in Ian's life, which threatened to knock his entire career sideways. 'I developed cancer of the colon,' he recalls. 'I had absolutely no idea what was going to happen when I went into hospital. It took me ages to recover from it, although superficially I got back into the swing of things quite fast. For example, I did a lecture within a few weeks of coming out of hospital, and within six weeks I did a concert at the Stables with Nucleus. But then I had to go back into hospital because the wound had not healed. It had to be reopened and cleaned, because it was suppurating during the concert at the Dankworths' place, and I knew I'd have to go back in.

'I had to have a colostomy, which took a huge amount to getting used to. I had a very, very good surgeon, called Northover, an impressive guy who knew I played the trumpet (and told me, by the way, that he had a hell of a time sawing through my stomach muscles). He cut the hole in a strong part of the stomach which didn't weaken my musculature for playing. I began playing by wearing a tight belt, which prevented any intestines from pushing through, but eventually my body adjusted, and now I'm stronger on the trumpet than I ever was before.'[12]

Physically, Ian's recovery was quick, aided by the care and concern of Sandy, Selina, and the many friends and colleagues who rallied round him,[13] but his condition has meant that ever since his life has been governed by a rigourous daily routine of irrigation and hygiene, which is not the easiest regime to follow when one is on the road. Clean, comfortable European hotels are one thing, but during the year after Ian's illness, Nucleus undertook what turned out to be the most ambitious tour of the band's career, a lengthy British Council-sponsored itinerary round South America, which offered no such certainties about his health. Taking in a whistle stop tour of almost the entire continent, the line-up of Ian, Phil Todd, Mark Wood, Dill Katz and John Marshall, undertook a complex programme of workshops and concerts, the former events giving the band the opportunity to meet and play with local musicians in several countries, and the latter bringing to the continent's audiences a style of jazz that was not particularly well-known there.

One aspect of Ian's life that I have hardly mentioned so far is that he has kept a fastidiously detailed diary during almost all his career, and although much of it makes interesting reading, and supports the remarkable detail and consistency that he brings to his spoken and broadcast autobiographical recollections, the South American volume stands out as a remarkable catalogue of the band's experiences. So rather than paraphrase it, here is an abridged version of Ian's own account of this 1984 tour.

10 May: Quito, Ecuador.
Superb climate for vegetation – gardeners' paradise. Very quiet city, no real danger. Almost 10,000 feet above sea level, and so higher than Bogota. Air very rare – shortness of breath. Sun can burn easily and quickly through the thin atmosphere. Our hotel in the quiet newer part of town. Population 40% Indian, 40% half-caste, 10% Negro, 10% European. Many very handsome men, and the women exude grace and sexuality. Heady stuff this.

11 May: Quito.
Taken round the old city by John Wright [of the British Embassy] and his assistant. Drove up the massive hill in the West...El Panecillo, with a gigantic kitsch metal statue of the Virgin Mary...We went down [again] into the old city, which was spread out below...and along a beautiful old street (La Ronda) with wrought iron balconies, window boxes of flowers, and leaded lights shining from their walls in hot sunshine. To get there we passed an open square where male and female prostitutes plied their trade in the middle of stalls and food stands. My radio interview was at an American (funded) Evangelical radio station. The school (again run by Americans) which is the *raison d'etre* of our workshop tomorrow is called the Cotopaxi Academy. Cotopaxi is the name of an enormous volcano to the East of Quito. Beautiful view of this from John Wright's house where we had lunch today. Most of the stuff in all shops here is of very high quality. In the old town we passed poky looking little shops, but all contained superb goods – leather, wool, clothes etc. John Marshall pointed out this was very different from the grey drabness and shoddy goods of Eastern Europe. Quito is the most foreign place I've ever visited, except perhaps for India. Virtually no European faces in the streets, all Indians and half-castes.

British and European newspapers are almost non-existent, and totally out of date.

After the war, Quito offered free land to European powers who wished to build their own cultural centre in Quito. The French and German governments did so, but the British declined. Now nothing much happens in the French and German centres, but the British Council is always busy!

13 May: Quito.
Drove in John Wright's Ford Escort north from Quito to Otavalo, a 2-hour trip during which we crossed the Equator. Hot and sunny day and we could see Cotopaxi from John's house before we set off. He said it was the first time it hadn't been shrouded in cloud for some months. We drove through stupendous Andes country – huge mountains and valleys, lusciously green for the most part. The mountains cultivated halfway up their sides. Stopped on the way to photograph the peak of Cotopaxi – snow covered and clearly visible, though ringed by clouds. Particularly beautiful cloud formations here. Climate seems to be perfect on the equator, when very high up. Warm, but not too hot, and enough rain for vegetation and people.

14 May: Lima, Peru.
Suddenly we're at sea level. Arrived Lima which is almost as dangerous as Bogota. Met by Tim Hibbert. He'd brought no subsistence for us, because he'd phoned Ecuador who said we had travellers' cheques. We have of course, but only for Ecuador and Mexico. Such messy organisation when we are tired and sweaty and dirty is a real dampener of the spirits...Arrived 7pm. Reached hotel around 9 pm. We're told that we leave for a flight tomorrow at 6 am. Spirits glum. I decide not to eat because I would have no time to irrigate. We have no days off in Peru.

15 May: Lima.
Smelling of sea and sewer and looking something like North Africa. No rain here – just mist and haze. The whole coastal strip a desert, watered by some rivers and wells. Dramatic change from luscious greenery, clean air and clean views of Andes.

16 May: Trufillo, Peru.
A dull cool morning, grey sky, very refreshing. Last night the twilight was superb. Blue grey sky with a yellow ochre tint, cut in half by flat roofs of clear washed houses. Today, the clear blue pool at the hotel with its beige concrete surrounds, palm trees (small), and box-like flat-topped buildings recalls David Hockney's Californian 'Bigger Splash' paintings.

17 May: Trufillo.
Yesterday a workshop in the morning, then we were taken to the beautiful main square of the town where we took photos. Particularly notable were the different patterns of wrought iron grid which cove the windows of various buildings both private and public...Then we drove

4 km. to the ancient and huge *adobe* ruins of Chan-Chan, which was the largest mud city in the world...in its heyday [it] was about 18 square km. and held about a quarter of a million inhabitants. It withstood several Inca attacks and was only taken by the Incas when they discovered how to cut off the city's water supply...South America in general very favourably disposed towards Britain and the British. But British business is economically off the map here, no British cars except the occasional Land Rover, and in Ecuador we saw (maybe six in all) Leyland double-decker buses.

20 May: 03.50hrs on Chilean Airways flight to Santiago.
Lima was an unhealthy climate. The Humboldt current from the Antarctic goes North as far as Ecuador and/or Colombia, and this cold climate stops any rain, and keeps Peru cold. So although there is no rain, there is frequent mist, and cool temperatures. But when it is warm, the humidity makes it an excellent breeding ground for bacteria, viruses and bugs of various kinds. The result is flu, frequent outbreaks of spots, typhoid, diarrhoea, and general ill-health.

20 May (later): Santiago, Chile.
We did a workshop in Lima on the morning of 18th, which was very well attended, mostly by people hoping for a free concert. However we got some musicians up playing with us, with much goodwill and open-heartedness. This was all a pleasing essay in human relations. None of the South Americans had played in 5/4 time before, but we soon had a drummer and his pianist brother playing in that time. By then, Phil Todd had been ill for two days with stomach cramps, John Marshall had aching joints, like flu, and Mark Wood came out in spots. It was a relief to arrive in Chile today and have seasons for the first time since we arrived in South America. It is now autumn, and cool, even chilly(!) and trees were losing their leaves. We looked around in pleasant nostalgia – it is very European.

21 May: Santiago.
Santiago plumbing is very good. Lavatories that flush efficiently and I also have a bidet. Mostly new buildings as earthquakes have destroyed all the old ones. Now people build down almost as far as they build up. Foundations go two or three storeys below ground. There was a tremor here last week. People very European here. Spanish, German, Irish etc. Very few Indians as they were driven out. In the far north of the country there are some little towns where only English is spoken...British people came here in the 19th century to mine nitrates and to build railways. In 1879 Peru and Bolivia declared war on Chile, but aided by the British, Chile won the war and gained territory, including Bolivia's only port.

Peter Schwartz, the arts officer, took us around town today in a VW van. He is of Austrian Jewish extraction and speaks excellent English as does his wife. Peter voted for Allende. He said that after Allende was elected, everything was wonderful for a year. Then Allende's two parties, socialists and communists, couldn't agree and soon there were 18 parties in parliament. Allende made a law keeping prices low, and so big business refused to produce goods. For almost two years there was nothing in the shops. Peter was offered a batch of 500 toilet rolls, when he only wanted a few, but he had to take them all or go without. So he used them to trade with his friends...He and his associates at the British Council took it in turns to queue all day for rice or work all day in the ofice. Peter got fed up with the chaos under Allende. Eventually everyone in Santiago, except Allende, knew about the impending coup.

22 May: Santiago.
Tonight's concert was under the auspices of the Beethoven Society. We played in a cinema (1200 seats?) and it was a sell-out. The crowd very responsive. We started at 9.30 pm after the film, and finished at 12.15 am with a 15 minute interval. There is a curfew in Santiago, no cars allowed on the streets between 1.00 am and 5.00 am. But before our concert the President of the Beethoven Society announced that the curfew would start tonight at 2.00 am. Much rejoicing.

23 May: Santiago.
There is an air of affluence here, people well-fed and well-clad. But this is a facade, Milton Friedman's monetarist policies are in full spate here. The well-off get richer, and the poor get poorer. Kept well out of the way are some desperately poor people.

Although our host Peter Schwartz, the British Council Arts Officer, is charming and sypathetic, we will be glad to leave Santiago, largely because of the unsympathetic nature of the main British Council representative. He holds himself very aloof from us, and I do not feel one iota of warmth flowing from him. He has curly grey hair, glasses and a silvery and very 'posh' voice. When he came backstage last night he was wearing a black cape, the ultimate in high camp snobbery. I believe he is a classical music enthusiast and can't respond to our music at all.

24 May: Concepcion, Chile.
Flew here today. In the air surrounded by huge mountain peaks projecting from the dense white fog. Breakfast of Nescafé (the tin is proffered by the waiter and you take what you want, then add hot milk or water), and scrambled eggs with ham at this very provincial hotel. Then ablution, irrigation, and an attempt to sleep. Two hours of warmth and rest but no sleep. My room resounded with a symphony of torrential rain. It drummed on the roof, rattled on the windows, roared in the distance, hissed onto the vegetation outside the window, trickled in shallow rivulets and gurgled darkly in the pipes and bellies of various receptacles.

26 May: Viñ del Mar, Chile.
Bougainvillaea and orange trees here, a pleasant little seaside town next to Val Paraiso on the Pacific coast. It poured with torrential rain

during the evening, and I got soaked going the 150 metres from the hotel to the theatre. We have had little sleep for two nights because of early flights and a long van drive. We arrived at 1.00 pm yesterday and all I wanted was some food and two or three hours in bed. But no, we were taken to a restaurant a twenty-minute drive away where everyone sat around drinking and eating snacks for forty minutes, while I sat there exhausted, and eating and drinking nothing. Then eventually we ate and I was back at the hotel by 4.00 pm. By this time I was very angry. So I spent an hour irrigating, bathing and shaving. (I'd not washed that day on account of the early flight.) Then I did my basic practice and cleaned the trumpet, by which time it was 6.00 pm. So instead of going to the theatre for sound check, I simply lay down on my bed and rested til 7.00 pm. This was the first time in this whole tour I had missed sound check, and only because our hosts had pushed me to the very limits of my energy and stamina. Done out of ignorance, not necessity.

However our concert was quite brilliant. I did not play so well, but the other members of the band were superb. The opera house was packed from the stalls right up to the Gods. A loud, volatile enthusiastic audience. They began by chanting some things against General Pinochet, because, as Peter Schwartz explained, they wanted us to know they CAN protest in Chile.

All the guys played superbly at this concert. Mark came up with many new phrases and ideas. Phil Todd pushed himself to the limit and John Marshall played a drum solo so powerful that before it ended I said to Phil, 'That's beyond the call of duty!' After the concert a crippled half-blind old lady came backstage to tell us how happy the music had made her.

Then the little cultural officer of Viñ del Mar took us to a club/restaurant where we were supposed to meet with local musicians, eat something nice and maybe have a jam session. This after we had given our ALL and drained ourselves at a concert that had totally bewitched the audience. After such an expenditure of energy and imagination, and after such a reaction, total happiness and joy, all a musician wants is to relax, listen to other musicians, and maybe eat and get drunk. But the club they took us to was vegetarian – John Marshall who'd not eaten all day wanted meat. He was ultimately (after much complaining from me) given a fish dish around 1.00 am. As we sat at our table, some local Chilean musicians played. No-one came up to us and said that they had been to our concert and would like us to play with them. No-one told us this, so when the short-assed organiser came up and said 'Would you like to play now?' I hesitated for moment, and then in a fit of anger said that I wouldn't like to play with the local gladiators. This caused a huge amount of bad feeling, and as we left the building, people hurled insults at us. So irrational is the course of music.

27 May: Montevideo, Uruguay.
By far the most European city we've seen to date. The population is nearly all European – and the atmosphere in the streets reminds me of Paris, Brussels, even Nice. Our hosts are Richard Cowley, the Director-General of the Insituto Cultural Anglo-Uruguayo, an immensely tall, easy-going man, and his assistant Jorge. Our concert tonight has had to be postponed because a power failure has blacked out the theatre.

28 May: Montevideo.
Revised plans are workshop this evening and concert tomorrow. Incessant downpour and heavy rain today. I got drenched shopping for shampoo and ineffectually for pedal bin liners which I need for my condition. Oddly such household items are hard to come by. Since the Falklands war, Uruguay has become very important to Britain, being our main ally and base on the Atlantic coast of South America. John Marshall complains bitterly about the diplomatic socialising we have to do at receptions and meals. I say I find them quite amusing and just get people to talk about themselves, which appeals to the failed novelist in me. John says no-one is interested in him.

29 May: Montevideo.
Rain continued today, accompanied by vast squalls of wind, blowing trees down and people off their mopeds. Richard Cowley, driving us back to the hotel after a shopping trip accelerated into some muddy water and smashed into something, destroying his left front wheel, and damaging his engine. We had to brave the immense gusts of wind and lashing rain and take a taxi.

Tonight's concert a triumph at the Opera House (Teatro Solis). Because of the cancellation of our first concert, and because of the atrocious and dangerous weather, there were only about 600 people in the theatre, but they made up in warmth and noise what they lacked in numbers. Afterwards I was told that they were SHOCKED at the high quality of the music. The band was brilliant and light-hearted tonight, with dynamics from a whisper to a roar. Much musical fun, high jinks and laughter. The band was on its mettle because some local musicians had shown a competitive spirit at our workshop on Monday and needled Dill and Mark in particular. Dill played superb bass on the concert, and his Uruguayan bassist/needler was captivated and generous with his praise.

31 May: Rio de Janeiro, Brazil.
Spectacular arrival at sea-level airport yesterday. Rio itself a seething mass of perpetual activity. Warm, humid and a sense of fetid and dense sexuality. Our driver goes at speed and he drove (albeit cautiously) through a red light. Later we discovered it is dangerous to stop at red lights because hidden thieves appear and put a gun to your head. As each day is an 18-hour day for us, and we have no day off in Brazil, rest becomes a priority for me. Yesterday after abluting and practising,

spent two hours doing an interview which was televised. Then after a light lunch and seeing to various organisational chores, I went to bed for one and a half hours, while the guys all were driven sight seeing. I saw nothing of Rio except the view from my hotel and the car en route to the theatre.

1 June: Londrina, Brazil.
To bed at 2.00 am last night and up at 5.30 am for flights to São Paulo and Londrina, so-called because it was founded by an Englishman.

2 June: Londrina.
50th anniversary of founding of Londrina coincided with the founding of the British council, hence our visit, which happens to be the first jazz concert ever in Londrina. A beautiful lush area, a highish plateau with low hills and rich vegetation – coffee and vines – warmer than the average Mediterranean climate but with a plentiful water supply. Great communication problems at our hotel. The staff spoke only Portuguese and couldn't understand Spanish. It was with great difficulty I made them realise there was no soap in my room, and I had to go down to the foyer and make gestures. Then there was no plug in the washbasin. Spanish for plug is 'taco', and this I asked for firmly on the phone. They brought me talcum powder! I improvised a plug by pushing a handkerchief down the hole. Portuguese for 'plug'is pronounced 'ploog' so a Yorkshire accent might have got results.

3 June: Curitiba, Brazil.
Superb concert at Curitiba last night with a lovely audience who gave us a standing ovation at the end. Many new ideas came to me, a brilliant fluency and inexhaustible 'chops'. This may have been because of having to rethink the creative act. Phil had been emotionally down for a couple of days and looked unhappy before last night's concert. He said he was totally stale and sick of his own phrases and couldn't think of anything else to play. In a moment of inspiration I said, 'Why don't you radically simplify your phrases and alternate them with the more complex lines you play. You can sometimes think of lots of new things to do with just three or four notes.' He thought for a few moments and then came up to me and said, 'You know, that's a marvellous idea and it's so simple. I can't think why it didn't occurr to me!' He played with renewed inspiration last night, with lots of new ideas, and during the interval I heard him telling the others what I'd said.

4 June: Curitiba.
Woken at 6.15 am, by a call from Sandy to say that John Marshall's father had just had a heart attack and died. I was to try and break the news to him before anyone else phoned. I threw some clothes on and went down to the foyer to find his room number, but he was there already. 'You've heard the news?' I asked, touching his arm. 'Yes,' he said, 'Maxie [his wife] just phoned.'

We went up to his room and sat drinking Coke and talking about what to do. My eyes kept filling with tears because I knew how close he was to his father. I never thought I'd feel grief at the death of anyone else's father. I felt nothing when my own father died. We weren't close and I hadn't seen him for years. John said, 'It hasn't hit me yet.'

John felt he would have to go back to London to give moral and emotional support to his mother. I told him to do what felt right – we could always play without drums, until a replacement was flown out. Nic France knows most of our repertoire and might be available. The first thing was to fix John's flight back to London. Meanwhile I'd go back to my room to irrigate and thus free myself for the day's business. I'd just finished when John came to my room.

'Look,' he said. 'Maxie and my sister are with my mother, and they're all right at the moment. So I won't go back yet. This tour's unfinished business and I'm really enjoying it. I'll have to go for the funeral of course, but maybe I can go in the three days next week when we don't have a concert? Or maybe just miss one concert? This is the happiest solution from my point of view.

5 June: São Paulo.
John is going back for the funeral in six days' time, and will fly out again the following day to join us in Mexico. That's his decision and I'm very happy about it. Yesterday was a very long day, we flew here and had no rest during the afternoon. Our workshops began at 5.00 pm. in the English Cultural Centre. It was full – maybe 250-300 people. We played and explained three pieces: the *7/4 Blues, Bouquet Pour Ma Belle,* and *Lady Bountiful* (5/4). We were given a prolonged ovation after *Bountiful*, then we answered lots of questions, and had some musicians join us to p;lay on some parts of the pieces. There were two or three spirited saxophonists and an American drummer, Bob Wyatt, who lives here. After three hours of very successful workshop there was a buffet supper. We are now into the sixth week of this tour.

6 June: Santos, Brazil.
Concert here last night: an almost full house and a very friendly audience. Lots of new and interesting things musically – my energy at a high level. This inexplicable. Tom Ponsonby phoned us at 6.00 am. Our insurance covers John's flight home, but not his or Nic's flight to Mexico. This latter flight is contractually my responsibility, but Tom says the British Council will help with it. John came to my room at 11.30 am. he now feels he ought to stay at home after the funeral. We had a long talk and the result is Nic will fly out to join us in Mexico City. He'll fly out on Sunday (10th) so he has the Monday – a free day – to acclimatise.

Today the Brazilian saxophonists who played at our workshop are going to Phil Todd's room for a sax seminar. Phil's incessant practising has often disturbed us, but he now takes a room well away from the rest of us, usually on a different floor.

7 June: São Paulo.
The concert here last night was a triumph. The theatre was totally full. A warm, discerning and vociferous audience. Tremendous feeling of warmth from them, so that we were really charged and excited. Standing ovations. We had to play an encore. The British Council people amazed and delighted. The people here the warmest and friendliest we have met in South America. This was also a sophisticated audience with all the best local musicians in it.

8 June: Recife, Brazil.
Climate hot and humid. We sweat profusely. Frequent cold showers.

9 June: Recife.
Yesterday took a taxi to the market in the old prison, in the heart of this old and beautiful town. In the middle of our visit, a small band struck up with a lilting, seductive rhythm. One very dark little kid on shakers, another dark young guy on tom-tom, which he played with a mallet, striking a resonant 'one' on the last half of the fourth beat, then for the rest of the bar muting the drum with his fingers and syncopating beats with the mallet. The snare drum player, a tall slim guy with a long impassive face, leaned against the wall and stood with his feet crossed. The epitome of relaxation, lovely lilting effortless rhythm. Then there was a singer, a dark woman with a half-Indian/half-African appearance. She sang in a minor key with a powerful voice of haunting feeling. Each verse was followed by a brief clarinet solo, played by an ancient and skinny Negro, wearing a straw hat...his clarinet tone was pure New Orleans – wide vibrato and acidic tone and slightly off-pitch all the time, with a mesmeric quality. The piece lasted a very long time, over 30 minutes, and gained in passion and power steadily until at the climax it was much louder and erupted in stop-time breaks. This was music of considerable magic, and totally hypnotic. The rhythm was so beautifully played that we didn't just hear it, we inhabited it and were taken beyond time by it. That's why the length of the music never became a bore. John Marshall was delighted with the rhythms played by this group, and borrowed my pen to jot down some of the time values.

10 June: on Mexican airways flight to Mexico City.
During this flight read my first book for over two months. *A Sort of Life*, the first part of Graham Greene's autobiography. Fascinating. The tour has been so demanding until now that I was unable to read a book. John Marshall left the hotel last night amid emotional farewells from us. He was clearly very moved. His flight was at 9.45pm, so he'll already be home. Nic France will already be in Mexico City.

13 June: Mexico City, Mexico.
The first concert with Nic last night was good and he did really well. There were about 1,000 people in a hall that held 2,500. Apparently the publicity had been poor. I was exhausted after a 1 hour rehearsal-cum-soundcheck and a 2 hrs 20 minute concert at this altitude. Woke up this morning feeling worn out, and so spent much of the day in bed. This did the trick and I was full of energy and ideas tonight, and the band was excellent.

14 June: Mexico City.
Went to Toluca, 66km SW of Mexico City. We were to give a one and a half hour concert in the Aula Magna there, but Mark Wood became ill before the concert – something he'd eaten. Mark tried manfully to play on *Dawn Choruses*, looking ghastly, white and drawn, but couldn't solo on it. We started *Bouquet pour ma Belle* without him, but he came back on stage and soloed beautifully, he stayed on for *Miles and Miles*, but again couldn't solo and went off stage. I called a 10-minute interval and told him not to come on. A doctor was on the way. We had to play as a quartet to a packed and sympathetic house. Our music was rapturously received.

16 June: Miami, Florida, USA.
Last night we played our final concert in the Auditorio Nacional in Mexico City. It had a capacity of about 5,000 but only 2,000 people were there. However they filled up the centre and were very responsive. Terrific enthusiasm. The entire concert was televised (Channel 13) and the group played brilliantly with many good ideas. Phil Todd started this tour a very good saxophonist, and is now, I believe, a great one.

The band arrived home on 17th June, having played thirty concerts and four workshops.[14] Ian was tired but satisfied with the music, and particularly proud that he had a fine group of musicians around him, who grew and developed as an ensemble during the tour, playing a core repertoire that was uniquely the product of the work done by Nucleus over the years. Reflecting on the experience later, Ian felt this hard-working, lengthy tour was the most musically rewarding of his career, although the three-week tour of India he had indertaken for the British Council in 1978 had been a more intensive travelling experience. In India, supported by the enthusiasm of Capitol, (through HMV India,) and by the Council, the band had played only six concerts in three weeks, and there was a much greater time for sightseeing and acclimatisation. However, musically, it lacked the cohesion and growth that came about in South America. This latest tour had also tested Ian's personal endurance far further, because he was still dealing with the after effects of his cancer and operation, yet managed to play at the highest level despite the demanding regimen his condition imposed on him. (Not least because it was often necessary to use mineral water – which had to be de-fizzed – for the irrigation, as the tap water was not sufficiently clean.)

Sandy and Selina greeted Ian warmly when he returned home, but the hugs and kisses were short-lived because Ian set off almost immediately for Germany, for the annual ten-day tour by the United Jazz and Rock Ensemble. Rehearsals began in Stuttgart only three days after he touched down in London after the transatlantic flight back from Miami. The band's German dates in Karlsruhe, Mainz, Göttingen and Heidelberg were packed with the usual enthusiastic vociferous crowds, but there were thinner attendances in Austria which slightly lowered the band's high spirits. However, when the UJRE returned to Stuttgart at the end of the month for two nights at the Theaterhaus, a vast, supportive crowd was in evidence. In front of it the band cut its fine sixth disc, *Live Opus Sechs*, with what is for most enthusiasts its definitive line-up, still at that stage including Charlie Mariano, Kenny Wheeler and Eberhard Weber, all of whom left during the following decade.

The German audiences, almost ten years into the life of the band, were still predominantly young, in the teenage to early twenties age bracket. Albert Mangelsdorff suggested this was because, far from looking like pop stars, the band 'presented the image of ideal parents'. Writing at the time, Wolfgang Dauner agreed, saying, '[a] pop star's time is over as soon as they develop a pot-belly [but it] is just when *we* get started!'[15] Tracing the history of the group through its albums, *Teamwork*, *The Break-Even Point*, and *Live in Berlin*, it was highly successful at bringing the formality and discipline of its studio work to its live concerts, yet paradoxically also injecting the informality of its live concerts to its studio playing. In other words, the band had the power to draw on its collective resources to use the language of big band jazz, or of jazz-rock fusion to put across a consistent message, whatever the setting.

Through this experience and the preceding Nucleus tour, the summer of 1984 saw Ian once again at a high point as an instrumentalist, in the wake of his illness. We can get a sense of his playing from the period (and the sound of the South American tour) when the same Nucleus line-up that had travelled across the continent came into the studio (reunited with John Marshall) and recorded *Live at The Theaterhaus* in Stuttgart for the Mood label, featuring much of the repertoire that had formed the backbone of the South American concerts and workshops.

Meanwhile, the other strands of Ian's career, as writer and composer, were also moving forward simultaneously, despite his triumphant refocussing on playing.

As I mentioned earlier, at around the time of his illness, Ian had contemplated the idea of following the Davis book by writing a biography of Sid Chaplin, the great Geordie writer. When this undertaking fizzled out for lack of publishing support, it was replaced by two very different projects. As an author, Ian's long term intention was to write about another highly individual musician, about whose work he felt almost as passionate as that of Miles Davis, namely Keith Jarrett. He had met Jarrett during his research on the Davis biography, and was to interview him again a year or two later, when BBC Radio 3 made a series of half-hour documentaries on Miles. They hit it off, and Jarrett was open to Ian writing about him.

But this was a long-haul project that would take several years to complete. In the shorter term, he joined forces with the traditional jazz trumpeter and broadcaster Digby Fairweather and the pianist and biographer Brian Priestley to create one of the most useful short biographical reference books in jazz, the *Essential Companion*, (which became the *Rough Guide to Jazz* in several subsequent editions). This was a major commitment, that brilliantly exploited the different spheres of experience of its three contributors. Fairweather's passion for traditional and mainstream jazz was matched by that of Priestley for Ellingtonia and the early bebop era, whereas Ian, building on his contacts for *Music Outside* and the Davis book, was ideally placed to cover contemporary British and American musicians. For the *Companion*, Ian wrote hundreds of short biographies combining detailed research with pithy critical assessments, and the book eventually appeared in 1987. At the same time, I was working as consultant editor on the *New Grove Dictionary of Jazz*, which involved a huge community of jazz scholars and writers around the world. Despite its comparatively minuscule authorial team, the original *Essential Companion*, matched the accuracy and usefulness of its larger cousin in almost every respect, and demonstrates what a truly remarkable feat of research and assessment Carr, Fairweather and Priestley achieved. They co-opted additional writers for later editions, but the original book was substantially all their own work.

The year before it was published, Ian flexed his muscles as a composer in a piece written for string orchestra and jazz musicians as a Bracknell Festival Commission. Called *Northumbrian Sketches* the piece was a musical tribute to Chaplin, in place of the previously planned literary biography.

It was not the first time Ian had written for strings. In 1981 Cologne Radio had asked him to arrange fifty minutes of his music and then travel over to conduct it with the Radio Orchestra. There were 32 strings, plus full orchestral brass, woodwind and percussion. 'I'd never written for big band before,' Ian recalls. 'And never for a string section, but I talked to Neil Ardley and Paul Buckmaster, and took it on. I thought "Maybe I won't finish in time," and so I asked Neil to write one or two arrangements of my pieces. I was also worried as to whether the German musicians would be able to handle assymetry. So I took Chucho Murchan and Nic France with me to handle that in the rhythm section, but actually the trumpets had most difficulty, and we couldn't use everything they recorded. The simpler things went better, including *Midnight Oil*, which had been the Television workshop piece. I'm not really interested in writing for big bands, but I do like slightly larger than normal ensembles, or different instrumentation.'[16]

The Cologne project, however, was largely a question of arranging existing music for different instrumental forces. Ian's *Northumbrian Sketches* was a vastly more ambitious work. It would fuse an essentially English style of string orchestration and writing with jazz solos and rhythms, while attempting to evoke the landscape of Carr's childhood, so beloved by Chaplin.

South Hill Park in Bracknell, Berkshire, had been the setting for some of the most adventurous British jazz festivals of the 1970s and 80s. Few of us who were there for incredible concerts by the likes of Gary Burton, Don Cherry, or such British stars as Trevor Watts, Graham, Collier, and the London Jazz Big Band, will forget its very special magic. Based in and around a rambling mansion (which had formerly belonged to the family of one of Ian's army officer colleagues) the garden marquee, Wilde Theatre, Studio Theatre and basement bar offered a variety of backdrops for simultaneous music-making, as well as providing an artistic focus for one of the more spread-out of the British new towns built and developed in the 1960s.

In 1986, the jazz festival – which had been in abeyance for the previous year, temporarily relocating to Pendley Manor, near Tring – joined forces with its sister classical event to commission Ian's new work for the Kreisler String Orchestra, a 17-piece group, conducted from the first violin desk by their founder Michael Thomas, with Ian and Phil Todd as soloists. It was to be performed at both the classical and jazz festivals, and was written in a mere five weeks.

Although it was extremely well reviewed at the time, it took another two years before it was recorded (apart from a broadcast on Danish Radio which was never issued commercially). When the album finally came to be made in the summer of 1988, it was a triumph, and ranks among Ian's finest artistic achievements, not simply because of his triumphant solo playing, but also his confident mastery of the instrumental forces for whom he was writing, and the fact that he has a genuinely new and individual set of ideas to express.

I disagree with the notion that such compositions are about bringing together two incompatible forms of music. Plenty of classical players are accomplished jazz musicians, and vice versa, and in much writing about jazz, it is the critical ghettoes insisted on by newpaper and radio editors that have fuelled an artificial separation between genres. It is also a canard that improvised jazz has little to do with composition. From the days of the Original Dixieland Jazz Band onwards, composed structures have been the bedrock of most improvisation, and such institutions os the Ellington orchestra could not have functioned without a massive element of composition. What is significant about *Northumbrian Sketches,* more than its use of what are traditionally thought of as 'classical' and 'jazz' elements, is that like so much of the jazz produced over the preceding decades by Ian, Don Rendell, and Michael Garrick, it is characteristically English. The suite epitomises what Duncan Heining has eloquently described as 'a search for non-American roots' in British jazz.[17] This is a view shared by Ian, who said at the time that the Kreislers were 'brought up with all kinds of rhythm, pop, ethnic, blues, gospel...so you can ask them to understand the rhythm and play it with feeling...my composition isn't just an ersatz experiment in trying to yoke two different musics together.'[18]

From the ethereal opening figure carried on the high strings at the start of the first movement *Open Country*, the piece commands the attention, and soon a slowly building countermelody, gently offset from the prevailing rhythm weaves its way on on the lower strings, captivating the listener as a preparation for the first of Ian's own extended, lyrical solos. Most remarkable of all, particularly for those who believe that it is impossible for strings to swing, is the third section, *Disjunctive Boogie* (a piece recorded in a single, jaunty, confident, take). By the simple expedient of mingling Mo Foster's incisive bass guitar with the pizzicato strings at the beginning, Ian achieves a rhythmic edge that maintains momentum throughout the piece. His own soloing and that of Phil Todd balance lyricism with a jazzy grittiness. Few critics have described it better than Keith Howell, who wrote of the 'subtle and emotive trumpet figures underlined by the spirited dancing lines of the string orchestrations'[19].

Richard Williams in *The Times* was a little less kind, suggesting that the final movement, *Spirit of Place*, showed the composer 'beginning to run out of ideas', only to be rescued by Phil Todd's bass clarinet. Nevertheless, Williams, a fellow Miles enthusiast, went on to recognise that *Northumbrian Sketches* was 'a very substantial work, in which [Ian] also manages to find a perfectly workable solution to the old problems of reconciling the pre-composed orchestral parts with the needs of an improvising soloist. He does it the hard way, too, without a rhythm section, gambling on his own ability to infuse his writing with sufficient rhythmic vigour, and on the ability of...the Kreisler String Orchestra to interpret it.'[20]

For the *Old Heartland* album, on which the suite was included, three additional tracks were played by the current Nucleus line-up – essentially the 'South American' band, with Geoff Castle added once more on keyboards. The confident assurance of this music, and the maturity of the writing show that in the decade after *Out of the Long Dark*, Ian had continued to develop and mature as a musician. The fears about his artistic worth that had so beset him in the late 1970s were long in the past, but ironically, the 1990s were to see him so immersed in other aspects of his career that he was seldom to capitalise on the artistic peak of *Old Heartland*. It stands as a beacon of musical promise, just before the point when he was inexorably drawn further away from actually making music to writing, broadcasting and making films about it. All these things were done with his usual passion and conviction, and there were many fulfilling musical interludes, including the revolutionary electronic band Zyklus, revivals of past triumphs, and continued tours and albums with the UJRE, but *Old Heartland* marks a fork in the road, and the end of a sustained period of musical growth, experiment and invention.

10 into the media

The final years of the 1980s saw a fine balance in Ian's work between music-making and his other interests as journalist, writer and teacher. The same period also saw Selina's departure from the family home to study textile design at Birmingham College of Art. A little later, his marriage to Sandy ended, and Ian moved from Kentish Town into a small Brixton flat, where he has, for the most part, lived alone with his voluminous collection of books and records ever since. However, this time his unsettled domestic arrangements did not have a deleterious effect on his music, and he continued to play and compose with flair and originality.

Following the publication of *Jazz – The Essential Companion*, he had started several years' work on his biography of Keith Jarrett, which eventually appeared in 1991, and this, together with the previously published Miles Davis book, would eventually lead him via BBC Radio into the direction of film-making. However, during the time he was writing and researching the Jarrett biography, he did not turn his back on performing live music, and most significantly he took part in a number of big band projects – one of his own, and the other two with a pair of the most innovative leaders of the 20th century, the Zimbabwean-born Michael Gibbs, and the veteran American theorist George Russell.

The first of these was Mike Gibbs's recording, *Big Music*, cut in December 1988 by an all-star ensemble, recorded in locations on both sides of the Atlantic, in which Ian joined a trumpet section that also included the American stars Earl Gardner and Lew Soloff.

Gibbs had arrived at the Berklee School of Music in Boston from his home in what was then Rhodesia in 1958, and once there, in company with such alumni as Gary Burton, he had made several forays into the world of jazz-rock fusion, as well as acquiring a reputation as a highly original composer and arranger. In the mid-60s, he had relocated to London, where he doubled as a big-band trombonist and an arranger, either playing with or writing for most of the principal musicians of the

British scene, before he again moved to America in the 1970s to take up a composer-in-residence position at Berklee.

As the 1980s went on, in between his various writing and musical-directing projects, Gibbs started to lead his own Anglo-American big band, an ensemble that drew together all his interests, and this was the basis of the line-up that put down the tracks for his *Big Music* album, produced by the writer and keyboard-player John L. Walters. The result is a typically Gibbsean mixture, in which some of his swaying African themes mingle with more contemporary fare. Indeed, Walters' intention was to produce an album that explored what he described as 'the missing link between *Out of the Cool* and *Bitches' Brew*, between Charles Ives and Salif Keita'[1].

In addition to Gibbs, the other key ingredient was the versatile drummer Bob Moses, who had worked with Gibbs in the 1970s on his *Only Chrome Waterfall Orchestra* album, and who had more recently been leading his own band Mozamba. His rhythmically adept playing underpins all the layers that Walters and Gibbs recorded – using the technique of overdubbing the base tracks with solos recorded independently by various American guests such as guitarists Bill Frisell and John Scofield, or trombonist Dave Bargeron. Nevertheless, one of the most impressive solos on the entire album comes from Ian Carr, who delves deep into his Miles Davis vocabulary for a feature on *Pride Aside*.

Ian and Michael Gibbs have remained close friends and colleagues ever since, and nowadays make a point of turning up to support one another's gigs. Indeed it was the paucity of gigs for his closest and most creative colleagues on the British jazz scene that launched Ian's own next venture, Orchestra UK, in the spring of 1989. This was a big band which had its origins in the research for the *Essential Companion*.

'When I was collating all the information,' Ian told Clive Davis of *The Times*, 'I noticed that all the British musicians I most admired all seemed to be doing most of their work abroad. They simply weren't getting the offers here.'[2] This was hardly a new experience for Ian himself, who as we know, for the previous two decades had done by far the greatest number of Nucleus gigs outside his own country. So, coining the name Orchestra UK, with a considerable amount of irony, he went about recruiting a band that would showcase the wealth of British talent that was too seldom heard at home. Kenny Wheeler joined Ian in the trumpet section, and the reeds were Tony Coe, Evan Parker, Alan Skidmore and John Surman. The rhythm section was John Taylor, piano, Chris Laurence, bass, and John Marshall, drums, with Norma Winstone added on vocals. A national tour began on 8 May 1989, and took in London, Aldershot, Swindon, Newcastle, Leicester and Eastbourne. Sadly, the

Orchestra UK, with Kenny Wheeler (Ian Carr)

band made no commercial recording, but Ian's intentions for it included 'modal themes, fusion, and ethnic sounds', comprehending a similarly wide range to the UJRE, a band of comparable size. In this case, his ceaseless championing of the British jazz cause led to a newly-created ensemble, rather than the books, articles and broadcasts that had preceded it, in order to bring his message in person to audiences around the country.

Nucleus had not been ignored either, during the early part of 1989, although – despite the brand recognition he had built up over eighteen years – Ian took the decision now to take the band out under the name of 'The Ian Carr Group', even though its line-up was unaltered from the South American tour by Nucleus, five years earlier. A Barbican concert received a rave review from that usually rather sniffy publication *The Wire*, which ignored the group's new name, and talked of how effectively the band combined 'top quality jazz with hard-driving rock...Nucleus allows the freer jazz spirit to breathe by utilising the punch and instant accessibility of rock only sparingly.'[3]

Important though Nucleus remained, and totemic as Orchestra UK's proselytising role was for his views on the lack of recognition of local jazz talent, Ian's most significant association in 1989 was with a veteran of the American jazz scene. George Russell is living proof that few boundaries exist between what we normally think of as 'jazz', 'classical' and 'rock' music. He bases his ideas on his own lifelong theory about modal jazz, the 'Lydian Chromatic Concept of Tonal Organisation', and his scores have brought the use of modal ideas into contexts as varied as Dizzy Gillespie's 1947 big band, Lee Konitz's 1951 'cool' jazz group, Miles Davis's late 1950s sextet, and his own Jazz Workshop, which at various times included Art Farmer and Bill Evans.

Russell spent several years in the 1960s working with European jazz musicians in Scandinavia, among them notably being Terje Rypdal and Jan Garbarek, and a decade later, he worked with the Swedish Radiojazzgruppen, interpreting a selection of his works. In the late 1980s a plot was hatched for him to do something similar in England, bringing over a collection of his scores and playing them with a predominantly British line-up, who would then undertake a short European tour, followed by a brief season at Ronnie Scott's club in London. As a trumpeter with a long experience of playing the kind of jazz-rock fusion beloved of Russell, not to mention a fascination with modes and unusual scales, Ian was a natural choice to be asked to join the line-up, although he had not been invited to work at Scott's since he parted company with the club's management venture during the early days of Nucleus. Indeed, Peter King, the club's co-owner and manager, had not been on speaking terms with him for much of the period in between.

'I'd forgiven Pete years ago, but I think that perhaps the rift had grown up because I'd left the family fold,' says Ian. 'In other words, I was the unrepentant prodigal son. I got to meet George Russell and to know him, when he came over before the tour, because I actually wanted to talk to him about his connections with Miles Davis. He knew that I would have liked to play in his band, and so he asked me. It was very hard work, because George wants so much from his players. He wants a lot, and then he wants more! Even when you've got almost nothing left to give, he wants more. So you've got to be in really good chops, which I wasn't because I'd been writing right up to the last moment. It was weird because he was using all these young guys like Andy Sheppard and so on, and here's the great Ian Carr coming in and sounding terrible. I sounded like shit, actually. It was really funny because he asked Andy to play up a bit, and Andy was scared he was going to get fired from the gig. I went over to George and said to him that I didn't think my chops were up to much and if he wanted to get somebody else in in my place it was fine by me. He said, "No, no, I want you. But what about this piece?" And he pointed to a particularly difficult bit I couldn't play. I said, "Oh, that's all right, I'll take it home with me, and have a look at it, it won't be a problem." In fact I couldn't see it properly, because

George's writing was very small, and I didn't have my strongest reading glasses. By the third day, my chops were right up, and it went pretty well.

'The first part of the tour was abroad, and then we came back to England. We had around four nights at Ronnie's where George wanted to make a record, and I went there for rehearsal on the first day, but I didn't see Pete King. Then we broke up, so that there was enough time to go home, have something to eat and change, and as I was on the way out I saw Pete standing with his back to me in the foyer. I said, "Oh, Pete, I must say hello!"

'He turned to me with a scowl, and said "Why?"

'So I said I heard he'd been ill. And he just flung his arms around me and said, "Oh Ian, we went wrong so long ago!" And over fifteen years of disagreement were wiped out just like that. I went back to the club later with my own band, and he always treated me very well. It was all over.'[4]

The *London Concerts*, recorded over a couple of nights at the end of August 1989, pointed the way towards Russell's several return trips to the UK over the following fourteen years, in which he combined a small core of American players with a predominantly British big band. And although small by the standards of some of Russell's later projects, this fourteen-piece group at Ronnie's plays with all the punch and fire that his later, larger ensembles managed, its solo strength heavily relying on Ian and Andy Sheppard, as well as the greatly underrated Steve Lodder on keyboards. Central to the two discs by this first British version of his Living Time Orchestra, issued on the French Label Bleu, is a performance of Russell's classic *Electronic Sonata For Souls Loved By Nature*. It is a piece which has a typical piece of Russellian philosophy attached to it, namely the notion that 'man...must confront technology and attempt to humanise it'[5]. Whenever I've spoken to Russell at any length, these Confucian nuggets tend to fall randomly into the conversation, but he is also capable of being a very direct and incisive commentator on music, and it was these latter qualities that Ian managed to draw out of him in a multi-part BBC radio documentary about Russell that Ian presented in the wake of his touring experience.

Ian's directness, his Northern blunt honesty, tends to cut straight through intellectual pretension, and get to the heart of a subject. His radio series on Russell was one of several he presented from the 1988 to the mid-1990s that showed his ability to combine probing interviews with a teacherly gift for making complex music straightforwardly accessible.

In the late 1980s, as a consistent, voluble spokesman for jazz, and an accomplished author on the topic, Ian had been co-opted onto the BBC's Central Music Advisory Committee. He used the position constantly to reiterate his view that jazz was underrepresented on the national radio and television networks, compared to its position on most European state broadcasters. In the late 1980s, RTF, for instance, featured jazz on a daily basis in France. Meanwhile, the WDR station in Germany funded one of the world's finest radio big bands, which Ian experienced at first hand during his many visits there with Nucleus and the UJRE. Equally, Scandinavian radio had recorded *Northumbrian Sketches*, at a time when the BBC made no overtures to Ian to record his extended work, despite its English focus. So, consequently, he brought the same passion and pent-up frustration that had fuelled *Music Outside* and the Orchestra UK project to his BBC advisory role.

'I'm like a kind of virus they've all been immunised against,' he told the *Guardian*'s John Fordham. 'They try not to minute what I say, so I just go on repeating it. They don't know anything about jazz, except that in their hearts they think it's inferior. I keep saying that until being a jazz producer is an honourable post with a salary to match – as it would be in a European station – nothing will change. And that's what they won't minute. But I'll keep saying it until they do something about it.'[6]

The BBC's solution, at a time when jazz was (as it still is) somewhat unevenly divided between the populist Radio 2 and the predominantly classical Radio 3, was to encourage Ian to make programmes for the latter network, under the aegis of the nearest thing the Corporation had to a producer of the type Ian mentioned, namely Derek Drescher. Although he also produced mainstream elements of the music output, such as *This Week's Composer* and *Concerto* (the latter for the Radio 4 speech-based network), Drescher was then in charge of Radio 3's entire jazz coverage, including fortnightly Saturday evening concerts, and a weekly half hour documentary or record recital slot. He had also worked with Charles Fox on *Jazz Today* and *Jazz In Britain*, which had been for some years the main outlet for contemporary British jazz on the airwaves, and, although it was frequently produced by a junior colleague, Drescher also had overall responsibility for Radio 3's most popular jazz programme, *Jazz Record Requests*, which was presented by Peter Clayton.

A consequence of producing fifty-two weekly half-hour jazz record or documentary programmes a year, which in those days went out at teatime on Friday with a late-night repeat during the following week, was that Drescher was always looking for new subjects for record-based programmes, and new presenters. One way of doing this was by keeping an eye on what new books were coming out, and just as he recruited me in 1989 to make a series about Fats Waller within a few months of the appearance of my biography of the pianist, so, too, had he recruited Ian the previous year to make a series about Miles Davis in the wake of his book.

As it turned out, Ian's first major project for Drescher was not about Miles, but a seven-part series of record programmes on Keith Jarrett. This was because they decided between them to go for an altogether more daring strategy with Miles and make a full-blown documentary series, complete with interviews, which would naturally take a rather longer time to set up. As a result, the two of them set off for New York in June 1988, to record as many interviews as possible about Davis.

'We were there for two weeks,' remembered Drescher. 'We had a pretty relaxed time, actually, and we'd set up a number of interviews in advance, plus some more while we were there, by making phone calls. Ian was very good at that, I think, because of the years he'd spent organising his own band. He had all the addresses and telephone numbers, and because he already knew most of the musicians we talked to, I left the actual organising of most of the interviews to him.

'In the middle of it all, we went out to see Keith Jarrett, who lived several miles out of town. We caught a coach, went as far as we could on that, and then called a taxi for the last ten miles or so. As well as doing an interview with him about Miles, Ian was already starting work on his book about Keith, so after we'd talked about Davis, we went on and I recorded another interview with him talking about Jarrett himself, ready for the book.

'We were there about three hours, but we were staggered because there were Jarrett and his wife in this lovely house, and the whole time we were there, he never offered us a cup of tea, a glass of water, or anything. Then we had to wait for quite a long time after we had done the interview for the taxi to come and pick us up, to take us back to the end of the bus line again. We were standing in the kitchen, and there was still no question of being offered anything to eat or drink. Ian got so embarrassed by this he had to go out and stand in the garden!'[7]

Nevertheless, Jarrett's was just one major contribution to Carr's first major radio documentary series, which went out in 1989. It was well received, and led to more series for Radio 3, which Ian presented and researched, including not only his lengthy exploration of the work of George Russell, but programmes on Thelonious Monk and the Native North American contribution to jazz. A greatly expanded version of the Davis series was written and presented by Ian in 2001, to mark the tenth anniversary of the trumpeter's death. During their years of working together, he and Drescher became firm personal friends, not least because, according to Drescher, 'I find him a joy to work with. It's jolly nice working with someone who really throws themselves into it with such enthusiasm. And because of that I like him very much, and we find we think alike on many things.'

The second part of the Jarrett interview which they recorded in June 1988 was of immense help in the underlying biographical research for Ian's next full length book, *Keith Jarrett – The Man and His Music*, which finally appeared, published by Collins, in 1991.

Ian himself was full of enthusiasm for his new literary project, telling the *Independent*, 'I always write about what I love, and I have had more enjoyment from Jarrett in the last 20 years than from anyone else apart from Miles Davis...Jarrett's a genius in a family of them – all five brothers have IQs over 140 – and his level of inspiration is unparalleled. Rhythmically he's simply the most exciting pianist I've ever heard.'[8]

Ian's fervent enthusiasm for Jarrett – something, incidentally, which is not shared by his keyboard-playing brother Mike – in some ways makes this a less satisfactory biography than the earlier book on Miles. Whereas Miles was examined warts and all, I get the sense that Ian deliberately glossed over aspects of Jarrett's life, not least in deference to Jarrett's wish to retain his personal privacy. Davis's life was lived very publicly, including his relationships, his well-documented addictions and his scuffles. Jarrett's has always been far less public, and having read the transcripts of his conversations with Ian, these tend to go into great depth about the philosophy of Gurdjieff and Hartmann, rather than exploring the highs and lows of life on the road with Charles Lloyd or Art Blakey.

A high proportion of the book consists of reviews of the pianist's copious output, and these seldom take anything but the most positive line. As a result, *Publishers' Weekly* was harsh in its criticism, saying 'This adulatory recap of jazz pianist Jarrett's work with Charles Lloyd, Miles Davis and American and European quartets will please his admirers, but others may wish for a more critical assessment.' Nevertheless, Ian's book found favour with its subject, and this was to prove invaluable in removing obstacles to progress in 2003-4 when he and the film director Mike Dibb were working on an television film about Jarrett and his music. But this is getting ahead of events.

As well as leading Orchestra UK, fronting Nucleus and doing the annual tour with the UJRE, 1989 saw the start of another quite different musical project for Ian. This not only brought him together with Mike Gibbs' erstwhile producer John L. Walters, but reunited him with Neil Ardley. Together with the software engineer Warren Grieveson, they formed a quartet using a complex sequencing device called the Zyklus

Midi Performance System, or Zyklus MPS for short. Midi technology (effectively a computer/music interface) was burgeoning in the early 1990s, and this system offered a lot of hitherto unexplored possibilities. The first experimental track by the band, John L. Walters' composition, *Before The Oil Ran Out*, was recorded at Yamaha's research and development department in late 1989.

'It's a sequencer you can improvise with,' Walters told me, a little later, when I introduced a Radio 3 broadcast by the group in 1992.[9] He and Ardley fed in musical material to the system as keyboard players, while Grieveson put in guitar and percussion parts. Performing via a series of linked computers, these musicians then created a real-time backdrop over which Ian played a trumpet or flugelhorn part, either written or improvised. For the most part, Ian preferred to listen to the output via speakers in the studio and to play acoustically over that, rather as one plays along to a record, and this seemed to fit the somewhat unpredictable nature of the output. For more complex pieces, such as Walters' *I. K. Brunel*, which uses a collage constructed of industrial sounds, built into a pitched and rhythmic framework, Ian donned headphones and played through an effects unit. But whether in this entirely artificially constructed landscape, or in the more conventional setting for the band's recording of Monk's *Round Midnight*, which featured Ian at his most Milesian, the quartet was exploring new musical territory that sat somewhere between the electronic soundscapes of Vangelis or Kraftwerke and the clever, if rather tricksy, sampling of real sounds that was being explored in the 1980s by classical composers such as Jonathan Harvey, or which has been exploited more recently, in the 21st century, by Matthew Herbert. Significantly, and in this respect closest to Herbert's work, it always focussed on live performance, and not sounds that were created entirely artificially in a studio.

'An aim I've always had,' Neil Ardley told me at the time, 'is to integrate composition and improvisation and to make musical sense...The ideas we put into Zyklus are not complete. They come out and create a different sound world, an electronic sound world, which I love. I find the mixture of acoustic and electronic sounds quite spine-tingling. The music you hear, from this rank of synthesizers and samplers, we can't actually play in a real sense. We control the routes the music takes through the different machines, we have at our disposal electronic orchestras, playing different combinations and sequences of notes. John L. Walters, for example, is quite good at creating counterpoint effects. Zyklus works so well for that.'[10]

Zyklus, as the quartet called itself, made a single album, *Virtual Realities*, in 1991, and it subsequently made a small number of live appearances and a 1992 *Impressions* broadcast for Radio 3. In my view, both on the album, and the broadcast, its most interesting piece was a reworking of *Rainbow 1* from Ardley's *Kaleidoscope of Rainbows*. Remembering his compositional technique, which involved building pieces from tiny fragments of musical information, I wondered if the Zyklus system helped Neil to write. He told me that not only did it allow him to build up performances using the motifs and scales of which he was so fond, but he actually used the system as a compositional tool. The year before the Zyklus broadcast, he had used it to test a new composition called *On The Four Winds*, written for the baritone saxophone player John Williams and his New Perspectives ensemble.

'Normally,' he told me, 'I always tend to compose at the piano. But for this piece, it was much more fun to use Zyklus to work out *On The Four Winds*. Although the eventual piece was going to be played acoustically by New Perspectives, this allowed me to have a go at the music in several different ways and to get an idea of the end result. Also, for music like *Kaleidoscope of Rainbows*, I think some musicians find sticking to a repetitive pattern somewhat frustrating, but Zyklus can do this automatically. *On the Four Winds* was built mainly on three Asian scales, from Japan, China and Bali, and as you know, *A Kaleidoscope of Rainbows* was built up in exactly the same way. I think this gives my music a kind of unity, whether it's being performed through a MIDI system or by a live group.

'I've also found it has revived a lot of my enthusiasm for music. In the 70s I was working at quite a rate. Then the music business really collapsed, and for ten years I took myself off into writing science and information books, and I didn't have much inclination to get back into music. I was fed up with the music business, so I made myself independent of it. Now I am, I can approach this project with a fresh appetite.'[11]

Certainly the Zyklus performances of Ardley's music became a stepping stone for the subsequent large scale 1990s revivals of *Kaleidoscope of Rainbows*, given in full by an enlarged version of Nucleus, as discussed in Chapter Eight.

There are some common elements between the aural backdrops of Zyklus and Ian's next solo recording project, *Songs and Sweet Airs*, a collection of his compositions inspired by Shakespeare, and played with as a duo with John Taylor at the organ of Southwark Cathedral in May 1992. In much the same way as Taylor coaxes unusual sounds out of the inside of the piano, he has the ability to create weird and wonderful exotic settings on the organ. On this disc, he does exactly that, putting

Shakespeare's Birthday 1993: Ian and Sam Wanamaker at one of a long
series of events for which Ian provided music (Peter Symes)

Don Rendell and Ian reunited, Royal Festival Hall, 18 May 2001
(Peter Symes)

Ian's trumpet or flugelhorn into a wide range of contexts, that illuminate and test the boundaries of the compositions.

The recording took place at a high point in the campaign, headed by Ian's old friend and fan, the theatre director and filmmaker Sam Wanamaker, to rebuild Shakespeare's Globe Theatre on London's South Bank. For several of the years since Ian's *Will's Birthday Suite* of 1974, there had been some kind of celebratory event either at Southwark Cathedral, or at the South Bank site where Wanamaker eventually saw the 'Wooden O' of the Tudor theatre rise again. In 1993, Don Rendell and Ian were reunited briefly on stage there at an on-site concert to raise more funds for the rebuilding of the theatre. There were to be more reunions between the two of them over the course of the next ten years, including a BBC *Jazz Notes* broadcast from BBC Pebble Mill in September 1996[12], and a Royal Festival Hall foyer concert in May 2001. If anything, these showed that Don's style had remained close to its 1960s mix of Lester Young and early John Coltrane influences, whereas Ian's had continued to keep pace with the development of his major idol, Miles Davis, and had travelled some distance from his bebop roots. However, whatever their stylistic differences, the Globe concert succeeded in bringing back together these iconic figures of 1960s British jazz, prefiguring a revival of interest in their music, which ultimately led to almost all of it being available on CD, as well as the appearance on the Harkit label of some previously unissued live sessions.

Wanamaker himself had first met Ian and Don when their mutual friend, the television actor Warren Mitchell, had taken him to a pub in Hampstead in the late 1960s to hear the Rendell-Carr Quintet. Soon afterwards, the Quintet had been invited to play on one of the first fundraising concerts in a temporary theatre that Wanamaker had built close to the Globe site. The group performed alongside those other indefatigable fundraisers, John Dankworth and Cleo Laine.

'Then at the start if the 70s, I had the idea,' recalled Wanamaker, 'that we should create an annual Shakespeare's Birthday concert, around the end of April each year. It would be celebrated in a contemporary way, so that the Globe could be seen as not just a backward-looking cultural institution, but one that looks forward. I began commissioning music from serious composers, and the first concert was a very long classical event, with too many new works conducted by too many conductors! It was a very lengthy evening in the Cathedral, which is not the most comfortable place to sit for several hours, nor acoustically ideal.

'In due course, I decided to add a second evening, which would be a jazz concert. Ian seemed to be the person who was most enthusiastic of those I approached for the first one,...and that developed into the *Will Power* recording.'[13]

Limited funds and the fact that as the Globe project developed, more energy was going on the theatre rebuilding than the supporting infrastructure of artistic events, meant that there were some years in the 70s and 80s when there was no concert, but overall, a sporadic series of events ran in a rather haphazard way through until the early 1990s, when *Songs and Sweet Airs* was recorded. Wanamaker valued Ian's commitment to the project considerably. 'There's a lovely genuineness and enthusiasm about him,' he said. 'There's nothing phoney about Ian or superficial. He's a very honest human being, and I found him to be extremely sympathetic to our aims. In a spiritual sense, we share a lot: the enthusiasms he has, and the integrity with which he approaches the things he cares about.'[14]

These are also the qualities that Ian brought to the most recent of his artistic projects, his collaboration with Mike Dibb on two outstanding jazz television films, the first on Miles Davis, and the second, aired at the end of 2004, on Keith Jarrett. It may seem that these projects are the logical summation of his years of investigative effort on both musicians' careers, but in fact the original intention was that the Miles film would be made during the late 1970s, to coincide with the first edition of Ian's biography. As it was, more than another two decades went by before it finally took shape.

Mike Dibb had originally met Ian when he made a short film for BBC Television about the Rendell-Carr Quintet in 1968. Following that, the two men had stayed in touch, and during 1976, when John Latimer Smith first encouraged Ian to write about Miles, the possibility of doing a tie-in film for television was floated.

'I was on the staff at the BBC,' remembers Dibb. 'At that time the mainstream television output really didn't touch jazz at all. But by persistent lobbying, I made some headway, and finally got the grudging admission that Miles was a player of such significance that perhaps he might be covered in some way. The next year, I got a remit from the BBC to explore some possible archive footage, and during Ian's tour with the UJRE, I went over to Berlin, where the festival had some good footage of Miles. Ian and I went and looked at it all, but coincidentally, he also introduced me to Jon Hiseman and Barbara Thompson, and in 1979 I ended up making a film about them instead.

'This was really because the whole Miles project was extremely tortuous. For reasons that it's not worth going into now, dealing with Miles's management, his record company, and the owners of the various pieces of film was highly complex, and all the time we were trying to keep the BBC warm to the idea.

'To try and kickstart matters, when I was in New York on another project, I decided to try and move things along. Now, you have to remember that during the late 1970s, it was widely believed that Miles would never play again. He had stopped performing, and was living in seclusion in his New York house. I spoke to Gil Evans, whom I'd met through Ian, and asked him if he could put me in touch with Miles. He gave me a number, and when I called it from my hotel, I was staggered to be talking to Miles himself.

'"Hello," I said, "you don't know me but I work for BBC Television in London."

'"What do you want?" said Miles.

'"I want to make a film about you, because you are one of the greatest jazz musicians in the world."

'"One of the...?" he said, somewhat menacingly.

'There was a pause, and then he asked if there was any money involved. I told him that there probably was not, because this was the

BBC and they didn't have big budgets to throw around. "You'd better talk to my agent," he said. And that was the end of the phone call.

'I tried to keep the negotiations going, but the problems were too huge, and eventually the idea collapsed.'[15]

Ironically, it was another friend of Ian's, Paul Buckmaster, the British arranger who had worked with Neil Ardley on recording the original *Kaleidoscope of Rainbows*, who finally gave Miles the help he needed to emerge from seclusion, and to begin the long haul back to playing in public. This, of course, changed the whole nature of the project. Despite BBC opposition, which meant that Miles was not filmed by or interviewed for the network during his last decade, Mike and Ian kept in touch, keeping discussions going about how they might eventually get round to making the film. Then Miles died in September 1991. Following a considerable expenditure of time on updating the *Rough Guide to Jazz*, Ian then spent his spare moments over the next few years adding copious additional material to his biography of Davis for a second edition. This was published in 1998.

'At that point,' recalls Dibb, 'the idea of the film surfaced again, still with the BBC, and I was back negotiating with Sony, with the Miles Davis estate, and with his former management. Just at the moment when I thought we had a breakthrough, I got a letter from the BBC saying they had decided not to go ahead after all. So immediately I contacted Michael Jackson at Channel 4, whom I knew from his time at the BBC, and who had a genuine appreciation of Miles and his music. The best part of twenty-five years had gone by from the first aspirations Ian and I had, but we eventually got to make the film, and when Jan Younghusband at Channel 4 saw a rough cut of it, she saw it had to be a lot longer than they had originally commissioned. The network was completely supportive, and created two slots so that the whole 124 minutes of film went out in two parts.'[16]

Ian's participation was vital in making this documentary. In just the same way as his address book and his reputation as a musician had opened doors for Derek Drescher's radio documentary on Miles, his integrity helped Mike Dibb gain access to all manner of Davis's associates, lovers, family and friends. 'He was the key to making it happen,'says Dibb, 'because everybody trusted him. He had an aura of trust and authority about him, so that when we were doing interviews, and the majority of them were done as a double act from behind the camera, we got helpful answers. Actually, in many cases, Ian himself already knew the answers, but I could ask more innocent general questions, once he had established that we knew our stuff.'[17]

Researching Miles, Ian interviewing Jack DeJohnette and Dave Holland for Mike Dibb's film, at DeJohnette's house near Woodstock. (Ian Carr)

Ian appears in the film, both in a round table discussion with Dave Holland, and Jack DeJohnette and his wife, and also as a 'talking head' in his own right. His investigation of Miles's professional life and work, and more particularly his tactful but probing revelations about Miles's tortuous personal life went a stage further in the film than they had in the most recent edition of his book. Dibb recalls nothing but praise from family and friends who attended a special screening in Davis's home town of St. Louis, where Miles's first girlfriend (and mother of his children) Irene Birth thanked him for the way that she had become 'part of the story'. The film went on to be released on DVD and to win an EMMY award.

Channel 4 was delighted with the success of the film, and was open to the possibility of doing a follow-up on Keith Jarrett. Ironically, there had been stirrings during the 1980s at the BBC about doing a film on Jarrett, but just as had happened with Miles, these came to nothing. As Ian relates in his second edition of the Davis book, during his last years Miles was clearly aware of both the biography and its author and treated Ian very favourably when they met subsequent to the appearance of the first edition at a London press conference. In the same way, Jarrett was equally aware of Ian's book about him, and remembered the interview with Derek Drescher that had been part of its genesis. In the wake of the Davis film, discreet overtures were made via Jarrett's manager, and it

Researching Miles: Ian with Miles Davis's nephew. (Ian Carr)

was agreed that Ian would go out and film a long interview with the pianist at Channel 4's expense. If this worked out, then there would be the money available to make a second full-scale film.

Jarrett can be a prickly interviewee, and he thinks very deeply about each question, sometimes querying the premise behind it, before attempting to frame an answer, as I have discovered in doing a number of interviews with him for the BBC and *The Times*. Fortunately, Ian's interview with him went extremely well, with Jarrett in relaxed mood, and enjoying himself to the extent that after the initial filming session, the team was invited to return the same evening and again the following day. Dibb and Ian returned to London knowing they had the raw material for another exceptional documentary. Through Ian's calming presence, Dibb was also able to film freely and extensively at a sound check by Jarrett's 'Standards Trio', putting on record one of the most thorough documents of the pianist' playing style, with none of the restrictions he usually imposes on cameras or photographers. *Keith Jarrett – The Art Of Improvisation,* was first shown on Channel 4 in December 2004, and like its sister film about Miles, was later released in a longer DVD version.

And it is the world of film that has finally begun to give Ian Carr and his generation of musicians the recognition that they have had almost everywhere but in Britain since the 1960s. Segments of Mike Dibb's 1968 film about the Rendell-Carr Quintet, and footage of early Nucleus

Researching Keith Jarrett: Ian and Jarrett at the pianist's house, for Channel 4 filming, 2004. (Ian Carr)

sessions were included in a BBC series aired in the spring of 2005 on BBC television under the title *Jazz Britannia*. Interviews with Ian (both historical and contemporary) were included, and his clear view of what he was doing and why was as apparent as when I first met him with Mike Garrick's sextet back in 1969. His blunt, Northern description of what Nucleus aimed to do – albeit from behind one of his very bushiest beards – was vintage Carr.

Yet these programmes subscribe to the myth that the British jazz of the 1960s and 70s is being 'rediscovered'. In the case of Ian Carr, who has led bands consistently since the 1960s, and a cross section of whose Nucleus output was reprised at a concert at London's Cargo club in the autumn of 2005, he has recorded, written and broadcast about jazz prolifically, and passed on his ideas to generations of younger players via Interchange and the Guildhall. Far from needing to be rediscovered, he has never really been away.

list of recordings

This recording chronology summarises the first issues of all known sessions on which Ian Carr plays. I am grateful to John Smallwood, Mike Carr, Andy Gray, and Roger Farbey (of the Unofficial Ian Carr Website: http://www.geocities.com/icnucleus) for help in compilation. Reissues and anthologies are not included, and I have used standard discographical abbreviations for instruments.

June 1961 Morton Sound Studios, Newcastle
EmCee Five
Ian Carr (t); Gary Cox (ts); Mike Carr (p); John O'Carroll (b); Ronnie Stephenson (d).

Lefty's Tune	Birdland MC 596
Blowin' The Blues Away	–
Dobson's Choice	–
Blues For Monk	–
The Bridge	–
Theme	Unissued demo
John O'Groats	–
The One That Got Away	–
Downbeat After Dark	–
Blue Sue	–

December 14, 1961 Lansdowne Studios, London
EmCee Five
Ian Carr (t); Gary Cox (ts); Mike Carr (p); Spike Heatley (b); Ronnie Stephenson (d).
Let's Take Five [EP]

The One That Got Away	Columbia SEG 8153
Stephenson's Rocket	–
Preludes	–

October 15, 1962 Club A-Gogo, Newcastle
EmCee Five
Ian Carr (t); Gary Cox (ts); Mike Carr (p); Midge Pike (b); Johnny Butts (d).

John O'Groats	Alpha Int. DB 92
Northumbrian Air	−
Mike's Dilemma	Birdland MC 587
Prayer to the East	Unissued

January 14, 1964 London
Clive Burrows
Bob Leaper, Ron Johnson, Ken Turner (t); Ian Carr (t, fh); Jeff Pritchard (frh); Henry Chapman, Terry Hellier, Paul Rutherford (tb); Les Carter (fl); Trevor Watts (as); Dave Gelly (as, ts); Brian Wales, Dave Tomlin (ts); Clive Burrows (bar); Paul Raymond (p); Tony Reeves (b); Jon Hiseman (d).

Sack O'Woe	Pye/Unissued
I Remember Clifford	−
Killer Joe	−
Work Song	−
Maria	−
Round About Midnight	−
Well You Needn't	−

January 22, 1964 London
Don Rendell Quintet
Ian Carr (t, fh); Don Rendell (ss, ts); Johnny Mealing (p); Dave Green (b); Trevor Tomkins (d).

There Is No Greater Love	Spotlite SPJ CD566
I've Never Been In Love Before	−
Blues By Five	−
You'll Never Know	−
Blues For Crazy Jane	−
Peace Talk	−
Waltz For Swingers	−
Blues For Sally	−
Downbeat After Dark	−

October 1, 2, 1964 London
Don Rendell/Ian Carr Quintet
Ian Carr (t, fh); Don Rendell (ss, ts); Colin Purbrook (p); Dave Green (b); Trevor Tomkins (d).

Shades of Blue

Blue Mosque	Columbia 33SX1733
Latin Blue	–
Sailin'	–
Garrison 64	–
Blue Doom	–
Shades of Blue	–
Big City Strut	–
Just Blue*	–

* Ian Carr out

February 1965 London
Roy Budd
Ian Carr (t); Dick Morrissey (ts); Roy Budd (p); Trevor Tomkins (d); other unidentified musicians; Harry South (arr).

Birth of the Budd	Pye 7NI5807
M'Ghee, M'Ghee	–

March 14, 1965 London
New Jazz Orchestra
Neil Ardley (ldr, cond); Bob Leaper, Mike Phillipson, Tony Dudley (t); Ian Carr (t, fh); John Mumford, Paul Rutherford (tb); Peter Harvey (btb); Nick Palmer (frh); Dick Hart (tu); Les Carter (fl, afl); Trevor Watts (as, fl); Barbara Thompson (cl, as); Dave Gelly (cl, ts); Tom Harris (ts); Sebastian Freudenberg (bar); Mike Barrett (p); Tony Reeves (b); Jon Hiseman (d).
Western Reunion

Big P	Decca LK4690
Shades Of Blue	–
So What	–
If You Could See Me Now	–
Tiny's Blues	–
Milestones	–
Django	–
Maria	–
Western Union	–
Black Nightgown	Unissued
Le Roi	–
Round Midnight	–
In A Mellotone	–
If You Could See Me Now (alt)*	–

* Lionel Grigson (p) replaces Barrett

May 27, 1965 London
Michael Garrick Sextet
Ian Carr (t, fh); Joe Harriott (as); Tony Coe (cl, ts); Michael Garrick (p);
Coleridge Goode (b); Colin Barnes (d).
Promises

Promises	Argo DA 36
Parting Is Such	–
Merlin the Wizzard	–
Second Coming	–
Requiem	–
Leprechaun Leap	–
Portrait of a Young Lady	–

May 28, 1965 London
Michael Garrick Quintet
Ian Carr (t, fh); Joe Harriott (as); Michael Garrick (p); Coleridge Goode
(b); Colin Barnes (d); Jeremy Robson (narr).
Before Night/Day

Cascade	Argo EAF115
Blues For The Lonely	–
Before Night/Day	–
Day of Atonement	–
Sketches of Israel	–
The Game	–

November 1965 The Highwayman, Camberley, Surrey
Don Rendell/Ian Carr Quintet
Ian Carr (t, fh); Don Rendell (ts); Michel Garrick,(p); Dave Green (b);
Trevor Tomkins (d).
Live In London

Blues By Five	Harkit HRCD 8045
Jonah and The Whale	–
Shades of Blue	–
Hot Rod	–
Garrison 64	–
Promises	–

Late 1965 London
Alan Price Set
Ian Carr, Kenny Wheeler (t, fh); Alan Price (org, v); + others

Any Day Now	Decca F12217

add John Walters (t); Nigel Stanger (ts);
    Never Be Sick On A Sunday   –

January 3, 1966 London
Michael Garrick Septet
Ian Carr (t, fh); Joe Harriott (as); Tony Coe (cl, ts); Don Rendell (ss, ts); Michael Garrick (p); Dave Green (b); Colin Barnes (d); John Smith (narr).
Black Marigolds

A Jazz Nativity	Argo DA88
Jazz For Five	–
True Story	Unissued

January 10, 11, 1966 London
Michael Garrick Septet
Ian Carr (t, fh); Joe Harriott (as); Tony Coe (cl, ts); Don Rendell (ss, ts); Michael Garrick (p); Dave Green (b); Trevor Tomkins (d).
Black Marigolds

Webster's Mood	Argo DA88
Good Times	–
Ursula	–
Shiva	Jazz Academy JAZA 6*
Sixth Seal	Unissued
Ophelia's Lay	–
Vishnu	–

* This single track was issued on JAZA 6 with a date attribution of "mid-60s" but the line-up is identical to the Argo session, and the studio sound is similar, so I have assumed that this comes from the same session.

January 25, 1966 London
Harry South Big Band
Harry South (dir); Ian Hamer, Hank Shaw, Les Condon, Albert Hall (t); Ian Carr (t, fh); Rick Kennedy, Chris Smith, Keith Christie, Bill Geldard (tb); Roy Willox, Alan Branscombe (as, fl); Ronnie Scott, Dick Morrissey (ts); Tubby Hayes (ts, fl); Pete King (bar); Gordon Beck (p); Phil Bates (b); Phil Seamen (d).
Presenting the Harry South Big Band

Costa Fortuna	Mercury 20081MCL
Last Orders	–
Afterthought	–
Alone Together	–

January 26, 1966 London
Harry South Big Band
Harry South (dir); Ian Hamer, Hank Shaw, Les Condon, Greg Bowen (t);
Ian Carr (t, fh); Marshall John, Chris Smith, Keith Christie, Gib Wallace
(tb); Roy Willox, Alan Branscombe (as, fl); Ronnie Scott, Dick Morrissey
(ts); Bob Efford (ts, fl); Harry Klein (bar); Gordon Beck (p); Phil Bates (b);
Phil Seamen (d).

Six To One Bar	Mercury 20081MCL
Lush Life	–
There and Back	–
North of the Soho Border	–

March 16, 17, 1966 London
Don Rendell / Ian Carr Quintet
Ian Carr (t, fh); Don Rendell (ss, ts); Michael Garrick (p); Dave Green (b);
Trevor Tomkins (d).
Dusk Fire

Ruth	Columbia SX6064
Tan Samfu	–
Jubal	–
Spooks	–
Prayer	–
Hot Rod	–
Dusk Fire	–

June 4, 1966 London
Ian Carr Quartet
Ian Carr (t, fh); Trevor Watts (as); Jeff Clyne (b); John Stevens (d).
Springboard

Ballad	Polydor 545007
Helen's Clown	–
Ou sont les neiges d'antan	–

August 27, 1966 London
Ian Carr Quartet
Ian Carr (t, fh); Trevor Watts (as); Jeff Clyne (b); John Stevens (d).
Springboard

Love Was Born	Polydor 545007
C4	–
Crazy Jane	–
Springboard	–
Ballad	(unissued)

November 1966, London/New York
Herbie Hancock
Collective personnel includes
Freddie Hubbard, Joe Newman, Ian Carr (t); Phil Woods (as); Joe
Henderson, Don Rendell (ts); Paul Griffin, Gordon Beck, Herbie
Hancock (kb); Jim Hall (g); Ron Carter (b); Jack DeJohnette (d) (and
others).
Blow Up (Original Soundtrack)
[The London sessions for this only appear to have been included on
Sony Special Music AK 52418, released in 1966. Subsequent issues only
include the American sessions recorded in New York, which do not
include Beck, Carr, and Rendell.]

February 23, 1967 London
Don Rendell/Ian Carr Quintet
Ian Carr (t, fh); Don Rendell (ss, ts); Michael Garrick (p); Dave Green (b);
Trevor Tomkins (d).
Phase III
    Les Neiges D'Antan (Snows of Yesteryear)   Columbia SX 6214
    Bath Sheba   –
    Black Marigolds   –

February 24, 1967 London
Don Rendell/Ian Carr Quintet
Personnel as previous day
Phase III
    Crazy Jane   Columbia SX 6214
    On!   –

March 18, 1968 London
Don Rendell/Ian Carr Quintet
Ian Carr (t, fh); Don Rendell (ss, ts); Michael Garrick (p); Dave Green (b);
Trevor Tomkins (d).
Live
    Voices   Columbia SX 6316
    On Track   –
    You've Said   –
    Pavane   –
    Nimjam   –
    Vignette   –

May 2/3 1968 London
Acker Bilk and the Stan Tracey Big Brass
Kenny Wheeler, Ian Hamer, Derek Watkins, Eddie Blair, Les Condon (t);
Ian Carr (fh); Keith Christie, Don Lusher, Chris Pyne, Bobby Lamb, Chris
Smith (tb); Acker Bilk (cl); Tony Coe (ts); Stan Tracey (p); Dave Green (b);
Barry Morgan (d).
Blue Acker

Royal Garden Blues	Columbia TW 0230
Stranger on the Shore	–
Festival Junction	–
Blues For Last Year	–
Tin Roof Blues	–
Baby Blues	–
Blues For This Year	–
Mood Indigo	–

July 23, 1968 Antibes
Don Rendell/Ian Carr Quintet
Ian Carr (t, fh); Don Rendell (ss, ts); Michael Garrick (p); Dave Green (b);
Trevor Tomkins (d)

Pavane	Spotlite SPJ CD 566
Hot Rod	–
Voices	–

August 20/21, 1968 London
Stan Tracey Big Brass
Derek Watkins, Paul Tongay, Kenny Baker, Eddie Blair, Les Condon (t);
Ian Carr (fh); Keith Christie, Don Lusher, Chris Pyne, Bobby Lamb, Chris
Smith (tb); Stan Tracey (p); Lennie Bush (b); Barry Morgan (d).
We Love You Madly

I'm Beginning To See The Light	Columbia SX 6320

Acker Bilk (cl); Joe Harriott (as); Don Rendell (ss, ts) added

Creole Love Call	–
Blues with a Feeling	–
Lay-By	–
We Love You Madly	–

September 17, 18, 1968 London
New Jazz Orchestra
Neil Ardley (ldr, cond); Derek Watkins, Henry Lowther, Ian Carr, Harry
Beckett (t, fh); Mike Gibbs, John Mumford, Derek Wadsworth, Tony
Russell (tb); George Smith (tu); Barbara Thompson (fl, ss, as); Jim Philip

(cl, ts, fl); Dick Heckstall-Smith (ss, ts); Dave Gelly (bcl, cl, ts); Frank Ricotti (vib); Jack Bruce (b); Jon Hiseman (d).

Dejeuner Sur L'Herbe

Dejeuner Sur L'Herbe	Verve VLP9236
Dusk Fire	−
Ballad	−
Naima	−
Angle	−
Nardis	−
Study	−
Rebirth	−

October 25, 1968 St. Paul's Cathedral, London

Michael Garrick Sextet

Ian Carr (t, fh); Jim Philip (cl, ts, fl); Art Themen (cl, ss, ts, fl), Michael Garrick (org); Coleridge Goode (b); John Marshall (d); Choir of Farnborough Grammar School; Peter Mound (cond).

Jazz Praises

Anthem	Airborne NBP 0021
Sanctus	−
Kyrie	−
Behold, A Pale Horse	−
Salvation March	−
The Beatitudes	Jaza 11
Rustat's Grave Song	Airborne NBP 0021
The Lord's Prayer	−
Agnus Dei	−
Confiteor	−
Psalm 73	−
Carolling	Jaza 11

November 1, 2, 3 1968 London

Guy Warren

Ian Carr (t, fh); Don Rendell (ss, ts); Amancio D'Silva (g); Michael Garrick, (p, hc, perc); Dave Green (b); Trevor Tomkins (d, perc); Guy Warren (perc).

Afro Jazz

Ours, This Is Our Land	Columbia SX 6340
That Happy Feeling	−
Yaw Barima	−
Builsa	−
Dearest Noelle	−

Souls of the Departed Have A Drink   —
African Jazz Dance No 1   —
African Jazz Dance No 2   —
It's A Long Way To Mampong   —
Burning Bush 1   —
Burning Bush 2   —
I Love The Silence   —
Africa Speaks, India Answers   —

Nov 1968 London
Joe Harriott
Ian Carr (fh); Joe Harriott (as); Amancio D'Silva (g); Dave Green (b);
Bryan Spring (d).
Hum Dono
    Stephano's Dance   Columbia SX 6354
    Jaipur   —

1968 London
Amancio D'Silva
Ian Carr (t, fh); Don Rendell (ts); Amancio D'Silva (g); Dave Green (b);
Trevor Tomkins (d).
Integration
    Ganges   Columbia SCX6322
    Jaipur   —
    Maharani (*)   —
    Cry Free (*)   —
    Joyce Country (*)   —
    Integration (**)   —
    We Tell You This (***)   —
* Rendell out; ** Carr out; *** Carr and D'Silva only

1968 Portugal
Don Byas Quintet
Ian Carr (t); Don Byas (ts); Mike Carr (org); Dave Green (b); Adrian
Rawsy (d); Earl Jordan, Amalia Rodriguez (v).
    unknown tracks   no issue details

March 20, April 16, 1969 London
Don Rendell/Ian Carr
Ian Carr (t, fh); Don Rendell (ss, ts); Michael Garrick (p, hc); Jeff Clyne*,
Dave Green (b); Trevor Tomkins (d), Guy Warren † (perc); Stan
Robinson ** (cl, ts)

Change Is
    Elastic Dream * † **   Columbia SX 6368
    Boy Dog and Carrot †   –
    Cold Mountain   –
    Black Hair   –
    Mirage   –
Mike Pyne replaces Garrick
    One Green Eye **   –

May 13, 1969 Farnham, Surrey
Michael Garrick Sextet
Ian Carr (fh); Art Themen (ts); Don Rendell (ss, ts, fl); Michael Garrick (p); Coleridge Goode (b); John Marshall (d), John Smith (v); Betty Mulcahy (narr); Choir of Farnborough Grammar School; Peter Mound (cond).
    A Jazz Cantata (For Martin Luther King)   Erase EO 254

June 22, 1969 Queen Elizabeth Hall London
Michael Garrick Sextet
Ian Carr (fh); Art Themen (ts); Don Rendell (ss, ts, fl); Michael Garrick (p); Dave Green (b); Trevor Tomkins (d).
    Children's Chorus   Unissued
    Ophelia's Lay   –
    Trane's Mood   –

October 12, 1969 London
Neil Ardley
Neil Ardley (arr, cond); Ian Carr (t, fh); Mike Gibbs (tb); Barbara Thompson (ss, as, fl); Don Rendell (ss, ts, fl); Karl Jenkins (ss, bar, ob); Frank Ricotti (vib, mar, perc); Jeff Clyne, Jack Bruce (b, elb); John Marshall (d); Jack Rothstein, Kenneth Isaacs (vn); Kenneth Essex (vla); Clive Tunnell, Amaryllis Fleming (vc).
Greek Variations
    Santorin   Columbia SCX 6414
    Omonioa   –
    Delphi   –
    Kerkyra   –
    Metrora   –
    Kriti   –

November 19, 1969 London
Ian Carr Quintet

Ian Carr (t, fl); Brian Smith (ss, ts); Chris Spedding (g); Jeff Clyne (b, eb); John Marshall (d).
Greek Variations

Wine Dark Lullaby	Columbia SCX 6414
Orpheus	–
Persephone's Jive	–

Late 1969 London
Adrian Henri
Adrian Henri (v); Andy Roberts (v, g); Mike Evans (ts, v); Percy Jones (b); Brian Dodson (d); plus Ian Carr (t); John Mumford (t); Karl Jenkins (ob, bar); Ian Whiteman (kb).
St. Adrian Co.: Broadway and 3rd.

Made in U.S.A.	RCA SF 8100
Uman Tapeworm	–
High Song	–
Bomb Commercial	–
Colours 4 Baby	–

January 12, 13, 16, 21, 1970 London
Ian Carr's Nucleus
Ian Carr (t, fl); Brian Smith (ss, ts, fl); Karl Jenkins (bar, ob, elp); Chris Spedding (g); Jeff Clyne (b, eb); John Marshall (d).
Elastic Rock

1916	Vertigo 6360.008
Elastic Rock	–
Striation	–
Taranaki	–
Twisted Track	–
Crude Blues, pt 1 & 2	–
1916 - The Battle Of Boogaloo	–
Torrid Zone	–
Stonescape	–
Earth Mother	–
Speaking for Myself, Personally, In My Own Opinion I Think...	–
Persephone's Jive	–

January 20, 21, 22, 1970 London
Michael Garrick Sextet
Ian Carr (fh); Art Themen (ts); Don Rendell (ss, ts, fl); Michael Garrick (p); Coleridge Goode (b); Trevor Tomkins (d); Norma Winstone (v).

The Heart Is A Lotus	Argo ZDA 135
Song By The Sea	–
Torrent	–
Temple Dancer	–
Blues on blues	–
Voices	–
Beautiful Thing	–
Rustat's Grave Song	–
Rest	Unissued

Early 1970 London
Blossom Dearie
Ian Carr (fh); Kenny Wheeler (t); Harold McNair (ts); Ray Warleigh (p); Jeff Clyne (b); Spike Wells (d); and orchestra; Brian Gascoigne (arr, cond).
That's Just The Way I Want It To Be

That's Just the Way I Want (it) to Be	Font 6309015
Long Daddy Green	–
Sweet Surprise	–
Hey John	–
Sweet Georgia Fame	–
Both Sides Now	–
Dusty Springfield	–
Will There Really Be A Morning?	–
I Know The Moon	–
Inside A Silent Tear	–
Yesterday I Was Young	–
I Like London In The Rain	–

March 31, April 1, 2, 13 1970 London
Chitinous Ensemble (dir. Paul Buckmaster)
Various instrumentalists, including Ian Carr (t, fh); Brian Smith (ss, ts); John Marshall (d); Frank Ricotti (perc.).
Chitinous

Mandible	Deram SML 1093
De Blonck	–
Mushroom dance	–
Was-Eye?	–
Aldebaranian song	–
Dance	–
Ronkproat'tn	–
8 fish-eyes	–

Rockrott   —
Loopild   —
Stoned   —

Mid-1970 London
Bob Downes Open Music
Bob Downes (fl, as, ts, lyricon, vcl, ldr); Nigel Carter, Kenny Wheeler,
Bud Parkes, Ian Carr, Harry Beckett, (t, fh); Bubba Brooks, (ts); Don Faye
(bar); Ray Russell, Chris Spedding (g); Herbie Flowers, Daryl Runswick,
Harry Miller (b); Denis Smith, Alan Rushton, Clem Catani (d); Robin
Jones (cga); Robert Cockburn (narr).
Electric City
    No Time Like The Present   Vertigo 6360.005
    Keep Off The Grass   —
    Don't Let Tomorrow Get You Down   —
    Down Until Dawn   —
    Go Find Time   —
    Walking On   —
    Crash Hour   —
    West (II)   —
    In Your Eyes   —
    Piccadilly Circles   —
    Gonna Take A Journey   —

September 21, 22, 1970 London
Ian Carr's Nucleus
Ian Carr (t, fl, narr); Brian Smith (ss, ts, fl); Karl Jenkins (bar, ob, p, elp);
Chris Spedding (g, bouzouki, v); Jeff Clyne (b, eb); John Marshall (d).
We'll Talk About It Later
    Song For the Bearded Lady   Vertigo 6360.027
    Sun Child   —
    Lullaby For A Lonely Child   —
    We'll Talk About It Later   —
    Oasis   —
    Ballad of Joe Pimp   —
    Easter 1916   —

December 14, 15, 1970 London
Ian Carr's Nucleus
Ian Carr, Kenny Wheeler †, Harry Beckett* (t, fl); Brian Smith (ss, ts, fl);
Tony Roberts (ts, bcl); Karl Jenkins (bar, ob, elp); Chris Spedding (g);

Keith Winter (syn); Jeff Clyne (b, eb); Ron Matthewson (eb); John Marshall (d), Chris Karan (perc).

Elements I and II †	Vertigo 6360.039
Changing Times †	–
Bedrock Deadlock*	–
Spirit Level*	–
Torso †	–
Snakehips Dream †	–

March 9, 1971 Studio 1, Kensington House, London
Ian Carr (t, fl); Brian Smith (ss, ts, fl); Karl Jenkins (bar, ob, p, elp); Chris Spedding (g); Jeff Clyne (b, eb); John Marshall (d).
Jazz London (BBC Transcription Service)

Song For The Bearded Lady	Hux 039
Elastic Rock	–
Snakehips Dream	–

May 7, 1971 London
Spontaneous Music Ensemble Big Band
Ian Carr, Kenny Wheeler (t); Chris Pyne (tb); Roland Czyzek (pco); Trevor Watts (ss, as); Ray Warleigh (as); Brian Smith (ts); Karl Jenkins (bar); Pete Lemer (elp); Mike Pyne (p); Ron Herman, Ron Matthewson (b); John Stevens, Keith Bailey, Laurie Allen, John Marshall (d); Julie Tippetts, Maggie Nicols, Carolann Nicols, Norma Winstone (v).
Live

Let's Sing For Him (A March for Albert Ayler) View VMS 015

May 25, 1971 Gondel Filmkunsttheater, Bremen, Germany
Nucleus
Ian Carr (t/fh/perc); Brian Smith (ts/ss/fl/perc); Karl Jenkins (ob/elp); Ray Russell (g); Roy Babbington (b); John Marshall (d)
Live In Bremen

Song For The Bearded Lady	Cuneiform Rune 173/174
By The Pool (Wiesbaden '71)	–
Kookie And The Zoom Club	–
Torrid Zone	–
Zoom Out	–
Snakehips' Dream	–
Oasis/Money Mad	–
Dortmund Backtrack	–
Bremen Dreams	–
Elastic Rock	–

A Bit For Vic   —
Persephone's Jive   —

June 1971 London
Keith Tippett
Ian Carr, Mongezi Feza, Mike Collins (t); Nick Evans, Paul Rutherford
(tb); Elton Dean, Dudu Pukwana, Jan Steel, Larry Stebbins, Brian Smith,
Alan Skidmore, John Williams (as, ts, bar); Keith Tippett (p); Jeff Clyne,
Boz, Brian Bleshaw (b); John Marshall, Tony Fennell. Robert Wyatt (d);
strings; voices.
Centipede
    Septober Energy Part 1   Neon NE9/1
    Septober Energy Part 2   —
    Septober Energy Part 3   —
    Septober Energy Part 4   —

July, 1972 London
Ian Carr's Nucleus
Ian Carr (t, fl); Brian Smith (ss, ts, fl); Gordon Beck (p*); Dave McRae (ep);
Allan Holdsworth (g); Roy Babbington (eb); Clive Thacker (d); Trevor
Tomkins (perc) †.
Belladonna
    Belladonna * †   Vertigo 6360.076
    Summer Rain   —
    Remadione †   —
    May Day * †   —
    Suspension   —
    Hector's House *   —

March 1973 London
Ian Carr's Nucleus
Ian Carr, Kenny Wheeler (t, fl); Tony Coe (cl, ts, bcl); Brian Smith (ss, ts,
fl); Dave McRae, Gordon Beck (p, elp); Paddy Kingsland (synth); Roy
Babbington (eb); Clive Thacker, Tony Levin (d); Trevor Tomkins (perc);
Norma Winstone (v).
Labyrinth
    Origins   Vertigo 6360.091
    Bull-Dance   —
    Ariadne   —
    Arena-Arena   —
    Exultation   —
    Nexos   —

June 22, 25, 1973 London
Neil Ardley
Tony Fisher, Greg Bowen, Henry Lowther, Ian Carr (t, fh); Chris Pyne, David Horler (tb); Ray Premru (btb); Barbara Thompson (f, af, ss); Ray Warleigh (f, as); Stan Sulzmann (f, as, ss); Bob Efford (ob, ts, bn); Dave Gelly (bcl, cl ,ts); Bunny Gould (bcl, bn); Peter Lemer (p, elp, syn); Alan Branscombe (vib); Chris Laurence, Ron Mathewson (b, bg); Jon Hiseman (d, perc); Neil Ardley (dir); Norma Winstone (v).
Mike Taylor Remembered - 1973

Half Blue	Issued in a limited edition by Neil Ardley. No number.
Pendulum	–
I See You	–
Son of Red Blues - Brown Thursday	–
Song of Love	–
Folk Dance No 2	–
Summer Sounds	–
Land of Rhyme in Time	–
Timewind*	–
Jumping Off The Sun	–
Black and White Raga	–

[* Recorded by Denis Preston for Record Supervision, the entire session was never issued at the time. However, Neil Ardley issued it before his death in a limited edition of CDRs, but *Timewind* was brought out commercially in 2004 on Universal's second anthology of Gilles Peterson's Impressed/Repressed. It has since been deleted.].

November 1973 London
Ian Carr's Nucleus
Ian Carr (t); Brian Smith (ss, ts, fl); Dave McRae (p, elp); Jocelyn Pitchen (g); Roger Sutton (eb); Clive Thacker (d); Aureo De Souza (perc); Joy Yates (v).
Roots

Roots	Vertigo 6360.100
Images	–
Caliban	–
Wapatiti	–
Capricorn	–
Odokamona	–
Southern Roots and Celebration	–

March 1974 London
Ian Carr's Nucleus
Ian Carr (t, fl); Bob Bertles (as, bar, bcl, fl); Geoff Castle (elp, synth); Gordon Beck (elp, perc); Jocelyn Pitchen, Ken Shaw (g); Roger Sutton (eb); Bryan Spring (d); Keiran White (v).
Under The Sun

Addison Trip	Vertigo 6360.110
Feast Alfresco	–
In Procession	–
New Life	–
Pastoral Graffiti	–
Rites of Man	–
Sarsparilla	–
Taste of Sarsparilla	

April 27, 1974 Southwark Cathedral, London
Neil Ardley, Ian Carr, Mike Gibbs, Stan Tracey
Kenny Wheeler (t, fh); Tony Coe (cl, saxes); Paul Buckmaster, Colin Walker (vc); Gordon Beck, John Taylor, Stan Tracey (p, el-p); Ron Matthewson (b); Tony Levin (d); Trevor Tomkins (perc); Norma Winstone, Peppi Lemer (v).
Will Power

Will's Birthday Suite (Carr)	Argo SZDA164/5
1 Heyday	–
2 Dirge (Fear No More the Heat of the Sun)	–
3 Fool Talk	–

NB The disc also contains compositions by Ardley, Gibbs and Tracey.

April 1975 London
Ian Carr's Nucleus
Ian Carr (t, fl, synth); Bob Bertles (as, bar, bcl, fl); Geoff Castle (elp, synth); Ken Shaw (g); Roger Sutton (eb); Roger Sellers (d).
Snakehips etc.

Alive and Kicking	Vertigo 6360.119
Heyday	–
Pussyfoot	–
Rachel's Tune	–
Rat's Bag	–
Snakehips etc.	–

December 1975 London
Ian Carr's Nucleus

Ian Carr (t, fl, synth); Bob Bertles (ss, as, bar, fl); Geoff Castle (elp, synth); Ken Shaw (g); Roger Sutton (eb); Roger Sellers (d); Trevor Tomkins (perc).
Alleycat

Phaideaux Corner	Vertigo 6360.124
Alleycat	–
Splat	–
You Can't Be Sure	–
Nosegay	–

Early 1976 London
Neil Ardley
Neil Ardley (arr, cond, synth); Ian Carr (t, fl,); Bob Bertles (ss, as, bar, fl); Tony Coe (cl, ts, bcl); Brian Smith (ss, ts, fl); Barbara Thompson (ss, as, fl); Geoff Castle, Dave McRae (elp, synth); Ken Shaw (g); Roger Sutton (eb); Paul Buckmaster (vc); Roger Sellers (d); Trevor Tomkins (perc).
Kaleidoscope of Rainbows

Prologue	Gull GULP1018
Rainbow One	–
Rainbow Three	–
Rainbow Four	–
Rainbow Five	–

1976 London
as above, but Stan Sulzmann (ss, as, fl) replaces Thompson

Rainbow Two	Gull GULP1018

1976 London
as above but Thompson returns in place of Sulzmann, and John Taylor (elp, synth) replaces McRae.

Rainbow Six	Gull GULP1018
Rainbow Seven	–

January 7, 9, 1977 Schützenhaus, Stuttgart-Heslach
United Jazz and Rock Ensemble
Ian Carr (t); Ack Van Rooyen (t, fh); Albert Mangelsdorff (tb); Barbara Thompson (ss, ts, fl); Charlie Mariano (nagashwaran, ss, as); Wolfgang Dauner (p, clavinet, syn); Volker Kriegel (g); Eberhard Weber (b); Jon Hiseman (d).
Live in Schützenhaus

Circus Gambit	Mood 22666
Hey Day	–
Steps of M. C. Escher	–

South Indian Line   –
Hypnotic Pignose   –
The Love That Cannot Speak Its Name   –
Be-cop Rock   –

February 6, 1977 Düren, Germany
Ian Carr's Nucleus
Ian Carr (t, fl, elp); Brian Smith (ss, as, bar, fl); Geoff Castle (elp, synth);
Bill Kristian (eb); Roger Sellers (d).
In Flagrante Delicto

Gestalt   CMP 1/Capitol ST 11771
Mysteries   –
Heyday   –
In Flagrante Delicto   –

September 14, 1977 Musikhalle, Hamburg
United Jazz and Rock Ensemble
Ian Carr (t); Ack Van Rooyen (t, fh); Albert Mangelsdorff (tb); Barbara
Thompson (ss, ts, fl); Charlie Mariano (ss, as); Wolfgang Dauner (p, syn);
Volker Kriegel (g); Eberhard Weber (b); Jon Hiseman (d).
NDR Jazzworkshop 1977

Bebop Rock   NDR 9666864

January 13-16, 1978 Stuttgart
United Jazz and Rock Ensemble
Ian Carr (t); Ack Van Rooyen (t, fh); Albert Mangelsdorff (tb); Barbara
Thompson (ss, ts, fl); Charlie Mariano (ss, as); Wolfgang Dauner (p, syn);
Volker Kriegel (g); Eberhard Weber (b); Jon Hiseman (d).
Teamwork

Gone With The Weed   Mood 33.618
Stumbling Henry's Divorce March   –
Sicilian Steal   –
Pale Smile   –
Albert's Song   –
Yin   –
To An Elfin Princess   –
Wart G'Schwind   –

July, September 1978 London
Neil Ardley and The Harmony of the Spheres
Neil Ardley (arr, cond, synth); Ian Carr (t, fl,); Tony Coe (cl, ts, bcl);
Barbara Thompson (ss, as, fl); Geoff Castle (elp, synth); John Martin (g);

Bill Kristian (eb); Richard Burgess (d); Trevor Tomkins (perc); Pepe Lemer, Norma Winstone (v).

Upstarts All	Decca TXS-R133
Leap In The Dark	–
Glittering Circles	–
Fair Mirage	–
Soft Stillness and the Night	–
Headstrong, Headlong	–
Towards Tranquility	–

November 1978 London
Ian Carr's Nucleus
Ian Carr (t, fl, synth); Brian Smith (ss, as, bar, fl); Geoff Castle (elp, synth); Neil Ardley (synth); Bill Kristian (eb); Roger Sellers (d); Richard Burgess, Chris Fletcher * (perc).
Out of the Long Dark

Gone With The Weed	Capitol ST11916
Lady Bountiful	–
Solar Wind *	–
Selina	–
Out of the Long Dark (Conception)	–
Sassy (American Girl)	–
Simply This (The Human Condition)	–
Black Ballad (Ecce Domina)	–
For Liam	–

NB: Names in brackets are those of Gerald Laing's sculptures which inspired each track.

April 12-15, 1979 Stuttgart, Germany
United Jazz and Rock Ensemble
Ian Carr, Ack Van Rooyen, Kenny Wheeler (t, fh); Albert Mangelsdorff (tb); Barbara Thompson (ss, ts, fl); Charlie Mariano (ss, as); Wolfgang Dauner (p, syn); Volker Kriegel (g); Eberhard Weber (b); Jon Hiseman (d).
The Break Even Point

Boorcet	Mood 33.619
Chateau Sentimental	–
Sparrhamlingslied	–
Alfred Schmack	–
Sidewalk	–
Amber	–
Song With No Name	–
One Sin A While	–

April 21, 22, 1979 Berlin
Ian Carr's Nucleus
Ian Carr (t, fl, elp); Brian Smith (ss, as, bar, fl); Geoff Castle (elp, synth);
Bill Kristian (eb); Roger Sellers (d).
Jazzbuhne Berlin '79
    Out Of The Long Dark   Amiga 8.55.749

September 1980 London
Ian Carr's Nucleus
Ian Carr (t, fl, elp); Brian Smith (ss, as, bar, fl); Geoff Castle (elp, synth);
Chucho Merchan (elb); Nic France (dr)
Awakening

Awakening	Mood 24.400
Midnight Oil	–
Mutatis Mutandis	–
White City Blues	–
Things Past	–
You Can't Be Serious/You must Be Joking	–

October 30, 31, 1981 Berlin Jazz Festival, Berlin
United Jazz and Rock Ensemble
Ian Carr, Ack Van Rooyen, Kenny Wheeler (t, fh); Albert Mangelsdorff
(tb); Barbara Thompson (ss, ts, fl); Charlie Mariano (ss, as); Wolfgang
Dauner (p, clavinet, syn); Volker Kriegel (g); Eberhard Weber (b); Jon
Hiseman (d).
Live in Berlin

Ausgeslchafen	Mood 33.620
Red Room	–
Storyboard	–
Out of the Long Dark	–
Freibad Sud	–
Des'sch Too Much	–
Simply This	–
Trans tanz	–
South Indian Line	–

February 10, 1982 Rome
Algemona Quartetto with Ian Carr
Ian Carr (t); Stefano Frosi (ts); Andrea Alberti (p); Toni Armetta (b);
Roberto Altamura (d).

Ohanaba	Mia JM 1598
For Miles and Miles	–

Penasando a un'anima   —
Canzona Per il Sud   —
The Human Factor   —
Erodani   —
Campo Primo   —

October 6, 1982 Maida Vale, London
Nucleus
Ian Carr (t, fh); Tim Whitehead (ss, ts); Mark Wood (g); Joe Hubbard (elb); John Marshall (d).
Jazz Today (BBC Radio 3, original broadcast introduced by Charles Fox)
    Easy Does It Now   Hux 039
    The Pretty Redhead   —
    For Miles and Miles   —

June 30, July 1, 1984 Theaterhaus, Stuttgart
United Jazz and Rock Ensemble
Ian Carr, Ack Van Rooyen, Kenny Wheeler (t, fh); Albert Mangelsdorff (tb); Barbara Thompson (ss, ts, fl); Charlie Mariano (ss, as); Wolfgang Dauner (p, syn); Volker Kriegel (g); Eberhard Weber (b); Jon Hiseman (d).
Live Opus Sechs
    Garberville   Mood 33.621
    Wendekreis Des Steinbocks   —
    Rip Off   —
    Die Wiederkehr   —
    Some Time In Silence   —
    Lady Bountiful   —

March 1985 London
Nico + The Faction
Nico (vocal, harmonium); James Young (kb); Graham Dids (perc); Ian Carr (t).
Camera Obscura
My Funny Valentine   Beggars Banquet BEGA63
Into the Arena   —
[Ian Carr does not play on the other tracks, some of which feature the producer, John Cale, on vocals.]

April 6, 1985 Theaterhaus, Stuttgart
Ian Carr's Nucleus
Ian Carr (t, fh); Phil Todd (ss, ts); Mark Wood (g); Dill Katz (b); John Marshall (d).

Live at The Theaterhaus
Dawn Choruses   Mood 28.650
Bouquet pour ma belle   –
For Miles and Miles   –
Easy Does It Now   –
Something For Mr Jelly Lord   –

1986 Stuttgart
United Jazz and Rock Ensemble
Ian Carr, Ack Van Rooyen, Johannes Faber (t, fh); Albert Mangelsdorff
(tb); Barbara Thompson (ss, ts, fl); Charlie Mariano (ss, as); Wolfgang
Dauner (p, syn); Volker Kriegel (g); Eberhard Weber (b); Jon Hiseman (d).
Live at the Stuttgart Jazz Festival
   Fireworks: Overture   MMGV074 [video]
   Funk   –
   African Dance   –
   Adagio   –
   Interview   –
   Loschzug 2   –

1987
United Jazz and Rock Ensemble
Probable personnel: Ian Carr, Ack Van Rooyen, Johannes Faber (t, fh);
Albert Mangelsdorff (tb); Barbara Thompson (ss, ts, fl); Charlie Mariano
(ss, as); Wolfgang Dauner (p, syn); Volker Kriegel (g); Eberhard Weber
(b); Jon Hiseman (d).
   The Voices   ZDF Jazz Club Mix [video]

February 1987 Tonstudio Bauer, Ludwigsberg
United Jazz and Rock Ensemble
Ian Carr, Ack Van Rooyen, Johannes Faber (t, fh); Albert Mangelsdorff
(tb); Barbara Thompson (ss, ts, fl); Charlie Mariano (ss, as); Wolfgang
Dauner (p, syn); Volker Kriegel (g); Eberhard Weber (b); Jon Hiseman (d).
Round Seven
   Feuerwerxmusik (Suite In 3 Movements)   Mood 33.606
   a) Ouverture
   b) Funk
   c) African Dance
   Seriously Deep   –
   Raga Yagapriya   –
   Balance   –
   Voices Behind Locked Doors   –

Midnight Oil	–
Randy	–
Ganz Schon Heiss Man	–

April 23, 1988 Abbey Road, London
Ian Carr
Ian Carr (t, fh); Phil Todd (ss, bcl); Steve Berry* (b); Mo Foster (elb); The Kreisler String Orchestra: Michael Thomas (ldr); Chris Brierly, Abigail Brown, Kathy Shave, Anne Solomon, Louisa Fuller, Richard Kosta, Sonia Slaney, Mark Pharoah (vn); John Metcalfe, Elspeth Cowey, Helen Kamminga, Mairi Campbell (vla); Robert Woolard, Mark Davies, Rachael Maguire (vc); Andrew Davis (b).
Old Heartland

Northumbrian Sketches	
Part 1: Open Country	MMC 1016
Part 2: Interiors *	–
Part 3: Disjunctive Boogie †	–
Part 4: Spirit of Place	–

May 1988 London
Ian Carr
Ian Carr (t, fh); Phil Todd (ss, bcl); Mark Wood (g); Geoff Castle (kb); Dill Katz (elb); John Marshall (d).
Old Heartland

Full Fathom Five	MMC 1016
Old Heartland	–
Things Past	–

December 1988
Michael Gibbs Orchestra
Michael Gibbs (dir, tb, p); Ian Carr, Earl Gardner, Allan Rubin, Lew Soloff (t); John Clark (frhn); Dave Bargeron (tb); David Taylor (btb); Jim Odgren (as); Chris Hunter (ss, as, ts, fl); Lou Marini (ss, ts, fl); Bob Mintzer (bcl, ts, fl); Dave Tofani (fl, pco); Dave Bristow, Brad Hatfield (kb); Kevin Eubanks, David Fiuczynski, Bill Frisell, Duke Levine, John Scofield (g); Kai Eckhardt (b); Bob Moses (d); Bad Bill Martin, Ben Wittman (d prog, perc).
Big Music

Wall To Wall	Venture VE 27
Mopsus	–
Almost Ev'ry Day	–
Pride Aside	–
Adult	–

August 28-31, 1989 Ronnie Scott's Club, London
George Russell Living Time Orchestra
Russell (dir); Stuart Brooks, Ian Carr, Mark Chandler (t); Pete Beachill,
Ashley Slater (tb); Andy Sheppard, Chris Biscoe, Pete Hurt (ss, as, ts);
Brad Hartfield, Steve Lodder (kb); David Fiuczynski (g); Bill Urmson (b);
Steve Johns (d); Dave Adams (perc).
The London Concerts

La Folia	Label Bleu LBLC 6527
Uncommon Ground	–
Electronic Sonata For Souls Loved By Nature	–
Listen To The Silence	–
Struggle of the Magicians	Label Bleu LBLC 6528
Six Aesthetic Gravities	–
So What	–

1989 Yamaha R and D
Zyklus
Ian Carr (t, fh); Neil Ardley (kb, Zyklus MPS); John L. Walters (kb, Zyklus
MPS, EWI); Warren Grieveson (g, eld, Zyklus MPS).
Virtual Realities

Before The Oil Ran Out	AMP CD017

June 21, 1991 ?
United Jazz and Rock Ensemble
Ian Carr, Ack Van Rooyen, Kenny Wheeler (t, fh); Albert Mangelsdorff
(tb); Barbara Thompson (ss, ts, fl); Charlie Mariano (ss, as); Wolfgang
Dauner (p, kb); Volker Kriegel (g, sitar); Dave King(b); Jon Hiseman (d).
European Jazz Night 1991

Capriccio Funky	[video n.d.]
Circus Gambit	–
Be Bop Rock	–

1991 Temple Music, London
Zyklus
Ian Carr (t, fh); Neil Ardley (kb, Zyklus MPS); John L. Walters (kb, Zyklus
MPS, EWI); Warren Grieveson (g, eld, Zyklus MPS).
Virtual Realities

Refracted Rainbow	AMP CD017
No Score	–
Rooms	–
Enchanted Isle	–
I K Brunel	–

Round Midnight   —
Remembrances   —

April, May 1992 Studio Bauer, Ludwigsberg
United Jazz and Rock Ensemble
Ian Carr, Ack Van Rooyen, Kenny Wheeler (t, fh); Albert Mangelsdorff
(tb); Barbara Thompson (ss, ts, fl); Charlie Mariano (ss, as); Wolfgang
Dauner (p, kb); Volker Kriegel (g, sitar); Dave King (b); Jon Hiseman (d).
Na Endlich
    Don't Follow the "Follow Me" Sign   Mood 6382
    Capriccio Funky   —
    Ode To Sappho   —
    Absage Albert Mangelsdorff   —
    Meise Form Fenster   —
    Plum Island   —
    Bebop Scat   —
    Echoes of Harlem   —

May 30, 31, 1992 Southwark Cathedral, London
Ian Carr
Ian Carr (t, fh); John Taylor (org).
Sounds and Sweet Airs
    A sea change rich and strange   Celestial Harmonies 13064
    Lulled in these flowers with dances and delight   —
    The sacred radiance of the sun   —
    Alas poor Yorick   —
    The prince of darkness is a gentleman   —
    Come unto these yellow sands   —
    We are such stuff as dreams are made on   —
    There is a willow grows aslant a brook   —
    Sounds and sweet airs (fh solo)   —
    Soft stillness and the night   —
    Such sweet sorrow   —
    Requiem (The rest is silence) (t solo)   —

January 1994 London
London Jazz Orchestra
Noel Langley, Andy Bush, Henry Lowther, Ian Carr, Sid Gauld (t, fh);
Scott Stroman, Paul Nieman, Brian Archer, Richard Edwards (tb); Dave
Stewart, Andy Lester (btb); Stan Sulzmann, Martin Hathaway, Tim
Garland, Pete Hurt, Jamie Talbot, Mark Lockheart, Alan Barnes (ss, as,
ts); Pate Saberton (p); Phil Lee (g); Alec Dankworth (b); Paul Clarvis (d).

Dance For Human Folk
  The Tradition (parts 1-4)   Hot House HHCD1016/7

1994 London
No-Man
Tim Bowness (v); Steven Wilson (misc.instruments); Ian Carr (t); Ben Coleman (vn); Mel Collins (ss); Robert Fripp (g); Chris Maitland (d); Silas Maitland (elb).
Flowermouth
  Angel Gets Caught In The Beauty Trap   Stone CD045

June 9, 1996 Mainz, Germany
United Jazz and Rock Ensemble
Kenny Wheeler, Ian Carr, Ack Van Rooyen (t); Albert Mangelsdorff (tb); Christof Lauer, Barbara Thompson (ss, as, ts); Wolfgang Dauner (p); Volker Kriegel (g); Dave King (b); Jon Hiseman (d).
Die Neunte Von United
  Double Bind   Mood 6472
  The Worm's Turn   —
  Postcard for F. W. Bernstein   —
  Drachenburg Fur R   —
  Lie In Wait   —
  In Memory   —
  Midday Moon   —
  Wounded Love   —
  Elongate   —

1996 London
No-Man
Tim Bowness (v); Steven Wilson (misc.insts); Ian Carr (t); Robert Fripp (soundscape).
Housewives Hooked on Heroin
  Where I'm Calling From   Stone CD 026

January 15, 17, 1999 Cotton Club, Kaierslautern
United Jazz and Rock Ensemble
Thorsten Benkenstein, Ian Carr, Ack Van Rooyen (t); Albert Mangelsdorff (tb); Christof Lauer, Barbara Thompson (ss, as, ts); Wolfgang Dauner (p); Peter O'Mara (g); Dave King (b); Jon Hiseman (d).
X
  United Funk   Mood 6582
  Flying Carpets   —

S'wahnsinn	–
Things Past	–
Tribute	–
Autumn Bugle	–
Burn Up	–
SWR2	–
Thompson's Tango	–

1999 London
Faultline
David Kosten, Dennis Hopper (v); Keith Bayley (g, hca); Kyra
Humphreys (vn); Emma Black (clo); Ian Carr (t); Mark Feltham (hca).
Closer Colder
> Mute   Thirsty Ear FABR 023

August 14, 2001 London
Ian Carr (t, fh); Don Rendell (as, ts, fl); Richard Busiakiewicz (p); Mario
Castronari (b), Robin Jones (d).
Reunion
> I Can't Believe That You're In Love With Me   Spotlite SPJCD 571
> Penthouse Serenade   –
> Bernie's Tune   –
> If You Only Knew   –
> Smoke Screen   –
> How Deep Is The Ocean   –
> Struttin' With Some Barbecue   –

2001 London
No-Man
Tim Bowness (v); Steven Wilson (misc. insts.); Ian Carr (t); Ben
Christophers (g); David Kosten (syn); Colin Edwin (b); Steve Jansen (d).
Returning Jesus
> Only Rain   Stone CD 038

October 2002 London
Solar Apple Quarktette
Richard E. (dj); Mr Christy (syn); Ian Carr (t).
> Kali Yuga   Further Out SAQ2

notes

1 northumbrian sketches

1. Ian Carr interviewed by John Smallwood, 1991
2. *History, Topography and Directory of Durham* (London, Whellan, 1894)
3. W.S. Gilbert: 'The Yarn of the Nancy Bell' (1866, abridged) in *Fifty Bab Ballads* (London, Macmillan, 1871)
4. Ian Carr interviewed by John Smallwood, 1991
5. Author's interview with Ian Carr for National Sound Archive, 20 June 2000
6. Taped recollections recorded by Ian Carr, 12 September 1990
7. ibid.
8. ibid.
9. 'Fate plays an electrifying hand', *Northern Echo*, 20 October 2002
10. Ian Carr interviewed by John Smallwood, 1991
11. ibid.
12. Author's interview with Ian Carr for National Sound Archive, 20 June 2000
13. ibid.
14. ibid, plus additional material from taped recollections recorded by Ian Carr, 12 September 1990
15. Rudi Blesh: *Shining Trumpets* (London, Cassell, 1949)
16. Author's interview with Ian Carr for National Sound Archive, 20 June 2000
17. ibid.
18. Alyn Shipton: 'Marian McPartland' in *Handful of Keys, Conversations with Thirty Jazz Pianists* (London, Equinox, 2004) (expanded, using original interview, from the printed version.)
19. Author's interview with Ian Carr for National Sound Archive, 20 June 2000, plus additional material from taped recollections recorded by Ian Carr, 12 September 1990

2 from king's college to queen's commission

1. Ian Carr interviewed by John Smallwood, 1991
2. ibid.
3. ibid.
4. ibid.
5. Stanley Eveling: 'Fame as no spur', *Northern Review, a Journal of Regional and Cultural Affairs*, Vol. 4, (Winter 1996) p. 31

6. Richard Cook: 'Garlic and Keystone Burgundy: Student Life in Newcastle During the 1950s', *Northern Review, a Journal of Regional and Cultural Affairs*, Vol. 4, (Winter 1996) p. 20
7. Ian Carr interviewed by John Smallwood, 1991
8. Stanley Eveling: op. cit. p. 29
9. Ian Carr interviewed by John Smallwood, 1991
10. Stanley Eveling: op. cit. p. 33
11. Author's interview with Ian Carr for National Sound Archive, 20 June 2000 and Ian Carr: 'Novocastrian Jazz: 1950s and Early 1960s', *Northern Review, a Journal of Regional and Cultural Affairs*, Vol. 4, (Winter 1996) p. 10ff.
12. Author's interview with Ian Carr for National Sound Archive, 20 June 2000
13. 'Ian Carr' in B.S. Johnson: *All Bull – The National Servicemen* (London, Allison and Busby, 1973) p. 103
14. Author's interview with Ian Carr for National Sound Archive, 20 June 2000
15. ibid
16. 'Ian Carr' in B.S. Johnson: op. cit. p. 103
17. Author's interview with Gerald Laing, February 2005
18. Author's interview with Ian Carr for National Sound Archive, 20 June 2000
19. ibid.
20. ibid.
21. 'Ian Carr' in B.S. Johnson: op. cit. p. 103
22. ibid.
23. Charlie Bourne recorded as a piano duo with Phil Ellis in the mid-1920s. He can be heard on Blossom Seeley's recordings from 1925.
24. Author's interview with Ian Carr for National Sound Archive, 20 June 2000

3 on the bum

1. Ian Carr interviewed by John Smallwood, 1991
2. ibid.
3. Kenneth Tindall: 'The Humanity of the Machine' [n.d.] is an article that summarises the intellectual circle of 1958 Paris and Heliczer's role in it. Heliczer's collected poems are to be found in P. Heliczer: *A Purchase in the White Botanica* (Granary Press). Heliczer returned to New York in the early 1960s where he became a leading light in the lower East Side literary underground scene, founding the Dead Language Press, and he also dabbled in music, recording with Lou Reed and Velvet Underground.
4. Ian Carr interviewed by John Smallwood, 1991
5. ibid.
6. ibid.
7. ibid.
8. Author's interview with Gerald Laing, February 2005
9. Ian Carr interviewed by John Smallwood, 1991
10. Author's interview with Ian Carr for National Sound Archive, 20 June 2000
11. Author's interview with Percy Heath, for *Miles Ten Years On*, BBC Radio 2, 2001
12. Author's interview with Ian Carr for National Sound Archive, 20 June 2000
13. ibid.

14. Ian Carr interviewed by John Smallwood, 1991
15. Shirley Deane: *The Expectant Mariner* (London, John Murray, 1962) A jam session is described in which Ian plays the trumpet.
16. Author's interview with Ian Carr for National Sound Archive, 20 June 2000

4 stephenson's rocket – the emcee five

1. Alun Morgan: 'Bebop from the East Coast 1960/62' [liner notes to Birdland MC 596, May 1987]; Peter Vacher: 'This Carr Has Driven The Best' *Jazz UK*, (No. 61) Jan/Feb 2005 p.13
2. Ian Carr: 'Novocastrian Jazz: 1950s and Early 1960s', *Northern Review, a Journal of Regional and Cultural Affairs*, Vol. 4, (Winter 1996) p. 10ff.
3. Mike Carr interviewed by John Smallwood, 1991
4. Ian Carr: op. cit.
5. Mike Carr interviewed by John Smallwood, 1991
6. Author's interview with Mike Figgis, 20 July 2004
7. Alun Morgan: op. cit.
8. Ian Carr: op. cit. p. 10ff.
9. ibid.
10. Author's interview with Ian Carr for National Sound Archive, 20 June 2000
11. Ian Carr interviewed by John Smallwood, 1991, and Ian Carr: op. cit.
12. ibid.
13. Geoff Harrison: 'Bebop from the East Coast 1960/62' [liner notes to Birdland MC 596, March 1996]
14. *Sunday Times*, 10 June 1962
15. I am indebted to Paul Adams of Lake Records, current licensee of much of the 'Jazz Today' and Lansdowne catalogue for this information.
16. Geoff Harrison: op. cit.
17. Ian Carr: op. cit.
18. Alun Morgan: 'Let's Take Five', *Jazz Monthly*, [n.d.] 1962
19. Ian Carr interviewed by John Smallwood, 1991
20. J.B. Walters: 'Blues Singer With Style' *Newcastle Journal*, 10 August 1962
21. Ian Carr: op. cit.
22. Ian Carr interviewed by John Smallwood, 1991
23. Ian Carr: 'Men With A Mission' *Newcastle Journal*, [n.d.] 1962 (from Ian Carr's personal scrapbooks)

5 affectionate fink – harold mcnair and 1960s london

1. Peter Guidi: 'A Short History of the Jazz Flute', *The Jazz Flute Vol. II* (Molenaar Edition, 1997)
2. Ronnie Scott (with Mike Hennessey): *Some of My Best Friends Are Blues* (2nd edition, London, Northway, 2004) pp 64-67
3. Simon Spillett: 'Yellow Birds – West Indian Jazz Musicians In London in the 1950s & 1960s' (jazzscript.co.uk) posted 2004
4. Author's interview with Ian Carr for National Sound Archive, 20 June 2000

5. Ian Carr interviewed by John Smallwood, 1991
6. J.B. Walters: 'Blues Singer With Style' *Newcastle Journal*, 10 August 1962
7. Ian Carr interviewed by John Smallwood, 1991
8. ibid.
9. ibid.
10. ibid.
11. ibid.
12. ibid.

6 shades of blue – the rendell-carr quintet

1. Philip Larkin: *All What Jazz? A Record Diary 1961-68* (London, Faber, 1970)
2. Martin C. King: 'British Jazzmen, No. 1: Don Rendell' *Jazz Journal*, July 1970, (xxiii/7) p. 7
3. Don Rendell interviewed by John Smallwood, 1991
4. 'Illness hits the jazz boys' *Melody Maker*, 12 January 1963
5. 'Britain', *Downbeat*, 28 February 1963
6. Author's interview with Ian Carr for National Sound Archive, 20 June 2000
7. Don Rendell interviewed by John Smallwood, 1991
8. Duncan Heining: 'Miles Ahead' [The Don Rendell-Ian Carr Quintet], *Jazz UK*, No. 58 (Jul/Aug 2004) p.14
9. Author's interview with Ian Carr for National Sound Archive, 20 June 2000
10. Martin C. King: 'British Jazzmen, No. 3: Neil Ardley' *Jazz Journal*, September 1970, (xxiii/9) p. 14
11. Charles Fox: 'Shades of Blue' [liner note to Columbia 33SX1733] October 1964
12. ibid.
13. 'Rendell's tenor has regressed back towards the Stan Getz period and there are few signs of Coltrane or the avant garde...' Bob Dawbarn: 'Rendell-Carr' *Melody Maker*, 17 July 1965; 'Rendell...uses the soprano sax and the sheets of sound principle with a fresh measured restraint' Ian Breach: 'New Jazz Records' *The Guardian*, 9 August 1965; 'The themes are restrained, tuneful and not too adventurous' Peter Sykes: 'Don Keeps Moving' *Oxford Times*, 2 August 1965.
14. Martin C. King: 'British Jazzmen, No. 1: Don Rendell' op. cit.
15. Charles Fox: 'Dusk Fire' [liner note to Columbia 33SX 6064] March 1966
16. Don Rendell interviewed by John Smallwood, 1991
17. Author's interview with Gerald Laing, February 2005
18. Don Rendell interviewed by John Smallwood, 1991
19. Ian Carr interviewed by John Smallwood, 1991
20. ibid
21. Jimmy Craig: 'Alexis Korner' *Record Mirror Special Issue*, 24 April 1971
22. Alyn Shipton: 'Michael Garrick' *Jazzwise*, May 2003
23. Ian Carr interviewed by John Smallwood, 1991; band personnel from Andy Blackford: *Wild Animals   The Story of the Animals* (London, Sidgwick and Jackson, 1986)
24. Dave Green interviewed by John Smallwood, 1991
25. Charles Fox: 'Phase III' [liner notes to Columbia SX 6064] February 1967
26. Bangor University flier, 4 March 1966

27. Philip Larkin: op. cit.
28. Ian Carr interviewed by John Smallwood, 1991
29. ibid
30. Charles Fox: 'Phase III' op. cit.
31. Ian Carr interviewed by John Smallwood, 1991
32. ibid
33. Trevor Tomkins interviewed by John Smallwood, 1991
34. Ian Carr interviewed by John Smallwood, 1991
35. Ian Carr interviewed by John Smallwood, 1991
36. Ian Carr: 'Live!' [liner notes to Columbia SX6316] March 1968
37. Mark Gardner: 'Don Rendell / Ian Carr', *Jazz Journal*, December 1969 (xxii/12) p. 36
38. 'The Don Rendell/Ian Carr Quintet opened the programme...their jazz is...a little too studied and the unreasonable restrictions gave them no time to relax', Barry McRae: 'Poll Winners' Concert' *Jazz Journal*, May 1969 (xxii/5) p. 17
39. Eddie Cook: 'Don Rendell' *Jazz Journal*, December 2000 (ciii/12) p. 9
40. Ian Carr interviewed by John Smallwood, 1991
41. ibid
42. Dave Green interviewed by John Smallwood, 1991

7 elastic rock – the formation of nucleus

1. Barry McRae: 'Jeff Clyne/Ian Carr: Springboard', *Jazz Journal*, Sept. 1969 (xxii/9), p. 27
2. Ian Carr interviewed by John Smallwood, 1991
3. Ron Brown: 'Ardley/Carr/Rendell: Greek Variations', *Jazz Journal*, October 1970 (xxiii/10) p. 26
4. Pete Gamble: 'Nucleus at the Phoenix', *Jazz Journal*, July 1970 (xxiii/7) p. 14
5. Ian Carr interviewed by John Smallwood, 1991
6. Jeff Clyne interviewed by John Smallwood, 1991
7. Martha Sanders Gilmore: 'Newport 1970', *Jazz Journal*, Sept 1970 (xxiii/9) p. 12; NB: in 1970, Armstrong's birth date was still thought to be July 4th, 1900.
8. ibid.
9. John Marshall interviewed by John Smallwood, 1991.
10. Author's interview with Ian Carr for National Sound Archive, 20 June 2000
11. Tony Hopkins: 'The Jazz Journal Interview   Ian Carr', *Jazz Journal*, February 1973 (xxvi/2), p.4
12. Ian Carr interviewed by John Smallwood, 1991
13. Richard 'Dig' Fairweather: 'The Problem of Pop', *Jazz Journal*, April 1970 (xxiii/4) p. 10
14. Barry McRae: 'Elastic Rock' [review], *Jazz Journal*, August 1970 (xxiii/8) p. 32
15. ibid.
16. Quote from panel advertisement for Elastic Rock, *Jazz Journal*, August 1970 (xxiii/8) p. 32
17. A.N. Roberts: 'Round the ankles?', *Jazz Journal*, September 1970 (xxiii/9) p. 21 [letter quoting *Melody Maker* report of Nucleus sales figures]
18. Author's interview with Ian Carr for National Sound Archive, 20 June 2000

19. Tony Hopkins: op. cit.
20. Ian Carr interviewed by John Smallwood, 1991
21. Ron Brown: 'Nucleus at the Notre Dame Hall', *Jazz Journal,* October 1970, (xxiii/10) p. 13
22. Ron Brown: 'Melody Maker Poll Concert', *Jazz Journal,* April 1972, (xxv/4) p. 26
23. 'The Jazz Men: Ian Carr' *Beat Instrumental,* (Nov. 1972) p. 36
24. Ian Carr interviewed by John Smallwood, 1991
25. 'The Jazz Men: Ian Carr' op. cit.
26. ibid.
27. Author's interview with Ian Carr for National Sound Archive, 20 June 2000
28. Tony Hopkins: op. cit.
29. Ron Brown: 'Jazz Views of Shakespeare', *Jazz Journal,* June 1973 (xxvi/6) pp. 8-9
30. Ian Carr interviewed by John Smallwood, 1991
31. Author's interview with Ian Carr, January 2003

8 united jazz and rock, and the long dark

1. Tom Callaghan: 'Out of the Long Dark / Old Heartland' [liner notes] (BGO CD420)
2. Neil Ardley interviewed by John Smallwood, 1991.
3. Author's interview with Neil Ardley, 14 April 1997. His observations about the Arts Council appear at first glance to be at odds with Ian's recollections in the previous chapter, which suggest that Graham Collier received the first Arts Council assistance for a UK jazz composer. However, Collier received the first composition bursary for *Workpoints*, written for 12-piece band in 1967, which was not recorded at the time, whereas Ardley received assistance the same year with the costs of his recording project.
4. Author's interview with Neil Ardley, 14 April 1997
5. Max Harrison: 'Kaleidoscope of Rainbows' in Max Harrison, Eric Thacker and Stuart Nicholson: *The Essential Jazz Records, Vol. 2* (London, Mansell, 2000) p. 612
6. Neil Ardley interviewed by John Smallwood, 1991
7. ibid.
8. Alyn Shipton: 'All the old fusion fire rekindled', *The Times,* 30 March 1999
9. Ian Carr interviewed by Barbara Thompson for BBC Radio 3: *Jazz Rock in Britain,* July 2000.
10. Jon Hiseman interviewed by Barbara Thompson for BBC Radio 3: *Jazz Rock in Britain,* July 2000.
11. Author's interview with Ian Carr for National Sound Archive, 20 June 2000
12. Ian Carr interviewed by Barbara Thompson for BBC Radio 3: *Jazz Rock in Britain,* July 2000; and Author's interview with Ian Carr for National Sound Archive, 20 June 2000
13. Jon Hiseman interviewed by Barbara Thompson for BBC Radio 3: *Jazz Rock in Britain,* July 2000.
14. ibid.
15. Ian Carr interviewed by John Smallwood, 1991
16. Alf Dodd interviewed by John Smallwood, 1991
17. Author's interview with Ian Carr for National Sound Archive, 20 June 2000
18. Tom Callaghan: 'Out of the Long Dark / Old Heartland' [liner notes] (BGO CD420)

19. Geoff Castle interviewed by John Smallwood, 1991.
20. Alf Dodd interviewed by John Smallwood, 1991.
21. ibid.
22. Ian Carr interviewed by John Smallwood, 1991
23. Brian Blain and John Fordham: 'Radio and TV Jazz – Still the Poor Relation?' *Jazz UK* (No. 61) Jan/Feb 2005, p. 16
24. Ian Carr interviewed by John Smallwood, 1991
25. ibid.
26. Author's interview with Ian Carr for National Sound Archive, 20 June 2000
27. Ian Carr interviewed by John Smallwood, 1991
28. John Dixon interviewed by John Smallwood, 1991
29. ibid.
30. Ian Carr interviewed by John Smallwood, 1991
31. ibid.
32. ibid.
33. Author's interview with Ian Carr for National Sound Archive, 20 June 2000
34. Ian Carr interviewed by John Smallwood, 1991

9 old heartland

1. John Dixon interviewed by John Smallwood, 1991
2. Author's interview with Ian Carr for National Sound Archive, 20 June 2000
3. Author's interview with Ian Carr for BBC Radio 3 *Teaching Jazz* series, broadcast November 2001
4. Chris Horne: 'Julian Joseph' in *Contemporary Jazz UK   Twenty-One Lives in Jazz* (London, Perspectives in Jazz, 2004)
5. Author's interview with Ian Carr for BBC Radio 3 *Teaching Jazz* series, broadcast November 2001
6. Ian Carr interviewed by John Smallwood, 1991
7. Ian Carr: *Miles Davis – The Definitive Biography* [2nd edition] (London, Harper Collins, 1998) p. 423
8. Ian Carr interviewed by John Smallwood, 1991, supplemented by Author's interviews
9. Clive Davis: 'Ian Carr, Riding an Old Wave', *The Times*, 5 May 1989
10. Author's interview with Ian Carr for *Pretty Redhead* liner notes, 2003
11. Mark Wood, having previously agreed his leave of absence from Nucleus, remained in the fold. His band with Merchan and France can be heard on Wood's 1988 album *La Meczla* (MMC 1015), produced by ex-King Crimson drummer Michael Giles, and with a guest spot for trumpeter Dave DeFries.
12. Author's interview with Ian Carr for National Sound Archive, 20 June 2000
13. Gerald Laing in the previously cited interview told me how friends from all walks of Ian's life visited him in hospital, and that he was truly amazed at the breadth of Ian's circle of friends from the arts, literature, and music. John Marshall equally expressed his amazement at the speed of Ian's physical recovery and the strength and will-power that was necessary for him to appear at the Stables within a month and a half of his operation.

14. Statistics from Ian's journal. I am grateful to him for permission to reproduce these excerpts, some of which were included in a much shorter travel diary published in *The Guardian* during June 1984.
15. Wolfgang Dauner, quoted on www.bremme-hohensee.de/ujre.htm
16. Author's interview with Ian Carr for National Sound Archive, 20 June 2000
17. Duncan Heining: 'Miles Ahead' *Jazz UK*, No 58 (Jul/Aug 2004) p. 15
18. Chris Parker: 'Jazz Diary', *The Independent,* 18 January 1989
19. Keith Howell: 'Old Heartland', *CD Review*, July 1989, p.65
20. Richard Williams: 'Heart Strings', *The Times*, 17 December 1988

10 into the media

1. John L. Walters, quoted in Richard Cook and Brian Morton: *Penguin Guide to Jazz on CD* (4th Edition, London, Penguin, 1998)
2. Clive Davis: 'Riding an Old Wave' *The Times*, 5 May 1989
3. Chris Parker: 'Ian Carr' *Wire*, June 1989, p. 24
4. Author's interview with Ian Carr for National Sound Archive, 20 June 2000
5. George Russell, quoted in Stuart Nicholson: *Jazz Rock* (Edinburgh, Canongate, 1998)
6. John Fordham: 'Tynesider with a reason to blow his own trumpet', *The Guardian*, 5 May 1989
7. Derek Drescher interviewed by John Smallwood, 1991
8. Chris Parker: 'Jazz Diary', *The Independent,* 18 January 1989
9. John L. Walters interviewed by Alyn Shipton for Radio 3 *Impressions*, 1992
10. Neil Ardley interviewed by Alyn Shipton for Radio 3 *Impressions*, 1992
11. ibid.
12. Session recorded 20 September 1996 and broadcast on 24 October, presented by Alyn Shipton, on Radio 3 *Jazz Notes*
13. Sam Wanamaker interviewed by John Smallwood, 1991
14. ibid.
15. Author's interview with Mike Dibb, 28 February 2005
16. ibid.
17. ibid.

index

Printed in the United States
51883LVS00001B/199-218

9 781845 532222